# ROMNEY'S WAY
## A Man and an Idea

by

T George Harris

Prentice-Hall, Inc.
Englewood Cliffs, N.J.

ROMNEY'S WAY: A Man and an Idea
by T George Harris
© 1967 by T George Harris

Library of Congress Catalog Card Number: 68–13399
Printed in the United States of America
T
Prentice-Hall International, Inc., London
Prentice-Hall of Australia, Pty. Ltd., Sydney
Prentice-Hall of Canada, Ltd., Toronto
Prentice-Hall of India Private Ltd., New Delhi
Prentice-Hall of Japan, Inc., Tokyo

Second Printing . . . . . February, 1968

*dedicated to Sheila and Luna*

# TABLE OF CONTENTS

v

# PREFACE

Get mad enough, and you do things you ought not to try. This book belongs to that order of error. I got disgusted with the know-it-alls of my trade, reporting. "If there's anything to learn from George Romney," quipped a New York writer, "you've got an exclusive as far as I'm concerned." As far as I could tell, nobody had tried to find out. The result was that instead of probing the serious problems raised by his political position, the press fluttered around the verbal fringes. This habit came to its absurd climax in the monumental flap over his I've-been-brainwashed gaff.

My purpose is not to promote Romney for the White House. That's his problem, and he may feel that the book makes it more difficult. My purpose is to look at him and the Mormon world he came from, to explore his criticism of today's way of doing public business and his alternative to the stock assumptions of orthodox liberals and conservatives. What he is may be more important than what happens to him.

At the risk of sounding cheerful, I find that he is well ahead of the standard-brand thinkers, not behind, and far enough out so that the locked-in language of present politics fails to work for him. "There aren't any words to say it with, unless you go back to John Stuart Mill," says Romney ghost Al Applegate in anguish. "Then people think they know all that stuff, and you're old-fashioned." The language problem reflects the real problem. In his basic critique of foreign policy, for example, Romney finds such a gap between what we do now and what he thinks we ought to do that he has serious trouble talking about it. In his 17-city tour of the domestic warfront, Negro militants dug his ideas better than the attendant press. From Rochester on September 16, the Washington *Post*'s William Chapman wrote wonderingly about the "peculiar rapport" between the black leaders of FIGHT and this blunt-spoken Republican.

A language that might help him is growing up in the New Right and the campus New Left, with their hatred of manipulative central power and their search for community in urban life. To both, "liberal" is a cussword. Romney avidly watches the student rebels, convinced that their demand for a piece of the action is a valid reassertion of American tradition. When I sent him a long, provocative letter from a Berkeley student leader, the Governor had it Xeroxed for each staffer. But he objects to radical method, and in his thought structure the student protest is only one symptom of the deeper difficulty. He does not tear down; he builds alternatives. For instance, he would not take welfare away from people; he wants to take people up from welfare.

A partisanship of ideas is implicit in my role as biographer. Had I not suspected that Romney was on to something useful, I would not have spent five months to find out what it was. You must also assume another kind of prejudice: I came to like him and enjoy our talks. When you jog around golf courses together in the chill of many dawns—the Governor pulling a cart and the reporter scratching at a notebook—it is

artificial to keep up the bearbaiting game of the press conference. And, finally, there is the bias caused by deadline: I
interviewed Romney's chief critics at length, left and right,
until their comments became repetitive, but still invested less
time in them than in the subject himself. You will have to
decide whether this method was limiting.

The work was more rewarding—and therefore more difficult—than I had expected. I had seen Romney once or twice
in his Rambler days when he unsettled Chicago bankers.
After he had won the 1962 governor's race in Michigan, I
still assumed that he was just another liberal Republican with
a salesman's spiel. Saul Alinsky, that cantankerous "professional radical," told me off. He said that he knew Romney
well, and found in him a unique political insight. From Saul,
the slum organizer, this was liberal praise indeed. In the ten
years since I had first run into Alinsky's unusual work, I had
never heard him call a businessman or a politician, let alone
a Republican, anything but a fink. It was an article of faith for
him, and Romney was the rare exception.

Some while later, after the Goldwater wreck of '64, I did
a *Look* article somewhat grandly titled "A New Conservative
Manifesto."[1] Instead of performing a post-mortem on the Republican body, then considered ready for burial in two graves,
the article reported on a new proposal for a distinctive party
program that undercut the liberal-conservative split. The proposal came from Richard C. Cornuelle, a former right-wing
undergrounder and Goldwater friend who had never been
comfortable with let-em-eat-cake conservatism. Cornuelle
argued that instead of trying to burn down big government,
Republicans could actually compete with it in public service.
Strange to tell, they could invent nongovernmental solutions
to problems like unemployment and pollution—largely
through the "independent sector," that forgotten zone of

[1] *Look,* December 29, 1964.

institutions between the public sector (government) and the private sector (profit-making business). Churches, unions, foundations and a few hundred thousand other organizations fit this category. Among them were the two great political parties. Before the rise of big business and big government, some such set of community forces had provided much of the education, culture, welfare and other public services, as well as subtle context for day-to-day government at each level. Cornuelle wanted to revive this independent way in the computer age. For an experiment, he had chartered a non-profit corporation, United Student Aid Funds, to reinsure bank loans for needy college students. These U.S.A. Funds served students in 49 states so well that it eventually forced the Federal program to retrench. Then he began on experimental cures for hard-core unemployment.

Romney read the *Look* article, telephoned Cornuelle and me. Could we fly out? Sure; we were out on a limb and eager for any company. We spent the first workday of his second gubernatorial term talking, just three of us in the morning and with seven of the Romney staff around his spear-shaped table in the afternoon. Cornuelle wrote about the meeting in *Reclaiming the American Dream*,[1] a book that has been quietly adopted as a manual by a new breed of candidate, usually Republican but sometimes Kennedy Democratic. Romney wanted to pump us for practical schemes, but he knew more about the subject than we did and had done more. His experiments with the independent approach went back many years. He talked knowledgeably, but in the archaic-sounding language of voluntarism, with its too-quick implication that citizens are eager to serve their communities without social pressure or compensation. As governor, he had founded a new branch of state government, the Human Resources

[1] Richard C. Cornuelle, *Reclaiming the American Dream* (New York: Random House, 1965), p. 153.

Council, to encourage nongovernmental attacks on public problems. The Council was not going well, but over the next couple of years he kept testing until he found a formula that showed promise.

As an on-the-road reporter, I soon found that most of the country was already doing, mainly by blind impulse, the same kind of thing that Romney was involved in. As the New Deal gave birth to alphabet agencies in government, the independent sector was spawning dozens of acronymic outfits—e.g., ACT, ACTION, OIC, SCORE, FIGHT, MIND—to take on the rising urban crisis. Though earnest, few workers in these organizations, whose politics ranged from Black Power to business conservatism, felt that they could do much without Federal funds.

It was black people, as many citizens are now proud to call themselves, who demonstrated the immediate danger of all-government programs. The civil rights movement had over the years proved the capacity of voluntary citizen groups to bring on change. But the movement was running into an ideological dead end. It had pushed Federal legislation to the limit, only to find black people trapped by the segregated blessings of the welfare state. Their cheated feeling made violence inevitable. I had covered many riots since 1949, and in the quiet winter of 1966 I went back to the major ghettoes, from Watts to Harlem, to ask what next. This time, I found a surge of ambition that meant one thing: the slums would be renewed from within, or burned down. Responsible militants, and burners, too, were in rage against the Federal practice of shooting programs at black captives. The militants also resented the patronizing rationale of their latest overseers, the city welfare politicians. For instance, instead of helping people buy their apartments and houses the way whites do, well-intended Washington and helpful city hall kept bulldozing with urban renewal, public housing and model cities projects.

The ghettoes were being turned into Federal prisons. Unless the residents could build independent community bodies, grasp control and ownership of their neighborhoods, they would, one said, "always be on somebody's plantation." The thought was intolerable.

Going back by Lansing, I sounded off at Romney. He picked up where I quit, and sharpened the focus on the danger ahead. A mutual friend had suggested that I write a book about him, but neither of us had been overly eager to spend the time on it. Now, we both thought a book might be worth the workout. He agreed to cut twenty or thirty talking hours out of his tight schedule—it actually took much more —and I put my family on short rations. We were to operate under strict rules. If I had a reasonable doubt about a fact, I would double-check it, as I would with any source on any story. No censorship, no control.

I suppose, then, that I am an authorized biographer, but this is not an authorized book. Nobody even vaguely associated with Romney or his campaign will read so much as a paragraph of the manuscript before it goes to the printer. The publisher agreed after discussion to an ironbound hands-off clause. With a tight deadline, and no insider to foolproof each sentence, I may have let minor errors slip by me, but the reader will be spared the major error of a campaign puff job. Except where Romney is quoted or cited, you can blame me for the content.

The arrangements for the writing of this book tell something about the subject. Not every candidate for the Presidency would open his personal files and income-tax data to a reporter without tying on some kind of string. Not many men have so lived that they would dare invite an outside audit. The members of the family, in Utah and in Michigan, responded to my questions with engaging candor. They talked like people who, having nothing to hide, delighted in the fullness of their lives. Mrs. Romney went into hours of interviews with such vivacity that some of the tapes honk with my laughter. Sample: When a future daughter-in-law sympathized with her over her loss of a son to marriage, Mrs. Romney said, "Oh, he was never mine in that way." The family took me to church, absorbed me into their Sunday and, when they went away, left me to roam around the house and browse in the library.

No subject, so far as I could find, was off-limits. After running back from the golf course one morning, Romney and I were taking off our wet shoes in the garage. He was as usual in baggy pants left over from a suit, with a heavy knit shirt and nylon windbreaker to make him sweat hard. His golf shoes, just cleated overshoes pulled over worn-out slippers, did not match. The right was red, the left black. As he pulled up his trouser leg to take off the right shoe, I noticed the bottom shank of a suit of long underwear. That settled the question I had been hesitating to ask: He *did* wear Mormon temple garments. I must have stopped in mid-sentence and stared. Catching on, he simply pulled the trouser leg a notch higher and resumed the conversation. We talked about those temple garments on the way to Lansing. He did not ask me to leave out anything.

---

In the thank-you corner, a writer ought to nod gratefully to his main source. But it might as well be said right there, Governor, that you have a thin skin. Though you enjoy a joke on George Romney, you expect excellence from yourself and resent the thought of less. You will, therefore, react to sections of this book with Romney "intensity." I hope that in time it earns your respect.

In this context, I want to add a concern that to me is serious. It does not begin by blaming you for the Detroit riot. You tried, the President tried, Mayor Cavanaugh tried, a lot of people tried, but it was too little, too late, or else it was wrong. After 350 years, America was too late. We could be too late, or wrong, all over the world. As a political leader, you are demanding a basic turn in domestic and foreign policy. Your insights are persuasive. But I'm not sure there is time to work out the consequences of your criticism and to make the careful, steady changes that would have to follow. You pointed up the desperate need for innovation by your search through the new experiments in the major ghettoes. In the campaign ahead, I for one will be watching for evidence that you would be prepared for specific acts, enough to make a difference, soon. If there is a better way, as you say, it's time to be about it.

Several dozen people took time from busy lives to help. Thank you: Al Applegate, Wendy Baker, David Bigler, Liz Boyd, Virgil Boyd, Joyce Braithwaite, John Byington, Janet Byrum, Sister Mary Catherine, Ed and Mrs. Cushman, Jack Dempsey, Walt De Vries, Richard Durant, Bishop Emrich, Zolton Ferency, Max Fisher, Henry Ford II, Ken Galbraith, Van Hadley, Chuck Harmon, Mrs. Willis Hayward, Grant Heath, S. E. Knudsen, Marybeth Koeze, Peg Little, Jane Marion, Bill McGaughey, Jack McIntosh, Harold McKinney, Elly Peterson, David Riesman; Charles, Jane, Janice, Junius, Lynn, Maurice, Miles, Scott, and Vernon Romney, and Mrs. Gaskell Romney; August Scholle, Mrs. John Scowcroft, William Smart, Gerald Smith, Bill Stirton, Jack Vandenberg, Dick Van Dusen, Hilary Whittaker. And Tom Mahoney, author of the 1959 book, *The Story of George Romney*, who turned over the files he had been keeping up to date.

The unthankable man is Martin R.R. Goldman, ever the editor-without-pencil, who believes that a book is a thing that comes out of a writer, not a something to be scribbled over by an editing machine.

# CHAPTER ONE

# THE UNORTHODOX CANDIDATE

---

"There's got to be a President who understands something other than Government," argues George Romney. "Our problems are too big for Government to solve alone."

Presidential candidates do not hustle votes door-to-door in the suburbs, or go open a string of neighborhood campaign offices in ghetto homes. But these and other odd doings will be seen in 1968, at least until the GOP convention. Many a roller-haired housewife is going to answer the front bell to face a rugged man with a notched nose and crowfeet eyes. He will look bigger than five-feet-eleven, 170 pounds. "My name is George Romney," he will say in that gravel baritone. "I hope you will support me."

The press and the pros will be sure he's wasting time, stumbling. In the mass age, Presidential candidates cannot throw away five minutes on one of 75 million voters. The modern rules say that parties must deal in economic categories of people, spray them in bunches with TV blurbs and press releases. But if Romney runs into an outspoken voter, he's apt

1

to stand toe-to-toe arguing for half an hour. Reporters, comparing notes, will keep shaking their heads and wondering, as one did to me, "How the hell this guy got to be Governor of Michigan, let alone a prospect for President."

Their dismay will turn acute when he singles out local do-gooder outfits for praise, or hustles over to study their projects. "We need such centers where people can go who need to be helpful," he will say, "as much as for people who need help."

He will be mighty eager to talk about the GOP, saying it ought to stand for a "Generation of Progress," but many a Republican will wonder if he hasn't got the wrong elephant by the tail. Romney's version of the party, while conservative in economics, looks suspiciously like a social movement in which them that have can't hide from them that have not. He will tell how his GOP back in Michigan, no longer "business-dominated," has not hesitated to use, and expand, the full powers of state government.

But he will preach that you can't limit party politics to government. During the Detroit riots of '67, paid GOP staffers and hundreds of Republican volunteers piled up truck-loads of food and clothes, and ran them through sniper fire to Negro victims of violence and arson. His state chairman has staked the Michigan organization's future on community service chores, from art shows to slum-housing renewal, as if a political party ought to be more than a vote-begging machine that you turn on every couple of years. Only people who get involved in the daily pains of the society, Romney suspects, can build a true party from the city block up to the White House.

Such "citizens-first" stuff, as he lugubriously calls it, will not make headlines. Some alert reporter will do better with a hot story on Romney's secret campaign tactics. Behind this apple-pie front, it will say, lurks Madison Avenue trickery. His Midwest political scientists, out-Kennedying the Ken-

2

nedys, have used three gubernatorial campaigns to perfect an electronic data-process (EDP) system for year-round politics. Every major politician plays with computers—it's the new thing—but if anybody else uses EDP in a more basic way than Romney, the fact has been hidden from technicians in both parties.

Prof. Walter De Vries, Romney's research chief from Calvin College, has expanded his formidable Michigan hookup to cover the other 49 states. His lease-time computers have been fed the voting history and Census profiles on the people in every U.S. county, and his pollsters now run their surveys from these benchmarks. The computers are integrated into the whole campaign. Programmed on an unorthodox but cogent concept of new voting habits, including ticket-splitting, the machines will select the exact neighborhoods where Romney will surprise housewives.

Computers will monitor each move. Local researchers with clipboards will pre-poll the area in advance, and come back again to be sure that Romney's visit has shifted the minimum two percent into his column, or pulled five percent of the anti's into the undecided list. The candidate, eager to walk rather than ride, will hit two houses a block and skip blocks in a checkerboard pattern so as to let gossip pass on the news to the other homes.

As the show goes on, a caravan of exhausted newsmen and haulers of TV gear will keep on reporting the visits as ritual, only vaguely aware that their doorstep vignettes are part of the program aimed at: (1) mobilizing thousands of volunteers (If Romney does it, why not me?) and (2) rousing millions of families in similar neighborhoods with the thought that the candidate may drop in. It's like Candid Camera. How can you be sure you won't be on next?

The Romney-all-around feeling will be reinforced by telectraphonics; if your neighbors are people whom Romney hopes

3

to switch, your phone may ring and his earnest voice come on with a taped message. Most people will say "Hello, Governor." His TV spots will not be desk talks. As in his 1966 race, they are apt to be unstaged scenes of people in stores telling Romney their views, and hearing his.

The methods are a deliberate extension of Romney's belief that the creative forces of the United States are widely diffused. That's the underlying theme, seldom fully stated, of his campaign. "There's got to be a President who understands something other than Government," he argues, stabbing away with his forefinger. "Our problems at home and abroad are too big for Government to solve alone. In my adult lifetime, there hasn't been a President who had serious experience outside the public sector."

The Big Brother implications of the electronic gear will have a fad run among witty columnists. Russell Baker of *The New York Times* will dig up Arthur T. Hadley's science-fiction satire, *The Joy Wagon,* on the computer that ran for President, or the late Eugene "Bud" Burdick's novel, *The 480,* based on John Kennedy's limited test of vote-bloc simulation, simulmatics. But Romney uses computers to fight the Big Brother trend. By taking in word of what people do (Census and vote data) along with what they think (polls), he "listens" to the electorate and tries for an active voter-candidate dialogue to replace the Big Daddy monologue of the politician. He is searching, with electronic help, for a specific group of voters. He has them defined; he knows they now control elections; he is convinced they are the key to the Presidency.

If Romney's door-to-door doings sound unorthodox for a would-be President, that's typical. As the campaign goes on, the voters will discover that he has consistently done the unexpected and made it work—when conventional wisdom said it wouldn't. When he took over a sick car company in

1954, his industry wrote him off as finished, especially after he turned to the small Rambler and had the nerve to attack the Big Three's "gas-guzzling dinosaurs." Bill Davidson of *Collier's* did a 1956 article saying that the Rambler had made it, but his editors feared that Romney's company would fold any day; they were still worrying over whether to run the story when *Collier's* folded. Financier Louis Wolfson let a fortune slip out of his hands by literally selling Romney's stock short.

Both Democratic and Republican party leaders in Michigan considered Romney to be just a foolish businessman when he set out in 1959 to organize a citizen drive for a new state constitution. In 1963, few expected him, as an untried governor, to break the two-party stalemate in the legislature. In the 1964 campaign, conservatives announced his political burial. In the 1966 race, Richard Nixon's friends in Washington informed the press that Romney would have to pull in at least three new congressmen on his coattails, upsetting strong Democrats, or be ruled out of the Presidential sweepstakes for '68. It was a good Nixon gambit, carefully pitched beyond the possible. Saul Friedman, political analyst for the Detroit *Free Press*, gravely predicted a Republican flop. "Barring a miracle," Friedman wrote, Romney would fail to win more than one or two—maybe none—of the five seats that he and his young "Action Team" were fighting for. The team looked odd anyway: it included a Ph.D. candidate out of Harvard Business School and a Yale Divinity graduate with a law degree. Next day, the Michigan GOP took all five seats, elected Robert Griffen to the United States Senate and, except for two state offices, picked up just about every job that was not nailed to some courthouse floor.

"On television, Romney looks harmless as the dove," says a wise corporate chief, "but is he also wise as the serpent?"

This question will, in one form or another, find its way into the minds of millions. Reporters looking for an answer will discover that Michigan has for some years been playing a parlor game of speculation about what makes Romney run. "He's a lavender-scented Sammy Glick," says a disgusted TV commentator. The Rt. Rev. Richard Emrich, Episcopal Bishop of Detroit, having served on Romney's advisory panels in business and government, says that his friend is not a natural politician because he thinks first in moral terms, but then with the wisdom of prudence takes account of the practical. That habit disturbs AFL-CIO president August Scholle, whose volcanic rages against Romney have long been the tourist attraction of Michigan politics. "Gorgeous George is the errand boy for the reactionaries," says Gus. "He has stood four-square on every side of every question." Gus has provided the Democrats with a basic reference document titled *Who is the Real George Romney?* To help right-wing Republicans fight Romney's bid for the GOP nomination, the Democrats also keep a handy supply of a '64 handbill. This document—sent out by Negro leaders in Flint and Detroit before Romney heard about it and called a halt—showed how to vote for Romney without voting for Senator Goldwater.

The Romney success in business and politics will be explained away, as in the past, both by angry foes and baffled backers. The explanations already on tap run all the way from lying to divine intervention. Democrats charge that "the Republican press has protected him." One newspaper columnist scratches his head over Romney speeches and hands all the credit to Mrs. Romney, whom the Governor calls "my secret weapon." The campaign will start in earnest, says the grizzled writer, "when George unleashes Lenore to round up the voters."

Even the Romney staff will keep on having trouble in the explanation department. Not always sure what the boss is after, or if he knows, some of the staff often feed the press stories indicating that their candidate has made mistakes by ignoring their wise counsel. He lets such stories go on and on before calling an aide down. Yet, the men and women around him share an almost mystical feeling that he will succeed at whatever he tries. "He hasn't failed yet," says Walt De Vries. Party Chairman Elly Peterson, the first feminine state boss in national GOP history, is tempted to humorous wonder—after fighting through one more narrow crisis—if maybe God is indeed playing politics. Old pros like Len Hall of New York pay considerable attention to "those crow-feet eyes. . . . He has more spirit in his little finger than most of us have in our whole body."

But as Romney closes in on the voters, his voice will hit that strident note and he will do again what he has been doing for years. He will try to stir people to the idea that they are not the helpless victims of the mass age, that they can bust loose and do something important. "He's tapping a deep vein of discontent," says a confidant. Romney does not deny the charge. He is, more than he cares to admit, resuming John F. Kennedy's "give me your hand" campaign.

The late President may have sensed the similarity, for he had a Romney theory. Around the White House one Saturday morning a few months before his death, Kennedy said to his wartime friend Paul B. Fay, Jr., then Undersecretary of the Navy:

> The one fellow I don't want to run against is Romney. That guy could be tough. . . . You have to be a little suspicious of somebody as good as Romney. No vices whatsoever, no smoking and no drinking. Imagine someone we know going off for twenty-four or forty-eight hours to fast and meditate, awaiting a message from the Lord whether to run or not to run. Does that sound like one of the old gang?[1]

[1] Paul B. Fay, Jr., *The Pleasure of His Company* (New York: Harper & Row, 1966), p. 259. Kennedy did not quite have the facts. Romney did not go off to meditate in the final hours of his '62 de-

Then, suddenly afraid he might have said too much, Kennedy warned: "That's a bit of information that is not to go any farther than this office. Let the Republicans choose their own candidate free of outside influences." Four years later, Lyndon B. Johnson went at the two-party problem another way: Some of his friends busily leaked word to Republicans—"this is off the record"—that LBJ had said he wanted nothing so dearly as a chance to run against Romney. The quote passed on was "let me at him."

Romney, again going against staff advice, began about then to hammer on his favorite slogan. "There's a better way than LBJ."

Even in the primaries, Romney's every impulse will force him to concentrate not on other GOP contenders but upon a project that to him has become a moral duty: the defeat of Lyndon Johnson. During the Detroit riot of '67, Johnson honed Romney's anti-Johnsonism down to a personal edge, and each morning's news out of Vietnam keeps it serviceable. The Governor's appraisal did not change during the months when the President, after Romney, like others, cautioned against all-out escalation, slowed down his Vietnam buildup. Romney respected Jack Kennedy, believing that he was trapped by the interest blocs in the Democratic Party, but he can barely conceal his belief that Johnson is rather like a vote-guzzling dinosaur with power steering.

Like the '60 race, '68 will have its dirty underside—the Mormon issue. To meet the early demand for sensational rumor, *Fact* Magazine devoted the lead article of its May-June '67 issue to the thesis that Romney is somehow the reincarna-

---

cision to run for governor. He fasts and prays within his normal 17-hour daily schedule. He goes to bed about ten, falls asleep in four minutes, gets up about five to read, heads out for golf when it's light. Under tension on a decision, he sleeps early and well but wakes after 2:30 A.M. and does his best thinking racked out on the bed.

8

tion of Joseph Smith, founder of the Latter-day Saints church. "On the outside, Governor Romney is mature, reasonable, and capable," says the headline. "Inside there's a screwball named Joe Smith screaming to be let out."

And to keep the Mormon issue boiling, a group of Michigan right-wingers have formed a well-financed committee to draft Ezra Taft Benson, former Secretary of Agriculture and one of Mormonism's 12 ruling apostles, for the Presidency. "I have not done anything to promote it, but it is a draft," Elder Benson tells me. "They showed me the brochure they are mailing out, and I certainly could not object to their purposes and reasons. They have mailed out I don't know how many hundred thousand copies." Benson, whose proposed running mate is Senator Strom Thurmond of South Carolina, suggests that Romney is out of step with Mormon leadership. "Most people who know him say he's pretty liberal. He opposes right-to-work laws and supports Federal aid to education, both of which the President of the Church has spoken on [taking the opposite side]."

Somewhat more seriously, many a voter will wonder whether to trust a man who talks piety, doesn't even drink coffee, and trots out for exercise at 5:30 A.M. And white liberals will insist that Romney leave his church until it lets Negroes into its priesthood. By fighting to prove that he is not a bigot, one Democratic planner believes, Romney will trigger the white backlash against himself. The Negro attitude, informed by subtle racism in many whites, will be somewhat different. In Michigan, Negroes who once voted 14-to-one against Republican candidates have, since Mormon Romney came along, reduced that predilection to three-to-one.

Through it all, a cheerful man of 60 will keep a schedule that makes young men swear. Though his temper boils at criticism, Romney's goodwill feeds upon the strains of the voter trail. If he develops a sore hand or some other physical

9

ailment, as candidates often do, a stubborn physical reserve will make him run harder. Last year, after he sprained his left ankle badly and tore ligaments in the calf, he insisted on leading GOP volunteers in a doorbell drive to win a legislative seat that Democrats had owned for 15 years. Four days later, with the ankle still swollen an inch out of size, he got up at 5:30, stomped to jar loose the muscles and cinched the swelling hard inside an Ace bandage. "Got to get back to golf," he declared. He laughed at the stab of pain on the first swing because it kept him from killing the ball, his usual mistake. He joyously drove four balls around 12 holes and, but for my argument that he might re-tear the ligament, would have gone for 18.

He will throw his inevitable surprises into the ritual, perhaps provoke others out of their stuffed shirts. In Michigan, he has made a practice of gumming around with rank-and-file workers at labor parades and picnics, to the wrath of union brass up on the platform. One union chief, told that Romney was about to climb a fence and appear uninvited, instructed the faithful to ignore the pest, along with the flies and mosquitoes. Young Congressman Don Riegle, coached by Romney, more or less picketed a union headquarters that endorsed his opponent without giving him a hearing. When, at a union political dinner, a burly host stabbed a cigar into Riegle's plate of food, the members resented the bad manners. One lady even tore off the opposition stickers that a prankster had pasted on his back.

What remains to be seen is whether the press will figure Romney out well enough to go beyond standard "image" reporting, then force him into a solid debate on his ideas. The result might be a campaign worth living through. Within the Rotarian gothic of his language, this ex-carpenter has nailed together a complex frame of thought. For instance, his case against industry-wide bargaining by unions has an obvious counterpart on the business side. He proposes to make corporations that dominate a market spin off divisions into new companies. A matching pair, these proposals are not unrelated to the tendency of political parties, Romney believes, to serve as branches of economic bureaucracy, be they union or management. And the subjugated parties in turn allow the government pyramid, local-state-Federal, to be stood upon its point with power at the top instead of the bottom. That top-heavy teeter, Romney thinks, has caused an American President to operate abroad more like a pharaoh than like a member of a movement dedicated to the last, best hope on earth.

Romney argues that the GOP can loosen the muscle-bound system at home and abroad. His campaign devices, from computers to do-gooders, are the first stage, and his political policies the second stage, of a general effort to end an era—an era in which people are treated as faceless, passive masses boxed by lines of economic interest. This new age of urban affluence, to be worth living in, has to be the age of the participating society. "People must again control the forces that influence their lives," he says.

To do that, however, you have to diffuse power again. Romney views the Federal Government, not as a separate area of human action, but as one of many institutions, and not always the most important, through which men bring out the best that is in them. But he says it all in the old-shoe language of the Constitution. Even in a country where a constitutional decision on race has set off a social revolution, people don't always know that a man means it when he quotes the founding document while hustling votes from door to door.

11

# CHAPTER TWO

# THEY SWIM
# UPSTREAM

---

"Romneys were not descended like other humans," said George's brother Mike. "We descended from the mule."

Once a man moves up in the political ranks, his private life is laid out for inspection on a blanket of newsprint. This ritual of democracy, while essential, often obscures more than it reveals. The glare of the flashbulb and the blaze of controversy flatten the lines in his face and fuzz the grain of character. He, pushed into controversy every day, cautiously vagues his views. No matter how mixed and rich the elements in him, he is turned into a bit of a cliché.

Even a George Romney, one of the more vivid characters since Teddy Roosevelt, somehow gets homogenized and imagized. For a clear definition, you have to look back to his early years and poke around the family closet to study the shape of the skeletons.

Romney skeletons all have heavy jawbones. Like the jut-jawed Governor of Michigan, each followed the family habit of working out the consequences of conviction no matter what

the neighbors had to say. A Mormon elder had to reach outside the dry land of Utah, Romney homeland, for words to
explain how often in six generations the men and women of
the tribe have been known to swim against the tide. "When
a Romney drowns," he said with genial certainty, "you look
upstream for the body."

Both of Romney's grandfathers were polygamists. Even
among Mormons, coping with more than one wife was recognized, in practice though not in theory, as a test of spirit
beyond the capacity of all but about eleven men in a hundred.
Both grandfathers were chased out of Utah Territory into
Mexico by United States marshals because both refused to
abandon their plural wives and excess children. George's
Uncle Miles Archibald Romney clung devoutly to The Principle of polygamy even after the Mormon church was driven
to renounce it. He took four wives. The family has always
been strong in the church. Marion George Romney, nephew
of the last polygamist and a genuinely humble ex-carpenter,
is now one of the 12 apostles who rule the Mormon establishment.

The sister of this apostle is a Roman Catholic nun. Fourteen years ago, she gave her Los Angeles home and all worldly
goods to the Church in exchange for the drab brown habit of
the Carmelite order. When I went to visit Sister Mary
Catherine, once Lurlene Romney, she greeted me with a shy
smile at the door of a farmhouse that is now her cloister, the
Carmel of the Immaculate Heart of Mary. It is not in some
distant state, where she would be safe from religious controversy, but on the southeast outskirts of Mormonism's own
Zion, Salt Lake City.

Her vows prohibited her from the ego-temptation of talking
for quotation. She quickly came to understand, however, that
the vows of my trade would prohibit the quoting of anything
she might say on a not-for-attribution basis. So she helped

with facts about the first cousin whom she had known when he was a prankish boy. To check dates, she referred to a thick manuscript on which she works away her free hours. In Romney style, the elderly nun was hewing along the grain of her belief that her whole LDS family lives in error. Her manuscript, an autobiography, bore a defiant title: *To Carmel from Mormonism.*

As in religion, so in politics. George's Uncle Vernon, a lawyer and robust at 71, has been a permanent mainstay of conservative Republicanism. He gets up at five in the morning on election days, and has for 44 years been the first man in line at his neighborhood polling booth. He served as Robert A. Taft's presidential campaign manager for the western states in 1952 and proudly delivered a seconding oration for Taft's nomination at the Chicago convention. He staged a private walkout. The moment Gen. Dwight Eisenhower piled up enough delegate votes to win, Vernon, on crutches from child-hood polio damage to his left leg, plowed majestically off the convention floor and headed straight west for home. There was no need, he felt, to witness any more of the party's fall from honor.

In 1964, Vernon Romney was still the core of the hard core of the Utah GOP's conservatism, and chairman of the state's delegation to the upcoming national Republican convention in San Francisco. His nephew, Michigan's governor, stopped in Salt Lake on the way to the Goldwater show asking support for his resolutions against extremism and for civil rights. Vernon's broad, hard face did not flinch as he and his dele-gates turned George down cold. With George properly put down, the delegates did decide that it wouldn't hurt to stand up when the hometown boy was nominated by Michigan as a favorite son, so long as everybody was careful not to clap too loud.

The Utah delegation's sullen performance in San Francisco

outraged Mrs. Mike Romney, George's sister-in-law. Janice Romney, too moderate a Republican to be trusted with a delegate's badge, was only an alternate. Besides, she had already slugged it out with extremists at home. As a sociology teacher in the city school system, she had fought back when Reed Benson, son of Ezra Taft Benson, first began showing rightwing movies to teachers and to Mormon ward organizations. At one meeting, she bluntly cross-questioned Benson. "If he's the arsenal of democracy," she said, "we're worse off than I thought." She had become more outspoken after young Benson, backed by the religious figure of his apostle father, revealed that he had answered a call to be a paid agent of the John Birch Society. The San Francisco convention merely confirmed Janice's fears about the politics of anguish.

"I decided then and there," she later admitted, "to come home and do something about it if I could." She wheelhorsed for the GOP's gubernatorial candidate that year. By 1965, she had moved up to state vice-chairman, the highest party office open to a woman. Next time George Romney came out, he got a different reception. On his five-state Western tour in 1967, it was party leader Janice who loaded his Salt Lake schedule with five major addresses in a single day, plus press conferences and a public grilling by Protestant, Jewish and Catholic clergymen. Until the Governor's staff vetoed part of her plan, she had George booked to talk while rotating slowly upon a merry-go-round stage in the Valley Theater's big auditorium.

"I don't know if he'll ever speak to us again," she said with a womanly chuckle, "after what we put him through."

Janice Romney's stand against the Right Wing came as no surprise to old friends. She and husband Mike[1] had been in

[1] Mike is the nickname by which people know Miles Pratt Romney. He is a mining engineer, a graduate of Columbia University and

15

arguments before. Mike shook up a Mormon ward (parish) meeting as much as ten years ago in a home-turf struggle on the race issue. A Negro family was bidding on a house near the church. The meeting was called to raise money to buy up the house and keep the neighborhood the way the Book of Mormon describes virtue, "white and delightsome." Mike does not seem like a contentious man. His face is creased by an almost ribald smile and a mule-kick scar, and he does not share brother George's aversion to a cigarette, a cup of coffee, or a convivial Scotch. But that night, Mike stood and preached like a prophet against the purpose of the meeting. He knew he could not win—he could enlist only one ally—but he had to fight. He now lives in a different ward.

"They say that the Romneys are stubborn," says Apostle Marion Romney with the humor hidden in his voice. "But we all say that the Romneys are determined to do the right thing —and everybody else is stubborn."

Then there's the final skeleton, by GOP standards: the family Democrat. Charles Wilcken Romney has, if anything, become more tenacious in his Democratic loyalty since his elder brother, George Wilcken Romney, became a national Republican figure.[1] A lawyer in the Utah attorney general's office, Charles went to the state Democratic convention in April 1967 when Salt Lake City's A. Wally Sandack was

---

executive director of the Utah Mining Association. He is the brother who has been closest to George Romney, and only three years older. I stick to Mike's nickname to keep from confusing him with assorted other Miles Romneys, among them the brothers' great-grandfather from England, their tempestuous grandfather, and the uncle who became the last polygamist on the family tree.

[1] The middle name comes from Charles H. Wilcken, grandfather of George's mother. A German immigrant, he enlisted in the United States Army and marched West in 1856 with the forces sent to conquer the independent and polygamous Mormons. Instead of fighting, he was converted and settled down in Salt Lake.

nominated chairman. One delegate, presumably about to nominate a competitor, took the microphone to attack Sandack on religious grounds. The speaker had barely delivered his first jab—something about a devoted Jew not believing in Jesus—before Charles lunged out of his seat and rushed down the aisle toward the mike.

"You can't do that at a Democratic convention," Charles bellowed.

The startled racist never got his candidate nominated, if he had one. He backed away from Charles. The convention unanimously elected Sandack to be its new state boss. Charles admitted the next week that he had lost his temper and acted on impulse before he had time to think how he might look. But, since religious prejudice dies hard around the Great Salt Lake, he still chewed out fellow Mormons over the thought that a man could be hurt in politics "because of the way he chooses to worship."

The stiff-necked stance goes back as far as anybody has been able to trace the Romney generations, and is today a humorous theme in family folklore. At a Sunday evening service in the Mormon mission at Cambridge, Massachusetts, in 1967, I was sitting with Scott Romney, the Governor's oldest son and a Harvard law student. His father, at Harvard to see the Kennedy School of Government faculty,[1] stood up to preach a brisk sermon. He led off with the story of how the family had tried to control Scott's tendencies to declare his opinions too flatly. The boy's mother once suggested that he preface his views with "In my humble opinion. . . ." Scott was

[1] The Kennedy School faculty found that Romney did not follow the script of the usual dignitary invited up to give opinions on world affairs. Urban expert Daniel P. Moynihan, Democrat and former Assistant Secretary of Labor, said, "Governor Romney is the first visitor who came and asked what *we* thought. He knew something of what each of us had written, and he asked questions."

17

dutiful. Next time, he said, "In my humble but correct opinion. . . ."

The same Scott, when asked if his strict Mormon rules didn't cramp his social style, turned on me with a big smile. "No, just the opposite," he said. "I think maybe people enjoy somebody who's different."

George Romney has been swimming upstream most of his life. As a lobbyist for the old aluminum monopoly, he developed an aversion to concentrated economic power. A leading official in a church that discriminates against Negroes, he has for a quarter-century been a persistent worker for civil rights. At the height of the auto industry's rush to bigger, more powerful cars, he bet everything on the compact (a noun he redefined for the language). At the lowest ebb of the Michigan GOP, he resolved to make it the majority party.

Behind this habit is more than a man of stubborn will trying to reform business and political institutions from within, a practice that earns you the maverick label. There is also, critics charge, a kind of "minority mentality." Romney does not believe that everybody ought to think and act alike so as to assimilate into the smooth mold of a uniform culture. His right to go where belief leads, he knows, depends upon the right of others to take a different route. So he stands for the virtue of human variety, for the richest possible mix of opinions, races, religions and ambitions. "The great achievement of this society," he says doggedly, "will come when we have reached the point that differences are cherished."

That would suit brother Mike just fine. "I have always operated on the premise that Romneys were not descended like other humans," he says. "We descended from the mule."

18

# CHAPTER THREE

# THE EXPERIMENTAL
# PAST

---

"All the weaklings of your tribe," said an exasperated businessman, "died on the trail."

No notion gives George Romney more inward pain than the one generally on sale at GOP functions: rugged individualism. This old reliable chant, either in its primitive purity or in some slickered-up version, induces discomfort that he cannot always hide. "It's nothing," he snaps, "but a political banner to cover up greed."

The spurt of anger means that Romney has been touched at a sensitive point in his complex body of ideas. For all his excitement about the human potential, he seldom uses the word "individual" without a balancing emphasis on "community." This harnessing of two apparent opposites is the key to Romney's thought, to his way of looking at life and of working. "Though the community cannot develop without the contribution of the individual," he says, "neither can the individual reach his full potential without the support, or at least the experience, of the community. Each owes a debt to the other."

19

The underlying discipline to his belief, then, is an ideological brand of double-entry bookkeeping. Many a reporter, brought up in a depersonalized world, has gone away from him puzzled or contemptuous. Romney has trouble putting across his community concept because it rises out of his Mormon experience, where it is obscured by exotic religious detail or by the rural idiom. Yet, in his curiously intense life of action and hard reading, he has entered the plusses and minuses of each new insight on both sides of the individual-community ledger.

That same approach may be the best one for getting at him and his kind. The willful Romneys told about in the previous chapter were not anonymous faces in *The Lonely Crowd*.[1] They were, and are, strong people because they grew in strong communities. And, Romney would add, strong families. Unless you keep this in mind, any report on the Romneys and what they took from their past will be superficial.

They were descended, not from Mike Romney's mule, but from a long line of English carpenters. Only a few of them, the chief family historian admits, had ever "climbed from the common level of the family to great heights."[2] The climbers included a 16th century Lord Mayor of London, inventor

[1] David Riesman, *The Lonely Crowd* (New Haven: Yale University Press, 1950). Mr. Riesman kindly let me use private notes he made during his brief encounter, at Brigham Young University, with the *communitas* concept that is implicit in Mormonism and explicit in Romney politics. Now a professor of social science at Harvard, Riesman continues his highly original search for institutional solutions to the urban identity crisis—in "other-directed" people—that he defined for a generation of researchers. He was, therefore, the first certified member of the intellectual establishment, so far as I know, who sensed how much might be learned from a study of George Romney's thought and action.

[2] Thomas C. Romney, *The Story of Miles Park Romney* (Independence, Mo.: Zion's Printing and Publishing Co., 1948) pp. 1–3.

John Romney, often credited with putting the first spokes in a wheel, 18th century portrait painter George Romney, plus an unidentified farmer who bred up a strain of sheep still known as Romneys.

There's not much to learn from these few success stories. Just about anybody could, with the help of an agreeable genealogist, find bigger fruit on his family tree. The London mayor got the customary good conduct medal for his job, a knighthood. The spoked wheel, obvious enough once somebody made the first one,[1] was lighter than the solid wood discs that people had been rolling around on since the Sumerians invented vehicles *circa* 3,000 B.C. Because the spoke led in time to prairie schooners, bikes and cars, inventor Romney may have done more to bring on the pains of mobility, some argue, than did the salesman of the compact car. Painter George Romney's contribution was less ambiguous. He and Joshua Reynolds and Thomas Gainsborough, the English Triumvirate, laid about as much elegance on canvas as anybody before or since. When Vice-President Hubert H. Humphrey paid a political call on French President Charles de Gaulle, he found a George Romney already there, hanging on the wall.

As for Romney rams and ewes, they still have big heads and a reputation for thriving through uncertain weather.

It is the carpenters, "the common level of the family," who provide the early hints into the inner workings of George Romney. They were literal-minded idealists who forever worked to make the lumber of reality follow the blueprints of belief, or the other way around. Take, for instance, the unholy

[1] John Romney's claim on the first spoke is, of course, a legitimate subject for scholarly contention. For our purposes, the point is that he found a way to make a better wheel than anybody had seen in those parts of England.

trouble Miles Romney, founder of the United States branch of the family, got into over a spiral staircase.

Born July 15, 1806, at Dalton-in-Furness, in northern England, Miles soon became adept at building stairs that coiled around and stood without a centerpost or visible underpinning. Clever though he was in his interlocking design, Miles seemed to be up against one serious problem: To stand right, his stairs apparently needed to complete a circle, 360°, from the bottom step to the top. This engineering quirk never troubled him until long after he became a Mormon convert and moved to the United States. At the order of Prophet Brigham Young, he eventually bossed the building of a new meeting house at St. George, Utah. His pride and joy, of course, was a spiral stair rising to the balcony, a big gallery. Young came to inspect, and declared that the gallery must be lowered two feet. Miles said no. That was a word seldom heard by Young, especially on one of the building programs that he had revealed as God's own spoken word. "So two immovable objects met," says George Romney, who has heard about this encounter all his life. Miles, more stubborn than dogmatic, hunted for a compromise between the laws of physics and the authority of the church.

He managed. He kept the staircase as it was, and dropped the gallery two feet as ordered. At the top of the spiral stairs, he installed two feet of ordinary steps marching back down to the lowered gallery. Generations of Mormons have climbed over this theological hump like sheep clearing a fence.

Miles Romney was George Romney's great-grandfather. He and his wife, one Elizabeth Gaskell, were among the first English converts to Mormonism. It started by chance. Walking to market in Lancashire one day in 1837, when Miles was 31, they wandered up to a street-corner crowd gathered around a strange new kind of missionary. His name, they later learned, was Orson Hyde. What seemed odd, in this otherwise plausible American, was the way he identified himself: He was a saint here on earth, albeit a Latter-day Saint, or LDS. Mormons have never liked to be called "Mormons." That name, all too easily confused with morons, was hung on them by non-Mormons, whom the Saints called "Gentiles" even if they happened to be Jews.

The Mormon church was then only seven years old. Founded at Fayette, upstate New York, in 1830, it had spread through converts to Kirtland, Ohio, and to a frontier community near Independence, Missouri, inside what are now the expanded city limits of Kansas City. Mormonism's founding Saint, Joseph Smith, needed thousands of recruits to build his vision of Zion in Missouri. So he had sent two of his original twelve apostles, Heber Kimball and Orson Hyde, to England on the first LDS foreign mission. Before Hyde sailed back to the States—and into church trouble—he had the Romneys on the way to conversion. Both were baptized in 1839, and within a year were ready to spend all they had on a chancy 51-day voyage aboard the *Sheffield* with five children to join the "gathering in" of the Saints.

Were they religious nuts? The doctrinal overlay of any religion generally prevents the outsider from sensing what it means to the believer. You see only the package. Whatever else Joseph Smith asserted, he was denying the pessimistic doctrines then widely preached, from original sin to infant damnation and human depravity. In their place, he set forth an unflinching belief in the grandeur of man—head, heart and good strong back. "The glory of God is intelligence," he announced on May 6, 1833.[1] If a man used his unlimited capacities in harmony with other turned-on souls, he would find that there were no practical limits on joy, accomplish-

[1] *The Doctrine and Covenants of the Church of Jesus Christ of Latter-day Saints* (Salt Lake City: The Church of Jesus Christ of Latter-day Saints, 1953) Section 93, Verse 36, p. 160.

23

ment and love. He could be an earthly saint, and take his acquired wisdom with him to higher exaltation in heaven. In the years when a young United States was lunging toward wild experiments and Manifest Destiny, the young Joe Smith preached the most blatantly hopeful doctrine of man ever to become the basis for an organized religion.[1]

So Miles Romney took his place near the end of the centuries-long line of religious groups who came here hunting a better place to be. Not yet a victim of religious persecution, he arrived with his tools to lend a hand in the first true utopia, he thought, and to grace it with magic stairways.

He was about to get more work than he bargained for. He and the next three generations after him had to help build, from bare sand up, not one but five new social and economic systems, each an embryonic city. And five times, they were driven out. In just sixty years, they tried several combinations of competition and cooperation—from rugged individualism to village communism—in experiments designed to resolve the puzzle of the person's role in the larger community.

The Romneys were landed at New Orleans by a mutinous ship's crew, and boarded a riverboat up the Mississippi. Miles caught a fever and was given up for dead, but Elizabeth had him carried ashore on a blanket litter and slowly nursed him back to consciousness. Epidemics of river fever and diphtheria were but one of the hazards ahead. The Mormons, they learned, had been burned and beaten out of Missouri. The Romneys joined them at the Illinois town of Commerce,

[1] Catholic sociologist Thomas F. O'Dea, head of the University of California's Institute of Religious Studies, is the leading non-Mormon authority on LDS. In his book *The Mormons* (Chicago: The University of Chicago Press, 1957), he richly documents the "peculiarly American" ambitions of LDS doctrines. In trying to teach me, a standard-brand Protestant, how to interpret the swinging things in the Mormon tradition, the dapper Dr. O'Dea resorted to both sociology and hippie talk.

which they were trying to turn into a great new city they called Nauvoo, meaning "a beautiful plantation." Worse yet, lynch mobs and murderers, to say nothing of the Missouri militia, had roused in the would-be saints a sense of outrage for which the only modern parallel is Elijah Muhammed's Nation of Islam, the Black Muslims. Indeed, Joseph Smith was reported to be comparing himself with the warlike "Mahomet," as the court documents spelled it. Two of the twelve apostles had apostatized and sworn in affidavits that Smith was using an adaptation of Mahomet's warlike slogan: "Joseph Smith or the Sword. . . ."

One of these two former leaders who testified against Smith was none other than Orson Hyde, the missionary who had brought the Romneys into the church. Hyde[1] and other peaceful men had been shocked by the organization of a secret blood brotherhood within the church known as the Sons of Dan, or Danites. They meant business. Sworn to defend Mormonism from Gentile mobs, these "avenging angels" were also pledged, rumor said, to kill any converts who tried to defect. The most famous Danite, Orrin Porter Rockwell, was a small zealot with a black beard and hair that fell down to his shoulders like a chain-mail helmet. He was a regiment. Once when arrested in Illinois, he was holed up with guns enough to fire 71 rounds without reloading, plus an array of knives. He became known as "The Immortal Mormon" because he gunned down so many foes—and was credited with many more—before a natural heart failure contradicted his nickname at age 65.[2] The Danites were ominously present in Nauvoo, though Rockwell was away for some months. He

[1] Hyde was disfellowshipped (excommunicated) but later accepted back into the fold. He then led a mission to Palestine.

[2] Harold Schindler, *Orrin Porter Rockwell: Man of God, Son of Thunder* (Salt Lake City: University of Utah Press, 1966) p. 362.

was in jail charged (but never convicted) with shooting the governor of Missouri.

In this lively atmosphere, Miles Romney went peacefully to work as a master builder on the Nauvoo temple. The incredible energy of the LDS, an entire community mobilized for results, transformed the sickly river village into a thriving little city of 16,000, bigger than Chicago, in less than four years. It was precisely the expansionist energy of the Saints—in farming, business and political bloc-voting—that always made their neighbors envious and nervous. And to make matters more tense, disaffectors spread the word that a few of the elders had expanded the institution of matrimony to embrace plural wives. You can imagine how the press worked over the little evidence it had. Nor did Prophet Smith pour oil on the waters by announcing that he would run for President of the United States—the first and only Mormon candidate until George Romney.

Smith did not live to see political defeat. On June 27, 1844, locked in a Carthage jail on a trumped-up charge of treason, he and his brother Hyrum were cornered by an Illinois lynch mob and killed in cold blood. The Saints, instead of going after revenge, buried their prophet and returned sadly to their Nauvoo labors. But, leaderless and splintering, they were soon under armed attack again by the enemies around. Brigham Young, Smith's successor, led the Saints, now 10,000 to 15,000 strong and growing in adversity, on the westward trek to the Great Salt Lake Basin. Here was a site so desolate that the Mormons could hope to build their own society without having to fight their neighbors. Though hundreds died along the way, the LDS column marched with a brass band and, when weather permitted, stopped to hold dances.

"I didn't figure it out for a while," an exasperated company executive once said to George Romney. "All the weaklings of your tribe died on the trail."

Miles Romney, too poor to outfit a wagon for the trip, went to work in Iowa and then Missouri, mainly in St. Louis. But in October 1850, stubborn as ever, he arrived with his growing family in Salt Lake City. He housed the children in his wagon frame and took his tools over to the site of the biggest Mormon temple of all.[1] He became foreman of the public workshop in Temple Square. He soon went back to England on a two-year preaching mission, came home and prospered. But in 1862 he sold his Salt Lake house to go on the last and worst job of his life. Brigham Young had "called" him to superintend construction of a tabernacle and a temple in St. George, a barren patch of alkali and quicksand in the southern end of Utah known as "Dixie." So he built the last spiral stairway, the one Young wanted him to cut short, and died at 71 after falling from a tabernacle window while working.

A few years ago, Miles' great-grandson George ran into a university researcher whose sociology team had studied the LDS projects in Dixie. The group had been trying to figure out why these tiny colonies succeeded against long odds. After reading the study, the Governor provided his own pat but accurate summary: "Basically, it was because they had faith in what they were doing and had goals that enabled them to work together."

So fortified, he knew, the Dixie colonies had been able to engage in uninhibited social experimentation. Few men had been more heavily involved than his grandfather, Miles Park Romney, son of carpenter Miles and also a builder. Miles

[1] The Temple, "built to last 1,000 years," sits in Temple Square opposite the Tabernacle, whence the Mormon Choir broadcasts each Sunday morning. The Temple, used for religious ceremonies, can be entered only by Mormons in good standing; the Tabernacle or meeting house is, like most Mormon buildings, open to anyone.

27

Park and other Dixie colonists braced themselves when, in 1874, the general authorities of the church revealed that the Lord wished them to organize their labor and property under the "United Order of Enoch." They knew the general theory. Like many other sects of that day, especially the Campbellites, the LDS church had for years cherished the ideal of a pure community where all productive property would be held in common by the faithful. No selfishness would be allowed. Like the Amana communities of Iowa, the United Order was religious communism, Mormon brand.

This Romney, a young man long on opinion and short on temper, showed little enthusiasm for the planned economy until Prophet Brigham Young, on a visit, persuaded him as to its merits:

"Brother Romney," said Young, "would you like to go to heaven?"

"Yes, Brother Brigham, I think I should like to go there."

"Then you must join the Order," said church president Young, "and take charge of all the building operations in southern Utah."

So the volatile Miles Park signed the Order's articles and moved his contracting business into a cooperative corporation owned by the St. George community. The system had to be total, rigid. "There are only two ways to discipline an economy," Miles Park's grandson later argued. "You have to rely on competition, or absolute authority." Miles Park, made a bishop in St. George, reluctantly became an agent of absolute church authority. He helped fix the prices for all labor and products. He organized every man in the building trades under a closed-shop labor union, with himself as superintendent. Sample articles in the strict union charter:

> Art. 2 The members of the Union will work by day or job, wages to be fixed by the Union and subject to a general scale

28

of price which may be established hereafter in the community . . .
Art. 8 All contracts for work shall be under immediate supervision of Superintendent.

Somewhat more radical was Miles Park's family commune. It, too, began with a strong hint from Brigham Young ("Brother Romney, I want you to take another wife."). His first wife, Hannah Hood Hill, was sturdy enough. As a girl of seven, she had walked barefoot and bareheaded from Iowa to Utah behind a column of horseless converts with push-carts. Hannah and her husband accepted their new marital duty as if it were another long march. "If anything will make a woman's heart ache, it is for her husband to take another wife," she said before her death, "but I put my trust in my Heavenly Father and prayed and pled with him to give me strength to bear this trial . . . that I might be of support to my husband."

Few husbands, and fewer first wives, went into polygamy with enthusiasm.[1] Though it was an extension of Mormonism's very non-Puritan belief in the goodness of the flesh, the principle was generally viewed as a final test of faith, much as Buddhist monks view self-immolation. Brigham Young had to exhort the reluctant. "We must gird up our loins and

[1] The famous exception was Joseph Smith himself, originator of the practice after the manner of the biblical patriarchs. He was timid about explaining this revelation of the Lord to his first wife, a stern soul named Emma. But, once started, he followed through with customary vigor. A present-day Mormon scholar, who has pored over the Temple records, has identified no less than 86 women who might have been married to Smith before his martyrdom. Other scholars settle for a modest 48. The score was difficult to keep. After Smith was killed, several hundred other religious ladies were married to him in "vicarious" ceremonies that would, they believed, let them join his big, happy family in "the Celestial Kingdom" that he envisioned.

29

fulfill this," he said, "just as we would any other duty." One of Mrs. George Romney's forebears begged off by asking to be assigned some equally dreadful chore; sent as a missionary to the Old South, he caught a fever and died. Monogamous Governor Romney, in high spirits at 6:15 A.M. on a golf course, discussed the burden his grandfather had taken up. "If a fellow were just looking for fun," Romney said, "he sure wouldn't marry extra wives."

Miles Park's second wife, Caroline Lambourne, was pretty and jealous, and resentful of the hard life at St. George. When Caroline skipped back to Salt Lake after her second child, Hannah and the shared husband followed her to beg in vain that she please come home. The third one, Catherine Jane Cottam, worked out much better. One reason: While Miles Park and his oldest daughter were away for a few days at the Temple wedding, Hannah worked herself to exhaustion—and a stillborn child—preparing the new bride's part of the house. "I preferred to have Catherine live with me," Hannah explained, "as I felt I could not have the father of my children away from our fireside at night."[1] With new rooms forever being added, the Romney place, known as the White House, kept growing.

And the family kept growing to fill it. The recorded total, perhaps understated, was four wives and thirty children. Governor George Romney is one of 207 grandchildren. Last time he counted, he told the 1963 Gridiron dinner, he had 237 living first cousins.[2] Adding the in-laws and children and

[1] "Three Pioneer Women Speak," *Our Pioneer Heritage,* ed. K. B. Carter (February, 1962) p. 268.

[2] He counted cousins while ribbing John F. Kennedy, who laughed at many a family joke during his last Gridiron dinner. "Mr. President, as we have been reminded again tonight, you have quite a family," said Romney. "As a matter of fact, the way the Kennedys are over-

grandchildren, he has a kindred force of 2,000 to 3,000 scattered from Boston to Tahiti. He seldom goes to church anywhere without shaking hands with a relative, often a stranger.

By 1881, things were going fairly well in St. George. Miles Park had several business sidelines: a planing mill, a contract to carry the mail and a lawyer's license. He rose in the Mormon militia from captain to colonel. He became president of the area's Mutual Improvement Association, helped found the public library and organized a drama group of which he was the leading actor. He staged anything from Shakespeare to *Uncle Tom's Cabin.* He was one of those joyous souls who hug life so hard that they upset the pale people. The local church records contain a few solemn grumblings against him, and hints that he did not teetotal every day of his life. On the dance floor, he was in celestial glory. The Saints frowned on ballroom "round dancing," but Romney was an alkali-flats Arthur Murray at doing the squares: quadrilles, minuets, lancers, French fours and Virginia reels.

As might be expected, once the living was easy, Brigham Young got some more orders from the Lord. So the Romneys pulled up stakes, sold what they could not load on wagons, and forded the mud-red Colorado heading southeast. They followed the jagged banks of the Little Colorado above Grand Canyon, pushed on south of the Painted Desert and Petrified Forest. It was better than 320 mountain miles to St. Johns, Arizona. The assignment: build a colony to help Bishop David K. Udall[1] hold Mormon strength against new Gentile

running Washington it is a good thing it was the Mormon Church and not the Catholic Church that practiced polygamy . . . if you thought it was tough finding jobs for Bobby and Teddy and the rest, just think of having to find jobs for 237 first cousins."

[1] Forebear of Democratic Secretary of the Interior Stewart L. Udall, who was born in St. Johns, Arizona.

31

immigration. Or, as Miles Park Romney wrote in one of his regular dispatches back to Salt Lake's *Deseret News,* to "redeem the waste places of Arizona, and lengthen the cords and strengthen the Stakes of Zion."

Everybody worked. First wife Hannah scrounged up beans, bread and gravy through the long, cold winters. Fourth wife Annie started a school. Miles Park bought land, built homes and a meeting house, took over and edited the weekly *Orion Era.* His sons set type and turned the hand press. With his all-purpose family, he was a sort of prefab colony. He and Bishop Udall struggled to hold land titles in hostile courts. Soon he persuaded the church to send in another 100 reinforcements. By then he had provoked a few Gentiles into the theory that he ought to be hanged.

But he had things going his way until the United States marshals, armed with the new anti-Mormon law, began to chase him with warrants charging polygamy, "lewd cohabitation." Though he was arrested, he was not one of the Saints sentenced to what they called "the American Siberia in Detroit," the hated Federal prison. He could not be convicted because his devoted wives outwitted the marshals who tried to capture them to witness against him. They lived in a sort of underground hidden by other Mormons. Once when a marshal knocked at the door with a warrant, Hannah quickly noted that the names were spelled wrong on the document. She stated that no such women were there—while the extra wives slipped out back and hid in a dry canal.

Hounded and helpless, Miles Park took some of the family back to Utah and on April 7, 1885, joined an exploring party to hunt land for a safe colony south of the border in Mexico. When they found a site, the redoubtable Hannah again had a few things to do. With a baby in arms and two young sons —one of them 14-year-old Gaskell, Governor Romney's father —Hannah drove two wagons 355 miles right across the burning warpath of Apache chief Geronimo. Several brave men prudently refused to make the trip. Coming upon three riders who had been killed by the Apaches, Hannah calmly had the boys pull the shoes off the dead horses, and shod her own lame animals. She was five-feet-two and wore seven petticoats. Her abiding worry in all-night vigils over the children was to keep them from sensing the reasonable terror she felt.

She reached Mexico, with her cookstove and the farm implements, in time for the men to plant their 1886 crop. Third wife Catherine came and wove rawhide chair bottoms. Fourth wife Annie arrived, had a child, and three weeks later opened school. Within a few years, the whole colony of Saints had combined their talents to get civilization going again. Miles Park staged his favorite Shakespeare, *Othello,* and claimed the privilege of playing the Black Moor's tragic lead.

The Mormon saga, for all its distracting oddities, provides the most recent United States success at deliberately creating vital communities, not just housing, on a wholesale basis. The gift has been lost. In the slums as in the suburbs of the expressway age, people seem unable to discover the underlying causes of social disorganization and how to cure them. Part of the fault lies in a too-willing assumption that the institutions of business or government now on hand are absolute and complete. In this sense, few of us have built a home of our own, and nobody feels at home. The intellectual furniture, a crude clash of Robber Baron individualism and program liberalism, no less tattered, has become too comfortable to change. Not many try.

George Romney, talking to Brigham Young University students a few years ago, raised the question as to whether the United Order might again be tested on a local level. Though no advocate of community property, he pointed out that in a country where the central government does not run everything, you can build a community of your own choosing. That sounds wildly ambitious in this age. But Romney, sensitized by his family's experiments, has been more or less consciously fighting to make habitable places for people inside big business, megalopolis and modern government.

# CHAPTER FOUR

# GROWING UP
# IN A FAMILY SQUAD

---

"One of the most serious problems we face as Americans," Romney decided, "is the envy of other people."

Born in a displaced persons' colony in Mexico, July 8, 1907, George Wilcken Romney started out with one handicap: He had to wear a girl-baby's clothes. His mother, Mrs. Gaskell Romney, had three boys already. Hoping for a change, she had whipped up nothing but frilly gowns with ruffled yokes. Now she had to get busy on something suitable for another blocky man-child.

Mrs. Romney was, in fact, to make her career out of boys. She bore six in all and did not have a girl until Meryl, her seventh and last child, was born in 1917. She had by then become so entangled in the boy business that she spent the rest of her life teaching and mothering any small males in reach. She had a formula: "Loads of honest, loving praise never hurt a boy."

The birth was more like a family hoedown than a hospital

delivery. In medical charge was Aunt Aggie Thurber, chief midwife of the neighborhood and a relative of the laboring mother. Among the other women on hand to help was Aunt Amy Pratt, Mrs. Romney's maiden sister. George's father, exercising his office in the Mormon priesthood, blessed and named the child in a ceremony like a christening. And Bounce, a jealous Newfoundland dog, was let in to inspect the new addition while the rest of the family held its breath. Bounce had fangs for strangers. But he accepted the intruder, gown and all, on one casual sniff.

Life was warm and happy. It was a place where healthy boys put their fat fingers down in vats of homemade cheese to scoop up the fresh curds. The pressures of exile from the United States had strengthened family bonds. As the next few years were to prove, the Romney households had become mobile squads able to survive hardship and radical change that would have crippled people who tried to stand alone. Out of it all came a Romney insistence that sounded, to news-hungry reporters, like a preachy platitude. People could survive the unprecedented strains of the late 20th century, the Governor kept repeating, only if we restore the living fiber of the family.

The Mormon colonies had prospered on rich tracts bought from the Mexican Government. In the 22 years since the hunted polygamists had found a refuge, they had built eight small but healthy communities well to the south of El Paso, Texas. Six were in Chihuahua, two in Sonora. Only in one had they suffered disaster, but made up for it.

The big trouble had come in the headquarters village of Colonia Juarez. George's grandfather, Miles Park Romney, had settled there—and been suckered along with everybody else. On the ruins of an ancient aqueduct system left by a lost tribe, the men had built a dam and canal to irrigate the crops. They had put up homes, Annie Romney's school, a tithing house and other public buildings. Then, without warning, a rich Mexican politico had invalidated their title survey and claimed the site. So they had been forced to evacuate, move on a few miles up the Casa Grandes River, and start again by digging a three-mile canal. Oppression always inspired the Saints, and they finished the formidable new project in one year.

Each family was assigned a section of the canal to cut. Miles Park, who had been reduced to rawhide sandals when he came to Mexico, now wore a fresh white shirt every day; his sons did his share of the canal, six feet deep and several rods long, with one of those old horse-drawn pond-scrapers. No man who ever wrestled with these monstrous, unhandy scoops could regret the day when the bulldozer would make them obsolete. While son Will drove the team, son Gaskell, 16, hefted the handles to set the blade and flung his body around to control the scraper's bucking.

Gaskell was the fifth of ten children that Miles Park had by Hannah, his first wife and, therefore, the one recognized as legitimate under United States statutes. During tough times, Hannah and her children moved up into the desolate beauty of a small valley in the Sierra Madre mountains. They farmed a place called Cliff Ranch along with its owners, the Helamen Pratt family. Dangers there were even greater than they guessed. Soon after the Romneys and Pratts moved back down to the warmer colonies, the Indians roving the high ranges massacred the next residents of Cliff Ranch. But danger breeds romance, and young Gaskell Romney married a Pratt girl, Anna Amelia. Both were of monogamy persuasion.

Anna Pratt Romney, George's mother, belonged to the bluestockings of the Mormon establishment. Though the Romneys had been at the local contractor level, the Pratts had written some of the wilder chapters of the Saint saga. Parley P. Pratt, grandfather to Anna and a great-grandfather to

37

George, had led the LDS equivalent of the charge up San Juan Hill. It was in the 1838 battle of Crooked River, where sixty Saints, mainly Danites, attacked a marauding contingent of the Missouri militia. When the LDS commander caught a rifle ball in the bladder, Parley P. carried on the charge and routed the plundering Gentiles. Pratt's triumph, one of the few the Saints ever scored in combat, scared the Missouri governor into calling up 2,000 more militiamen from five divisions. His orders: The Mormons "must be exterminated or driven from the State. . . ." At Haun's Mill a few days later, 240 militia butchered 19 Mormons. An official exterminator let Sardius Smith, age 10, beg for life before he blew the child's brains out. "Nits," he said, "make lice." That's when Pratt and the rest had moved over to Illinois.

Parley P.'s brother, Orson Pratt, had led the scouting party that picked Salt Lake Valley to be the next Zion. He was also the apostle chosen to announce the polygamy doctrine in public. Formerly a Campbellite (Lyndon B. Johnson's denomination) preacher, Orson became the author of "As the Dew from Heaven" and other popular Mormon hymns, and the prolific theologian of the early church. Some of his works, such as an essay very close to the present notion of evolution, were considered too heretical and destroyed. But his chief philosophical thoughts were published—and given the practical test that most philosophers only dream of. He was the intellectual architect of "The Kingdom of God," the highly developed concept of a God-run but equalitarian government called "theo-democracy." The Mormons planned their separate nation of Deseret on this model before they really accepted a place in the Union. Pratt also belonged to the Council of Fifty, an inner ruling body so secret that its existence has only lately been proved by skeptical Mormon scholars. Since the Council was designed to take over the United

States in the fullness of time, Orson might be considered as much a traitor as my Confederate great-uncle.

"The Kingdom of God is an order of Government established by divine authority," Pratt wrote. "It is the only legal government that can exist in any part of the Universe. All other governments are illegal and unauthorized. God, having made all beings and worlds, has the supreme right to govern them by his own laws and by officers of his own appointment. Any people attempting to govern themselves by laws of their own making and by officers of their own appointment are in direct rebellion against the Kingdom of God."[1]

Descended from such fiery brothers, by way of a calm and genial father, Anna Pratt Romney would stint on food and clothes to buy books and music lessons for the children. "My husband has this terrific drive, and I'm sure it comes from his mother," says Lenore Romney. "She was a wonderful woman."

She had the distinct air of a patrician—and solid skills as a seamstress and cook. When Gaskell went on the usual two-year mission, to preach in Pennsylvania and New York, Anna supported the children by selling cream-filled candies and peanut brittle. She sold enough, in fact, to send her husband pocket change. Her homemade bread, however, provides the clearest insight into her value system. Proud as any cook of the brown loaves she lifted out of the oven, filling the house with a bakeshop smell, she did not drive away the sons who came with watering mouths. She would tear the hot crust from a perfect loaf and slather it with butter.

By the time George was born, Gaskell had built a two-story house of home-kiln brick in Colonia Dublan, 12 miles northeast of Colonia Juarez. On the same half-block, he operated a planing mill making window frames and doors. More im-

[1] Orson Pratt, "The Kingdom of God," *Series of Pamphlets* (Liverpool: Franklin D. Richards, 1851), Part I, p. 1.

portant to the colony's boys, he had a turning lathe that could spin out baseball bats. And, a mile and a half from town, he had a good farm.

The Saints were still improving their social and economic system by conscious decision and practice. They slowly untangled the tight red tape inherited from the United Order. Their cooperative scheme still made it possible, as in Utah, to build and make optimum use of canals. But the land, originally held as a communal tract, had been bought in pieces by individual farmers. Businesses like Gaskell's mill operated under the profit discipline. The colony co-op, Union Mercantile, was now expanding through individual ownership. While preserving a close community life, and building a college in Colonia Juarez, they were gaining the higher production of private enterprise and the variety of personal choice.

The most affluent family in town bought a car, a chain-drive Buick. After it broke down beyond repair, George and the boys threw lassoes over the radiator and pulled it around by horsepower. Now and then, there would be an excursion by train up to El Paso. "I tasted my first store bread there, and saw my first motion picture," recalls Romney. "The picture was a comedy with bathing beauties. The bread tasted like cake."

When he was four, George had a pony of his own, a small Indian cayuse called Monte, so fat that the boy's chubby legs stuck straight out to the sides. Most of the standard biographical material on the Governor plays up the day Monte threw him. Knocked cold, he was taken to the house and tenderly laid on a bed. While his mother went out to fix a comforting bowl of ice cream, he slipped away and climbed back on Monte.

George's brothers are puzzled over why this event has been considered unusual enough to merit mention. "What else would you expect a farm boy to do?" asks Mike. Douglas, the second-oldest brother, was thrown against a fence post when riding out to get the cows. He caught his horse and herded the cows home before he stopped to bother about the arm that the post had broken.

There was room in this busy little world for broad comedy, as when Junius Romney was caught drinking a bottle of hard liquor. Like the Methodists and Baptists of that day, the Saints had not yet gone to hardline teetotaling.[1] The admonitions against whiskey, tobacco, tea and coffee were still considered Words of Wisdom in LDS doctrine, not strict requirements for anybody allowed in the temple. Junius, one of George's 14 uncles, worked for a store and lived in Colonia Juarez. He went home one day with a flu virus so mean that he accepted a friend's offer of some medicinal alcohol, a bottle of tequila. He was 29, and he'd had only one drink in his life up to then, during a typhoid epidemic. About the time he had manfully downed most of the flu medicine, an unexpected knock drew him to the door.

There stood Anthony J. Ivins, president of the whole stake (diocese) in Mexico. (At 89, Mr. Romney still shuddered as he recounted his horror to me.) "You couldn't have come at a worse time," said Junius, holding forth the bottle so as not to add hypocrisy to his sins. "But since you're already here, Brother Ivins, come on in." His dismay deepened when he discovered that Ivins, now an apostle and called to Salt Lake, wanted Junius to take his place as president. Junius, accepting the honor, knew in a second of dazzling clarity that no matter how sick he might ever get, his second drink had also been his last.

[1] That happened soon after the Temperance Movement possessed Methodism and other denominations. But Mormonism has stayed abstemious, just as it has held to the practice of excluding Negroes from a place in its priesthood.

41

On the morning of March 5, 1911, the crash of distant cannon announced the end of the good life in Mexico. Francisco I. Madero, an idealistic aristocrat educated in the United States, was starting his revolution six miles from Colonia Dublan at Casas Grandes, a town known in Mexican history as the customary place to start a revolution. Madero had a bad first day. While Aunt Amy Pratt tried to keep the older children's attention at school, George was home peering at rebel stragglers retreating through the village streets. "They were slouchily dressed like the Viet Cong today," he remembers, "armed with pistols, guns and ammunition belts." He also remembers that they won.

The rebels and Federals seesawed back and forth across the colony three times before Madero won a decisive victory up near El Paso. He boarded a train for a triumphal tour to take over the government down in Mexico City. When he whistle-stopped through Dublan, he patted George and other kids on the head.

Much as the colonists admired reformer Madero, he let loose the forces that would put them out of business. In February 1912, Pascual Orozco, a Marxist and disappointed Madero lieutenant, organized counterrevolutionary units called "Red Flaggers." The northern states were soon crawling with Flaggers led by chiefs such as General Jose Inez Salazar and the legendary Pancho Villa. The irregulars raided Mormon homes and stores, butchered cattle and stole horses. Nine men and women were murdered. Parents tried to keep their fears from infecting the children. "They weren't talking it around the kids," Romney says. Gaskell's sons herded their 14 head of horses into a thick clump of trees down by the Rio Casas Grandes. George sometimes got to help carry food down to his brothers—picnic-like—and check on Monte. As it happened, Monte was one cayuse able to take care of himself. Even if his front legs were tied together by a standard

42

foot-long leather hobble, he had the knack of loping along without a stumble. The rebels finally made off with him; next morning, Monte was waiting at the Romney stable in a pair of bandit hobbles.

Uncle Junius Romney, the sober president, had the burden of power. Night and day he rode the region to keep in touch with the colonies, to stand up to rebel General Salazar and to help hold off raiders. Not satisfied with his supply of shotguns and hunting rifles, he sent two men, one a Romney, back to the States for 47 new Mauser rifles. All the while, Salazar was demanding that all Mormon guns be turned over to his troops, a move which would have left the men helpless to defend their families and property. Salazar had obviously come to the same conclusion. Suddenly, while he negotiated with Junius in Casas Grandes, his cavalry surrounded Dublan on three sides. From the cattleyards above the town, Red Flaggers trained down four cannon and seven machine guns. Junius, rushing back, maneuvered for time to get the women and children out of harm's way. He made a show of surrender. The Mormons turned over all their guns—all, that is, that they didn't have to have. They hauled from their attics a collector's dream of elderly flintlocks, plus enough modern firearms to imply compliance, but many kept their best personal rifles and all the Mausers.

That night, Saturday, July 27, 1912, the exodus began. A few families caught the Mexico Northwestern train for El Paso. They became the first of 2,300 refugees to reach Texas in three days. Gaskell Romney's eldest son Maurice carried the family's quota of baggage—three bedrolls and two suitcases—to the Union Mercantile platform down by the Dublan railroad station. All day Sunday, Mrs. Romney, very pregnant with sixth son Charles (the future angered Democrat), stood with hundreds more waiting for a train that didn't come. Finally, she got on a chair car early Monday with eight-

year-old Mike, five-year-old George and two-year-old Lawrence. The children feasted quietly on beef and homemade
cheese. Maurice, 14, and Douglas, 11, rode up front on a
flatcar. The family had $25 to start a new life.

Gaskell and 234 other men of the colonies stayed behind
with Junius hoping to hold off looters until Mexican Government troops put down the rebellion. No luck. About a week
later, Gaskell and a friend volunteered to ride rear guard for a
retreating column of armed Mormons with 500 horses. The
two fought off pursuing rebels and rode 150 desert miles in
two days to join their families at DP camps in El Paso.

The colonists had made the mistake of planting their few
stalks of plenty in a field of poverty. "We were the first displaced persons of the 20th century," believes George Romney.
"I was run out of Mexico with my parents because of the envy
of the Mexican people. My people were as poor as they were,
but through knowledge and industry made the deserts bloom
as the rose. But we didn't communicate and help others ade-
quately and just got run out. One of the most serious problems
we face as Americans is the envy of other people. . . .
With our national wealth and power, we have to be very careful how we throw our weight around."

Pancho Villa, operating out of the colony area, eventually
provoked the United States by a raid into New Mexico. General John J. Pershing headquartered at Colonia Dublan when
he led American troops in pursuit of the Villiastas, only to
find that the guerillas faded into the landscape and were protected by other Mexicans. Childhood experience with guerillas
later caused Candidate Romney considerable trouble. Much of
his discomfort over the United States role in Vietnam came
from a realization, out of years of family discussion, that regular armed units from an alien country face a near-impossible
hunting job against native terrorists. When a French-
Canadian reporter, aware of Romney's background, asked why

the United States had not learned from Pershing's failure, Romney finessed the question. He later told aides that, while the situations were not exactly parallel, the reporter was on to a line of questions that would be hard to answer.

After the exodus, the family automatically went into survival drill. Maurice ran telegrams. Douglas carried newspapers. Mike, the eight-year-old, begged his mother for a nickel carfare to go job-hunting, too. She would not insult his pride. He came proudly back that afternoon as a department store cashboy drawing $2.50 a week. By the time Gaskell, bearded and dusty, found his family, they were in a borrowed home, and every boy more than five years old had become a breadwinner. George was still in Hannah-made blouses that were striped like bed ticking.

Like the generations before him, Gaskell took up the carpenter's tools. He earned enough to transport his brood—six boys after Charles' birth—to a rented house in downtown Los Angeles, at Twenty-first and Main. They discovered among their neighbors such urban luxuries as bathrooms. When George brought home a strip of toilet paper given him by a friend, his mother thought he had stolen it. "She whipped me until I admitted the crime, though I hadn't committed it," he says.

For the next ten years, Gaskell combined forces with his brother, George Samuel Romney, science teacher but also a carpenter, of course, and head of a large family. The two fathers did house repairs. Their oldest sons served them as carpenter's helpers while the younger children went to school and hunted odd jobs. Mike, a paperboy again, sold the extra for Woodrow Wilson's 1912 election. Both sets of parents were hunting for a better scene in which to raise the children. In the fall of 1914, George Samuel found a teacher's job at Cassia Academy, a small church school up in southern Idaho, at Oakley (population 600). He soon spotted a potato farm that looked just right for Gaskell, who authorized him to buy it for him on a mortgage.

"George, this is the worst farm I've looked at," Gaskell said as soon as he saw the Idaho place. The boys lined up to help build a frame house, and to fight a losing battle with the dry, sour soil. The first winter was tight. About all they had to eat other than "Mormon gravy" (flour, grease and water) was their own potato crop—for breakfast, high-noon dinner and supper. "We had potatoes coming out of our eyes, ears, nose and other places, too," the Governor says with the unmistakable look of a man recalling childhood joys. Next summer, George was in charge of raising a garden. When his father did carpentry for a neighbor, the pay was a wagonload of overripe tomatoes. Mrs. Romney, sickly with allergies and asthma, worked through two nights turning soft red blobs into potato supplements—canned tomatoes, ketchup and chili sauce.

But the debts kept piling up. In 1916, Gaskell moved to Salt Lake to build houses; his brother came and finished his bachelor's at the University of Utah. (He later took his Ph.D. in educational psychology at Stanford.) Both families marched back to Idaho, this time to Rexburg (population 4,000). George Samuel became president of Ricks Academy (now Ricks College) at $80 a month, and Gaskell built houses near the school. When school president Romney got sick, Gaskell, who had one year of college, taught his brother's history, English and math classes. The two families—21 people—made it through the winter of 1917 on $72 a month. They paid their tithe, of course, off the top. Marion Romney, George Samuel's oldest son and now an apostle, remembers the tithe only because, having no coat, he used to get chilly walking to the bishop's house with the $8.

Through boom and bust, Gaskell kept on building with the equanimity of a man who could laugh at himself. "You can always tell an Englishman—but not much," he would say.

The houses he built—at least the ones I tracked down—were sturdy if not fancy, and had one fingerprint: He made use of every cubic foot of space by installing closet shelves, hat racks and storage cabinets. As his son was to build compact cars, so did he build compact houses. "I don't build much for pretty," he said, "but I build like hell for stout." He gave the boys a perspective on the excitements of growing up, such as the discovery of girls. "No need to get excited about the feminine form," he said. "There hasn't been a sport model in six thousand years."

The human animal, a hardy and adaptable species, can survive a hostile environment. Many citizens who scuffled through the farm depression, me among them, had it about as rough as the Romneys did in Idaho. The less common part, however, is how the family warded off the shakes of insecurity and the stunting of ambition. Mrs. Romney, the tone-deaf descendant of hymn-writers, saw to it each of her children studied a musical instrument whether they wanted to or not. Only daughter Meryl, while tone-deaf as her mother, kept up her music (piano) in adult life. George's cornet lessons left him with little more than a talent for playing taps on a Boy Scout bugle.[1]

Looking back into the kaleidoscope of his boyhood, Romney has to make a conscious effort to focus on its grim side. He mainly remembers items like the first fishing pole he rigged at Oakley, and the big suckers (carp) they waded after when the irrigation ditches went dry. Of course, he won't forget the scary instant when he, age eight, fell forward off a clod-busting mule drag. He rolled into a furrow so that the drag bruised but did not maim him. He breaks out in a laugh at the thought of the tricks played on a neighbor family of red-

[1] Like most good Mormon boys, George was a Scout. He made it up to Star rank, two notches below Eagle, before he devoted his time and trail talents to Lenore La Fount.

headed kids: Romney boys would start a game of Run-Sheepie-Run so as to hide in the neighbor's chicken coop and snitch an egg or two. An egg could be traded at the store for a penny's worth, and sometimes more, of Golden Crumbles (like Butterfingers) or licorice.

In Salt Lake, he remembers four of the boys finding a dollar and splurging it on merry-go-round and shoot-the-chute rides. "We went on the darndest binge," he says. There were the books his mother read and left around so the boys would find them, and there was the exciting teacher from back East who introduced him to Jack London's *White Fang* and James Fenimore Cooper's *The Last of the Mohicans*. Miles says George was the family's avid reader. And in Rexburg, George taught a scrawny collie named Bill to wear a work collar and pull a sled. Bill hauled him to school and came back when school was out to pull him home, or dump him in the snow.

The family could not dodge its share of real grief and pain. When brother Lawrence began to weaken from rheumatic fever, George, two years older, stubbornly refused to scamper off ahead of him. Lawrence kept fading and died when he was eleven. Douglas died some years later of a ruptured appendix. The other five lived to see George considered for the Presidency.

Being competitive, Romney remembers boyish triumphs. At hide-and-seek, he hit upon a trick of pinning his necktie so it fluttered at the corner of the house—while he raced around to come in home-free. He reveled in the two-and-a-half-minute talks that young Mormons give in church from age five on. As he grew older and talked longer, a friend decided that "George will likely be as good an orator as Senator Borah [Idaho's champ] one day." At age 12, he was drafted by family regulations to serve a three-year hitch as mother's helper, sweeping and cleaning house and changing diapers for baby Meryl. He protected his manly dignity that year by making a dollar a day chopping out sugar beets and shocking wheat.

A steady student in public schools and reliable in history and spelling, he finished eighth grade at the head of his class. He asked his parents what to say in his valedictory address, but had a second thought: "If you told me, then the speech wouldn't be mine, would it?" In later life, he took a similar view of ghost-written material; most of his ghosts in business and in politics eventually despaired of drafting a text, even on a repetitive theme, that he would not rewrite in his looping hand or reshape from the podium. He would pick up an idea anywhere, from anybody. But he would not handle it well until he had chewed it up and digested it into his personal system of plain, dogged prose, delivered in jagged-edged baritone with Karate chops of the right hand.

Out of the scratch-and-grabble boyhood came a proud, sometimes diffident man. When first confronted by smug Easterners, he used to remember the country saying, "A man ain't nothin' but a barrel of water and a bucket of ashes." He once had a way to deal with human pretense: Imagine everybody in sight with no clothes on, until you break out laughing. Today, he is apt to mutter contemptuously of "those sophomores," know-it-all newsmen, who have never had to dig their ideas like potatoes out of the dry dirt of experience.

If his talk often sounds quaint to intellectuals, theirs sounds narrow to him. A typical example can be found in a widely quoted United States Department of Labor study, *The Negro Family*. Its summary sentence says: "At the heart of the deterioration of the fabric of Negro society is the deterioration of the Negro family."[1] In Romney's view, this thesis would make sense—if the twice-repeated word "Negro" were

[1] *The Negro Family*, Office of Policy Planning and Research, United States Department of Labor (Washington: Government Printing Office, March, 1965), p. 5. The document is often called

taken out. He knows that whites have a family problem, too, even though the Federal sociologists recognize it only in black people. He has one experiment going in which volunteer pairs of families, one on welfare and one in affluence, strengthen themselves by working on each other's flaws. But he is, he admits, still short of a way to help today's urban families match the strength of the mobile family units he saw in action. His hang-up shows almost daily in the ceremonial duties that take up much of any public official's time. For instance, in handing out excellence awards at a radio press association banquet, he had the wives come up to be honored (and photographed) beside their husbands, joking the while about which had the brains. To a reporter with a bright wife, he said, "They'll talk about you the way they do about me."

Though he is not sure how Government can or ought to strengthen families, a first step would be to change programs (e.g., certain welfare rules) that tear families apart. With other Republicans, he believes that rental housing, private and public, has denied Negroes the standard United States opportunity for building a family financial base in one piece of real estate. He set up a state housing authority, albeit a poorly funded one, hoping by state initiative to turn the public slave quarters built by Federals into projects in which people own their apartments as co-ops or condominiums. To prove what can be done, his 1964 campaign manager, utilities executive Tom Hart, has brought the United States Gypsum Co. into Michigan to plan renovation of slum apartment houses. Such renewals have in other states been rented back to the tenants, but Hart is determined to sell the apartments to the tenants at monthly payments comparable to rent. The new owners would, like suburbanites, not only build a family

---

"The Moynihan Report" after Daniel P. Moynihan, then Assistant Secretary of Labor.

equity but benefit financially from their own efforts to make their high-rise neighborhoods into decent living places. Backed by Romney, Hart knows that slums will be prisons until the residents take over.

The Governor tracks down anybody who seems to understand the family crisis. Perhaps he is too much impressed by the survival techniques he watched as a boy. But until the basic social unit can be toughened up, maybe by doing heavier duty, he doubts that the United States can get on with its own self-renewal and its work in the world.

51

# CHAPTER FIVE

# NEVER GO TO BED
# ANGRY

---

"There's nothing under the sun I can't do if you'll be my girl," George, 17, told Lenore, 15. "Why, I could even be President."

Mrs. George Romney—people think of her as Lenore—has on occasion outshone her husband. Vivid and quick, she has a serious problem: She has to fight the impression that she, as a newspaper put it, is smarter than George. This view aggravates the Governor, not because of rivalry with his wife, but because "it's another way of trying to say I don't know anything." One reporter, playing for that angle, asked Mrs. Romney if she believed there was a great woman behind every great man. She instantly answered with an innocent smile: "I think that behind every great man there is a very surprised mother-in-law."

Her answer, while witty, hit near the family reality. In their man-wife setup, he is all masculine, and she very much the woman. She echoes, and echoes well, but the basic insights are his, and she works within his thought structure. He dotes;

52

she praises. Yet, they have a case of puppy love that never grew old. Their married daughters tease him over a show of jealousy at a dinner guest, a doctor, who seemed too damned attentive to Lenore. As an ambitious young man he once risked his business hopes to pursue her. And, after years of marriage, his face broke out in fever blisters because he could not be with her one afternoon when she needed him. In Michigan, where they keep a home in Lansing and one in suburban Detroit, plus a summer place, she juggles her speaking dates so as to spend each night at the same house he will reach. They argue policy but only in private and she follows a lifelong rule: "Never go to bed angry."

They are strong, plain people who operate a 24-hour-a-day political partnership. Since he first ran for governor—when she campaigned to keep the GOP hold on 64 outstate counties so that he could fight full-time to crack Democratic power in 19 heavyweight counties—she has been considerably more than a first lady. Her tight speaking schedule is typed up daily by the staff and coordinated with his. When a state crisis forces him to break a major date, like a speech to the Young Republicans national convention, she flies off to be his stand-in and on the way reshapes his prepared text into her "my husband believes" formula. She not only knows his ideas better than any aide, but unlike the aides she seldom misses an outstate trip with him. "He needs me," she says, "and I need to be with him."

The Romney match was made by chance one weekend in the fall of 1924. Lenore was a 15-year-old junior and George a 17-year-old senior in Latter-day Saints University High School and Junior College at Salt Lake. They were social miles apart. George's family, then deep in debt but always too stubborn to duck into bankruptcy, had moved down from Idaho three years earlier, after brother Lawrence's death and the postwar construction crash. Lenore, one of four pretty daughters of an earphone manufacturer, Harold Arundel La Fount, was a member of the most social LDS girls' club, the Seagulls.[1]

About 25 Seagulls and their chaperones went off one Friday night for a slumber party at a lodge in the Brighton Canyon resort 20 miles south of town. Before sundown Saturday, the girls giggled happily to see cheerleader Occi Evans roll up in his father's new Nash. Occi had brought along his football buddy George Romney and another boy. They offered to drive five or six of the girls home. Because she was a friend of Occi's girl, Lenore piled in, and without knowing it hooked the Romney boy for the rest of his life.

The high-school pictures of Lenore La Fount suggest why. A brunette, she had the dewy beauty of excited innocence. "She was so gentle and sweet," recalls a schoolmate, "that you could just choke her. She looked like Kathryn Grayson." The night she met George, she played the ukulele all the way home. Besides "Bye, Bye, Baby" and the standard pops of the day, she kittened with a family tune, "My Father's Whiskers," that she later passed along to their children:

> I have a dear old father for whom I daily pray
> But he has such great whiskers
> And they're always in the way.
> When he comes down for breakfast
> And the family's in a group,
> My father's great long whiskers
> Get tangled in the soup.

[1] Sea gulls are golden in Saint symbolism. In 1848, the first Mormon crop at Salt Lake was nearly destroyed by a plague of crickets or, some say, locusts. As grizzled pioneers were still telling the story when George was a teenager, they knelt in their fields to pray—and looked up to see thousands of sea gulls from the Lake fly in to gorge upon the insects, then vomit and come back for more. The Lord, of course, got the credit.

They're always in the way.
The cows eat them for hay.
My mother chews them in her sleep
She thinks she's eating shredded wheat.
They hide the dirt on my father's shirt
But they're always in the way.

Having worked too hard to have polished himself into a ladies' man, George could only sit in astonished awe. "People have trouble believing it now," he says, "but I was shy then." He made Occi drive Lenore home last. Then he badgered another friend into making a date with her—and arrived at the chosen hour himself. "When he showed up," Lenore says, "I was amazed." The La Fount house was at 1512 South Ninth Street East (Salt Lake addresses read like map coordinates), only a dozen blocks from the Romney home. Lenore's father, like many wealthy Mormons, served as a bishop; instead of living with the well-to-do on The Bench above an ancient watermark left by the receding Salt Lake, he had built a generous brick house down in the flats among his congregation (ward). Bishop La Fount closely questioned the boy about his family, then pointedly informed him that the chastity light would be burning out front. The kids took a streetcar to a movie. It was months before George got up the gall to match Lenore's songs with a serenade of his own:

I love to hold your teenie-weenie hand in mine.
It sends the prickly-wigglie feelings down my spine.

At school the day after the first date, George fell into his lifelong ritual of delivering Lenore a present and/or love note just about every 24 hours. He bought her a piece of coconut cake at the school cafeteria. He ate his own lunch out of a paper bag from home, as did other kids who did not have money for the cafeteria or the ZCMI department store's lunch counter, but kept on buying her daily cake out of money he earned. With a woman's acceptance of tribute, she never wondered, until asked about it recently, where the cash came from. He also found she had a weakness for candy crystals smaller than Red Devils, and kept her well supplied. And, like generations before and after, he passed her notes on gum wrappers: "You're my queen."

Years later, if she were not well and slept late, her early-to-work husband would pick a fresh rose and leave it on a breakfast tray outside the bedroom door. "I can get out of the bedroom quieter than a cat," he says. The rose became one of their symbols; he eventually bought her a gold one at Tiffany's.

Lenore's three sisters—Elsie, Connie and Ruth—kept track of the courting at close range. Connie and Ruth, the younger two, hid in the corner behind the brocade couch in the low-lit living room, about as close to George and Lenore as the couple were to each other. "I was the brat sister," says Constance, now a merry grandmother, Mrs. John Scowcroft, in Ogden, Utah. "It seemed to me he was always holding her hand, and his whole life was dedicated, almost, to the thought that she couldn't go out with anyone else." Connie followed unseen one evening when the breathless pair walked three blocks to the Snelgrove ice cream stand for butter-pecan cones. "There's nothing under the sun I can't do if you'll be my girl," said George. "Why, I could even be President." That shook Connie. "I came home and told my mother, 'How corny can you get?'"

Mrs. La Fount, a leader in social charities, already had her reservations. "A distant relative of mine lived next door," explains the Governor. "He beat his wife, and she entertained the milkman. Lenore's mother thought, 'Oh, no, not another one of those Romneys.'" No, say the La Fount sisters, but Lenore's mother did consider George too domineering, and wanted her daughter to have a theater career before she married. Lenore's grandmother raised the most unsettling question of what George would be like as a husband: "A man runs hard for a streetcar, but once he catches it . . . ," the old lady said, letting her voice trail off like a departing trolley.

George's secret advocate turned out to be Lenore's father, the businessman-bishop. (La Fount later became the first to have lawyers check out Romney's eligibility for the Presidency.) The family lineup became clear to the sisters after George insisted on playing in a basketball game when he should have been in bed treating a cold. He had a postgame date with Lenore, who remembers, "We went straight home the long way." Next day, he was flattened by pneumonia, about two months worth of it. Father La Fount sent flowers knowing that the patient would assume, in ecstasy, that Lenore sent them. She did not tell him any different for 41 years.

She had dates while he had pneumonia, but when he got his strength back a strange thing happened. One by one, her dates mysteriously stood her up. George had sought out each boy and taught him the better part of valor. Lenore wondered why she had become unpopular.

Unaccountably, she had never thought of herself as beautiful. As a little girl, she had stayed away from school, pretending sickness, because her small-boned legs were so thin that her laced boots overlapped at the top. She was baffled by George's admiration. When another boy slipped past his guard and took her to the movies, Romney suddenly appeared in the seat behind them loudly chewing popcorn. He trailed their bumper home in his father's car with his lights on high beam, and waited as if he had nothing else to do until Lenore vanished safely inside the door. Counting the girls he took out before he met her, and those she urged him to date, he went out with less than a dozen different girls, lifetime total.

At a garden dance held by one of the Seagulls, Lenore's little sister Ruth and a friend, Margie Riley, served the pink punch and cookies—and witnessed the most thrilling scene of their girlish lives. George had, as usual, written his name into most of the 12 blanks on Lenore's dance card. Like his grandfather Miles Park Romney, he was a bug on dancing but, unlike the polygamist, cared for just one partner. "He'd only trade as many dances with us as he absolutely had to," remembers Occi Evans. "Usually he'd trade the bonus dances, hoping the orchestra wouldn't stay and play them." He further discouraged the stag line by standing against the wall watching each Lenore step. The night of the garden party, however, she defied him. "I danced with another boy three times," she says. "George left the dance floor, and then came back and got me. He said, 'This is it. It's my responsibility to get you home.'" He lifted her up in his arms and marched red-faced to a borrowed car. "He put me safely in the back seat, and I slammed the door." So chauffeured, she was delivered home like a sack of groceries. Meanwhile, back by the punch bowl, Ruth and Margie swooned over the romance of it all. Now the wife of Dr. Willis Hayward, a gynecologist in Logan, Utah, Ruth still says, "That was the end!"

This pair of teenagers had an ethereal thing going. Both believed in Sunday school absolutes like truth and purity. Neither was ready to settle for less than beauty in the basic contract. "I never saw him kiss her," says Occi. On double dates in the Nash, Occi generally said, "George, you get in the driver's seat and let me in the back." Now a deputy sheriff, Occi was then an enthusiastic necker. But he found he could not devote full attention to his girl because George "would be all over the road . . . I'd have to yell, 'Look out— the curb!'" George and Lenore, holding hands and worshiping each other's hazel eyes, were absorbed in talk about the future. "I was so naive," Lenore says, "I thought that's the way everybody acted."

The wooing worked. The brat sisters caught on when

Lenore came home from school in tears because George, in an unethereal way, had lost his temper. They all knew another man like that. "My father was a man of temper and drive," Lenore says. "He'd blow up. We'd hear Father coming up the stairs, and we'd kneel down to pray or run to the bathroom." The sisters delighted in teasing George for his precipitous ways. When he crunched the fender of his father's old touring car, they ran out squealing, "Not again!"

In his hot pursuit, young Romney had the look of a man who would never give up once he'd set his mind to a job. After he locked on a target, businessmen and politicians later discovered, no amount of embarrassment or punishment would stop him. He was that way, Lenore saw, in sports. Not a natural athlete, he still went out for football, basketball and baseball, as well as field hockey. Besides, he had a family name to hold up. First cousin Mitt Romney had made All America on an Amos Alonzo Stagg team at the University of Chicago. Brother Mike was Inter-Mountain Amateur Welterweight boxing champ in 1922. And many a Utah team, then as now, had mesomorphic Romney kin stacked like blocks in the lineup.

He had got off to a bad start with the Fighting Saints teams of LDS High. When he first reported for football, he was a 112-pounder among 160-pound players. Coach Vadal Peterson, having no uniform small enough, suppressed a laugh at the sight of grim, pint-sized George in tan practice pants that did not stop at the knees but flopped on down to his ankles. The kid tied them up with shoestrings, and for three years sweated it out as a scrub tackle, meat for the regulars to grind up. He was an average player, Peterson says, except in guts. He lunged in the scrimmage lines and crashed himself against the bigger ball-carriers until his cowcatcher nose got rubbed raw from digging dirt. "He had heart," says Peterson. "I'd see him get mad and his face start to redden up, but he controlled his temper. He was a gentleman." In his senior year, sore-nosed but heavied up, he made halfback on the best varsity LDS High ever had. It won six games, scored 151 points to the opposition's 21 and fought to a scoreless tie in the state championship game.

He also earned three years of bench splinters in basketball, but finally willed himself up from the scrubs in his senior year by more or less taking charge of the team. The chance came on a bitterly cold night at Bear River City, sixty miles north of Salt Lake. As coaches sometimes do, Peterson decided to keep his first team fresh for a few minutes while the scrubs wore down the Bear River five. So George, the faithful substitute, got to start as a guard and acting captain. Gerald Smith, the scrub center, can still hear the pep pitch Romney made in the huddle before the first toss-up: "Let's play so damn good the coach can't take us out." That was the way it was. Though the coach substituted two forwards and one guard, Smith and Romney hustled the full four quarters, and won. From that night on, both were regular starters.

"He played it rough," remembers Gerry Smith, now boss of the big ZCMI (Zion's Cooperative Mercantile Institution) store near the Temple in Salt Lake. "Sometimes, you thought he was playing football. A lot more body contact was allowed then." In recent years, at basketball workouts with his sons, Governor Romney has been charged under soft modern rules with excessive fouls. Scott needles his father for being a hacker, who chops you across the arms when you try to shoot a basket.

Romney earned his third letter in right field for the Fighting Saints baseball nine. His tireless grit and rugged face made him an LDS hero. At a hen party, playing heart-to-heart confessions, two girls named George as their dream boy before Lenore's turn came. J. Kenneth Bennett, one of several young men who resented his monopoly of the angelic Lenore, had a set-to with George in the office of the student yearbook, *The Gold and Blue.* "He was a little stronger and more perfect than the rest of us," says an unforgetting Kenny Bennett, now an Ogden jeweler. "So naturally we resented it."

The teachers had their fun with the incredible Lenore + George situation. Coming back from game trips to talk to the student body, Coach Peterson drew laughs at devotional assembly with his accounts of George hunting telephones for calls back to the La Fount house. Drama coach Marion Redd entertained the faculty with her troubles in the class play. They were doing *Bab,* an Edward Childs Carpenter adaptation of a Mary Roberts Rinehart novel. Lenore, already hopeful of an acting career, played the part of an eloping daughter. Because George was hanging around rehearsals anyway, Miss Redd put him in the cast, as Lenore's father. But he did not lose himself in the plot's make-believe. When the eloping couple practiced a kissing scene, Romney hotly broke it up: "There's no need to be so realistic."

Just how he found time for his night-and-day courtship is still a mystery. Aside from school courses, at which he was steady but undistinguished, he had three sports, plus the Mormon teenager's standard church duties and extracurricular activities like the Ciceronia debating group and the Ink Slingers, a writing club identified by a spilled-ink button. And through the years, he earned his clothes and pocket money not only on odd jobs—he and brother Mike sold lightbulbs door-to-door—but on fairly regular pay as a carpenter. He kept only part of the cash. "Practically everything we earned went to Father and Mother," says the oldest brother, Maurice. Even before they had moved down from Idaho, George had joined Mike as a lather. On a new house, they nailed up the rows of sticklike wood laths over which the plaster was to be spread.

The brothers Romney prided themselves on being lightning lathers. They made the job a race against time. Each would grip a bundle of laths between his thighs, fill his mouth with nails and push the nails out point-first between his lips. Grabbing laths and feeding nails, they beat a fast, unbroken rhythm with their hammers. Each could put up 3,000 laths a day, against a standard rate of 1,600, and with the help of little brother Charles they could finish a house a day. In school months, George often worked nights. "He'd come in for football practice many a day when I knew he'd taken a lantern and worked until after midnight," says Coach Peterson, "but he never asked to be let off." On dates, Lenore caught him rolling nails around his mouth.

George's nose took more beating at carpentry. Jumping down from an unfinished house, he slipped and landed more or less headfirst, with a sprained ankle that laid him up for several days. "It's the first time I ever saw a man land on his head and sprain his ankle," said Mike. His nose was also sprained enough to leave a permanent notch, slightly off-side.

The boy's diligence was noticed even among Mormons, to whom a wasted hour is a missed opportunity to boost yourself a rung in the eternal progression toward a better celestial suburb. The secular symbol of the LDS society is the beehive. Brigham Young had called his Mormon nation Deseret, after the busy bee, and a huge beehive wrapped in blue-white neon now flickers over Salt Lake from the top of the church-owned Hotel Utah. Romney was a bee most of the time. He shot a little forbidden pool at a hall operated by a Japanese, and he played poker for matches with Occi and others of the Sensible Six, his gang. The Six sometimes called him "Gas," after his father's name. He never, one of the Six says, "had much time like the rest of us had. He was a working fool." And when he went up into the Wasatch Mountains with a crowd of boys on a cabin weekend, he was the genial nondrinker who mopped up after somebody drank more than he could hold.

People like that get elected to office. George stayed on at

LDS for a year of junior college—no need to let Lenore out of sight—and was elected president of the student body. Occi, ticketed to run for the same job, withdrew on grounds that "nobody would have a prayer against him." His chief duty was to hold the devotional assemblies every Friday morning. Unknown to him, Mrs. Gaskell Romney often boarded a streetcar, slipped into the back of the auditorium to watch her son preside and introduce visiting speakers. When Lenore spotted her, the proud mother begged the girl not to tell George she had been there. The sons of the poor feel more embarrassed by their parents than do other teenagers.

His mother died February 3, 1926, of cerebral hemorrhage while combing her hair before a masquerade ball. "My father's business had picked up, and her life was just getting better," Romney says. But at 49 she had, Lenore says, worn herself out working. At the next assembly after the funeral, the boy was on hand with a program ready, keeping the grief inside and tucking his head as usual to cover shy moments. One student, startled at her own tears, looked around the room to find that the faculty and student body were silently weeping. The fresh-scrubbed young man with the bulldog jaw had somehow come to be a part of what was in them. *The Gold and Blue* staff, writing a caption for his picture, fumbled for words like "noble."

With her home-baked bread and "loads of honest, loving praise," Anna Pratt Romney had raised her sons and built her aspirations into them. Mike never really wanted to be an architect, but he almost missed being a mining engineer because he could not escape guilt over his mother's belief that he must learn to do fine buildings. It was the earnest George, however, who went to his mother's fresh grave and promised to be the man she had expected him to be. "I said I was sorry," the Governor told me, "that I hadn't been better to her."

So he drove himself harder. With his nineteenth birthday

coming up in July, he wanted to get on with his two-year stint of mission work, expected of young Mormon men. The missionary, or his family, pays the expenses. Mike was away proselytizing in South Africa, and their father could not put up any more money. So back George went to lathing for the summer. To save every nickel, he even scrimped on dates with Lenore; he took her driving in his father's car, or dancing where it cost little. But he seemed unable to wait for the dating hour, and tended to drop by her house on his way home from lathing. Lenore's sisters got used to him, sweaty and smelly, in a pair of overall pants and a knitted shirt. By summer's end, he saved $700. He paid the $70 tithe, and in October boarded the train for the East—and England. He could not leave, though, until he had settled a deal with a University of Utah freshman named Lenore. "He made me promise never to kiss anybody," says Mrs. Romney. "I kept it, but it took some fast footwork getting in the door. . . . One boy did kiss me, but I didn't cooperate."

On his way East, he squandered the first of his $630 subsistence fund on a present for her, a pen and pencil set from Marshall Field's. In England, he splurged on a blue satin robe with a down collar. The letters flowed back at least twice a week, along with presents. Lenore's father took a picture of her in a bathing suit and in manly sympathy sent it to George. By then, La Fount had been appointed to the first Federal Radio Commission (now the FCC) and moved his all-girl family to Washington. Lenore became an English major at George Washington University, rushing through a three-year B.A. so as to spend a year in drama school. She crimped her sorority style at Chi Omega by letting out word that she was waiting for a missionary, but she still dated. She and a girl friend were photographed in long beads, short skirts and goggles, ready for a hop in an Army biplane. This news clipping did not comfort George. Soon after his mission ended, he cut short the customary tour of Europe, headed for Washington to resume Project Lenore. "He looked seedy when he first got back," the sisters decided, "but pretty soon he was his old self—zippy."

And broke. Going zippy in Lenore's Washington was expensive. The Wardman Park Hotel, now the Sheraton Park, turned him away from a New Year's dance because he didn't have a dinner jacket. In January 1929, he had only a quarter, a dime and four pennies in his pocket when he boarded the train for Salt Lake. Rather than let the La Founts know his poverty, he made the three-day trip on that 39 cents. "I got off at a stop and bought a big bag of peanuts—with the shells on so I didn't have to pay for shelling." The bag ran out a day before the ride did, but he had practice in not eating. "It wouldn't have done me any harm to fast four days," he says. "I'd put on too much weight abroad."

Lathing again with brother Mike, he earned tuition for the University of Utah, then for a summer course at night in Speedwriting. The Speedwriting money went down the drain because Lenore came out for summer vacation. He courted her so hard that he made it to only six classes. He was also courting disaster. That fall he landed a stenographer's job in Washington—she went back home—and proved utterly incompetent at taking dictation.

"I guess nobody will ever believe that I didn't move to Washington because of Lenore," Romney said recently. He's right; nobody will, even though he had long wanted to go to an Eastern school. He persuaded Mike, who had a Chrysler 50 roadster, to drive East and sign up with him for courses at George Washington University—Mike in architecture, George in liberal arts. "I never attended a class," says Mike, laughing. "I've always suspected that he sold me a bill of goods because he wanted to be near Lenore."

The worst was yet to come. Lenore went off to New York's

American Laboratory School of the Theatre. Under the "method acting" discipline of Madame Maria Ouspenskaya, she flung off stage inhibitions to bury herself, on order, in new identities. She had to be a sea animal swimming in the deep, a melting chocolate ice-cream soda and a mother pouring real tears over a sick child. She played Ophelia in *Hamlet*, Portia in *Julius Caesar*, and parts in Ibsen's *A Doll's House* and Chekhov's *The Cherry Orchard*. N.B.C. talent scouts offered her parts in a Shakespeare series on radio, and M.G.M. handed her a Hollywood starlet contract to sign. George Romney, shaken by the good news, left his Washington desk on the run for the next New York train. He was up the creek. As a day-worker and night-student, with plans to go from a B.A. to Harvard Business School, he would not be able to support her for years. She might by then be involved in too many roles other than the one part he wanted her to play: Mrs. George Romney.[1] "It was unreasonable," he says, "to ask a young girl to wait four years."

He was stuck with a weak hand, and worse luck. He kept riding the trains back and forth each weekend, taking the Saturday midnighter to Manhattan to get excursion rates and sitting with her wherever he could. "I guess we courted in more hotel lobbies than anybody you know," he says. They had lunch one Sunday with Lenore's roommate and some of her Utah friends. Saying they had to go to a show, the couple slipped back to her rented room to talk Hollywood. They were embarrassed to hear her roommate and friends coming down the hall, so they hid in the closet. For the next two

[1] The Romney way of total courtship became a political figure of speech in 1967. An undeclared candidate for President, he described his campaign trips as "a red-hot courtship with the public." A staff wag, vaguely aware of George's relentless wooing, suggested that the public ought to be warned to prepare for a siege. He may turn up behind you in the movies chomping popcorn.

hours, they sat side-by-side in forced silence while the group took turns saying what a schnook George was. "They said I was stiff-necked and pigheaded and selfish," he says, reddening, "and went on about what a great career Lenore would have if I would only get out of her way."

She went to Hollywood. She took the hot lights as a stand-in for Lily Damita in *Fifty Million Frenchmen,* and stepped aside for the fiery star when the cameras rolled. Moving up to bit parts, she played a chic French girl in a Greta Garbo film and another ingenue part in William Haines' *The Taylor-Made Man.* M.G.M. was about to offer her a three-year contract that would, if all went well, move her up to $50,000 and a bid for stardom. But the whole thing seemed a little cheap to her. The studio wanted her to pose for cheesecake. Her Mormon proprieties were also ruffled by "the riff-raff of extras that were around and did nothing but gamble." There was no acting satisfaction in the chopped-up shooting of a few lines at a time. She felt that the system wasted and demeaned people. She brought Tolstoy and Dostoyevsky novels to the set so as to be busy between shots on material that dealt with human dimensions above the cheesecake level. Besides, George wrote her every day and called on Sunday at 6 P.M. "We had special times when we would both think about the same things," she adds.

Back in Washington, Romney was pushing his way out of the trap. He found a chance to short-circuit his educational plans, and landed a job in Los Angeles a few months after she settled there. Though working days as a trainee for the Aluminum Company of America (Alcoa) and taking night courses as a junior at University of Southern California, he managed to be waiting at the set many an evening to drive her home, in a five-year-old Oldsmobile that had no first or second gear. He would leave starlet La Fount standing at the curb while he went for the car—always parked on a hill so it could start in high—and come chuffing by slowly enough for her to leap aboard.

He was not cut out for the hanger-on role. "He'd come out there, and didn't want to be known as my date," Lenore says. "In an acting career, I would have been upstaging him, and he couldn't stand that." Faced with M.G.M.'s alluring contract offer, she knew she could not have both the glamour and the man. "It was never either *and*; it was always either *or*."

She settled the either or. On July 2, 1931, in the Mormon Temple at Salt Lake, she married "for time and all eternity" the man who, though an aluminum paint salesman, gave substance to her sense that existence ought not to be cheapened. A practical romantic, the bride was proud to learn later that the groom had financed their honeymoon by selling paint—he had samples hidden in the car—to Salt Lake officials between the wedding parties.

# CHAPTER SIX

# A MISSIONARY'S
# LONG UNDERWEAR

---

"To me it is inconsistent to think that God would reveal truth to men at one time in history," Romney said in church, "and then quit at a time when truth is so needed."

The Governor of Michigan wears peculiar drawers. They are the kind of long johns that Mormons call "temple garments." He earned the right to them when he was 19, and put them on at a ceremony in Salt Lake's home temple of the Church of Jesus Christ of the Latter-day Saints. He does not buy any other kind of underwear.

Should he smoke, drink or give less than ten percent of his gross income to his church, he would by his lights forfeit the privilege. They are sort of holy BVD's, a cynic would say, for they have stitched marks across the front copied from symbols used in LDS temple oaths. These signs on fresh-laundered underclothes remind him that his muscular body is a tabernacle of God and that his actions and motives will one day be judged by a court that has all the evidence. The real significance of those garments, however, takes a second thought:

His personal religion, worn next to the skin, is as plain and serviceable as cotton knit.

Any other politician would have thrown every pair into the trash, back about February of 1962. That's when he learned the political price of piety. While working days as a company president and evenings as a vice-president of Michigan's Constitutional Convention, he quit eating for two days—a fast to help him pray over whether he ought to run for governor. He is careful to hunt all the help he can get on decisions, big or little. A reporter, noticing that Romney did not touch food, asked about his well-known habit of "seeking guidance beyond that of men." Both Romneys refused to comment, but the United Press dug the story, ran it. It all looked peculiar. August Scholle, hard-nosed president of the state AFL-CIO, roared from the front pages: "He's a big clown. This business of trying to put on an act of having a pipeline to God . . . is about the greatest anticlimax to a phony stunt I've ever seen." Romney's soft answer dealt with the implication that he was unfairly calling Upstairs: "The same pipeline is available to Mr. Scholle, or anyone else who chooses to use it."

The religious war never quite died down, in part because Romney never hesitated to say a few kind words, or a few hundred, for any brand of worship. Mrs. Claire Boothe Luce, who had sniped at candidate John F. Kennedy on grounds that he was (she said) "not a good Catholic,"[1] decided that Romney's belief was not quite up to her standards. Many blasted him because his church does not bring Negroes into its priest-

[1] When I dared argue on Kennedy's behalf that Mrs. Luce was proposing a religious qualification for political office, she raised the ante. Whatever a Presidential candidate's religion, she declared, he ought to have the deluxe model of it. But as an evangelistic convert to Roman Catholicism, she kept falling back on her demand that "the first Catholic President *must* be a good Catholic" to represent her faith in a good light. JFK flunked her tests.

hood. He had anguished over that rule for years and, unable to change it, tried like a guilt-hit Southerner to compensate. As president of American Motors, he had written the first fair-employment and fair-promotion clause into an industry-union contract.

The heavy weapons did not come into play, however, until the polls set him up on the Presidential target range. In the February 1967 issue of *Harper's*, a brilliant liberal, William V. Shannon, judged Romney an able governor but made fun of his religion. Under a killer slogan, "Holy and Hopeful," Shannon poured down the prose: "Michigan Democrats have long ridiculed this nearer-my-God-to-Thee complex. One of them commented, 'It's all right for George to want to be President, but I object to him using the White House as a stepping-stone.' . . . If America is yearning once again for the old-time religion, George W. Romney is ready and has the faith."

As the censors of the past castigated the impious, today's enforcers require a lukewarm secularism. *Life* followed *Harper's* with a textpiece, "The Puzzling Front-Runner," that amounted to a curious advertisement of writer Brock Brower's own Oxford-bred puzzlement. Brower grew strangely disturbed because Romney had pointed out an LDS angel's statue without wings, to suggest the down-to-earth quality of his religion.

About then, not yet well educated on Romney, I imagined that he would hunt a theological excuse for a less distinctive fashion, say boxer shorts. Visual symbols have always been dangerous in Presidential campaigns, especially if they somehow sum up the man. Among the disparaging symbols recently hung on campaigners—from Tom Dewey's "little man on top of a wedding cake" to Richard Nixon's dog Checkers, Adlai Stevenson's old shoe and Lyndon Johnson's wheeler-dealer Stetson—none has invited ridicule like a pair of saintly long johns.

Romney knew this. Democrats were already tagging him Batman to deride his earnest manner. They sure would wave the drawers. But when I happened to learn that he had not given up the garments, he simply tried to make me understand why. "You saw me receive an honorary doctorate the other day, another degree [he had 17] that I did not earn," he said. "But people are proud to wear the robes for degrees they earn. Though not visible, the garments are something I earned by living up to certain standards."

That's only a hint. To see why a sensible, vote-loving politician would risk public ridicule, we have to go back again to his Salt Lake years. He was an ambitious teenager. Raised a poor boy, he wanted to make money, plenty of money. "I used to be working on houses for doctors and people like that," he says. "I'd see them drive big cars and take vacations. That was what I wanted." He also wanted more than money. For instance, his five-year pursuit of Lenore La Fount marked a yen for romantic commitment, a following of the grail. He now admits that she was, in literal flesh that danced and sang, the purity ideal that he had read out of *Lorna Doone* and Sir Walter Scott's novels.

But he saw no contradiction between dollar desires and loftier hopes. Even an angel might like a good meal, and he eventually waxed rather explicit in promises, more to himself than to Lenore, that his sweat would fulfill her every whim. He said, "I'll build you a round house with seven bathrooms, along the Hudson River."[1] She says she never doubted.

He asked his father if he could find a better break as a doctor, or a businessman or a lawyer. Gaskell Romney, having

---

[1] Why seven baths? "I guess that's the finest house I could think of," Romney answered not long ago. He went on deadpan to explain that Mrs. Romney now has three houses, one circular living room and ten bathrooms. He finked out on the Hudson River part, but for water substituted a summer place on Lake Huron.

not been a money success, felt like a poor example for his aspiring son. So the father began to tell tales of other men, the local success set. Gaskell did not eulogize the prosperous, but showed how each seemed to fit a pattern. Each had gone East to college, come home to find opportunities apparently filled up, then in time found a useful role that paid. George, urged on by his father, went to visit these men. The interviews squelched the doctor idea, but left "the feeling that there was opportunity, and things could be changed." What things? He was on the prowl, as today's student generation says it, for "his own thing," for a chance to do more than type a carbon copy of what the parental generation had done.

The need to do something that matters takes a particular form in religious cultures, and infects a few young people in a specific way. No matter what they ever do, they are driven on by a feeling that unusual service is required of them. They must find their job, and be about it. Catholics speak of vocation, Protestants of a sense of mission. George Romney admits when pressed hard that he had the uncomfortable call of mission. "After all, it was all around me," he explains like a man telling how he caught the flu.

George's earnestness might have been heavy as lead but for his father's household humor. Confronted by a dogmatic Saint, Gaskell would say, "That fellow would rather be sure than right." While George was in LDS Junior College, three days before his mother died, his father was named bishop of their ward. In the excitement of that Sunday, Mrs. Romney burned the chicken dinner. "Mother," said the new bishop, "I see you've celebrated correctly—with burnt offering." Aunt Amy remembers George breaking up in relieved laughter. "Father, I was afraid that when you became a bishop," he said, "you wouldn't be able to joke anymore."

The character of Bishop Romney's humor comes clearest in an incident that took place years after George left home. He

invited a scholar to lecture his ward on the history of polygamy,[1] a delicate subject most Mormons had been trying to
forget since 1890. The bishop seemed, as the evening rolled
on, to be moving with the scholar toward serious doubts that
God had ever ordered polygamy by revelation, as Prophet
Joseph Smith had claimed. Pressed to explain his rank heresy,
the elder Romney chuckled and went all the way. "I'm afraid,"
he said, "Brother Joseph just had a weakness for women."[2]

Though George could never match his father's wit, he absorbed the religious attitude associated with it. A humorous
man cannot be a fundamentalist. Be he LDS, Baptist or
Buddhist, the fundamentalist[3] clings grimly to the hard shell
of belief rather than risk the confusions further down. Gaskell
pushed his son toward the deeper view. By the middle of his
business years, George was set for life in orthodox observances
but finding pleasure in such works as biochemist Lecomte du
Noüy's 1953 *Human Destiny*, a substantial contribution to
Catholic and Protestant thought. It foreshadowed Teilhard de
Chardin's *The Phenomenon of Man*.[4] Du Noüy reworked

[1] The precise term is "polygyny," the marital state in which one
husband serves several wives. "Polyandry" is the reverse arrangement,
in which one lady is shared by several husbands. "Polygamy" is the
take-your-choice word covering multiples of either variety, but the
proud Saints were hostile to any form of wife-sharing.

[2] Wallace Turner, *The Mormon Establishment* (Boston: Houghton
Mifflin Co., 1966), p. 58. Turner, a *New York Times* correspondent,
recounted this unusual incident without identifying George Romney's
father.

[3] "Fundamentalist" is used here in the general religious sense, not
in the strictly Mormon application to splinter sects that still practice
polygamy. In spite of stern church measures to stamp out the embarrassing reminders of its past, there are, by some estimates, as many as
30,000 polygamists still practicing their belief in Utah.

[4] Romney later followed up with De Chardin. After writing this
chapter, I happened on a copy of *The Phenomenon of Man* (New
York: Harper & Brothers, 1959) in his Lansing library. He had under-

74

evolutionary data to account for sudden mutations and suggested that man's post-biological jumps by social invention have made him a co-creator with God. Romney found these insights compatible with his Mormon notion of co-saints whose daily labor is God's work. As usual, he showered his friends with copies to provoke discussion.

Young George was still a long way from any durable belief, however, when he grew old enough to leave on his two-year missionary hitch. "I didn't know what I really believed," he says. "Unless you have to teach others, you rely on the church and other people and never have to make up your own mind." He felt, in the country phrase, sent for and couldn't get there. His mother's death, his search for a career, his fear of losing Lenore—all tore at him. He had plunged into carpentry to earn his missionary fund, and prepared for the "endowment" ceremonies that would mark his church step into manhood. Ever since he was eight years old, the responsible age in LDS, he had been a church member and since 12 had been working his dutiful way up through the three stages of the lower LDS priesthood. Now, ready or not, he would be an elder in the first of the three adult priesthoods.

At daybreak one morning in 1926, he walked into Mormonism's main temple, which his great-grandfather had helped on as a carpentry foreman. Romney was bathed by elderly temple workers, and anointed with oil. The oil went on his head first ("that I might have knowledge of the truths of God"), then on the other significant body organs down to his size eight-and-a-half feet ("that they might be swift in the paths of righteousness"). The Saints, in their joy over the fullness of life, do not, of course, fail to dedicate the procreative parts. Young Romney, fully dedicated, could now put on the

---

lined where De Chardin had written about the kind of wisdom that "sees."

temple garments, for life, and add white shirt and pants for the long day of rituals.[1]

After a good-bye party and dance, the boy put on his black missionary suit and headed for England. He sailed from Montreal aboard the Canadian Pacific liner *Montclare*, landed at Liverpool November 4, 1926. His boat was met by James Edward Talmadge, geologist and theologian and member of the Royal Scottish Geographical Society. Dr. Talmadge, former president of the University of Utah, was head of the LDS European missions. Not a narrowly religious mind, he was there to give the young men and women from Utah two years of preparation for college and for a coherent life. The Mormon mission experience is more like the Peace Corps than like a freshman course in philosophy, but it is calculated more to teach the missionary than the Gentiles he or she chases.

Romney floundered for months. As he was to prove several times in later years—notoriously in the start of his Presidential run—he is not gifted at faking a new role. He can be clumsy to the point of comedy until he is fully convinced of what he is doing and has used the specifics of that conviction to work out his own way of doing it. He was sent first to Glasgow. The penny-wise Scots, exporters of whiskey, had never encouraged this bone-dry preaching. Glasgow's 250 Mormons, total, had not even risen to the status of an oppressed minority. Working door-to-door in the slums, George and a teammate would try to get a leaflet into a housewife's hand before she slammed the door on a Mormon hand. It still hurts his pride to admit that he resorted to the "box stuffing" tradition of timid missionaries: He got rid of tracts by slipping them into mailboxes, which did not talk back.

"Four people at Sunday School," he noted in his diary, "was little to cheer one who is spending money and time to bring

[1] The temple's small, brightly-lit rooms have been photographed for the public. See *Fortune*, April 1964.

a gift to these people." Worse yet, he was less than sure of the gift. He was going to his room to pray, and to Glasgow's public library to read comparative religion, while he tried to settle doubts about a Creator and the divinity of Christ. Nor did his problem end there. To the Old and New Testaments, Mormonism adds a chapter that dates from the revivalistic fervor of Protestantism's "Second Great Awakening." Gist of the story: In 1820, Jesus and His Father visited a praying teenager, Joseph Smith, Jr., in a clump of trees outside Palmyra, New York, a boom town along the newly opened Erie Canal. The deities advised Smith not to join any of the splintering denominations and new sects then blazing at each other in such a "war of words and tumult of opinions" that the area was known as the "Burned-out District." Next came the angel Moroni, son of Mormon, who located a set of mysteriously inscribed gold plates from which Smith[1] translated the "restored gospel" called the Book of Mormon. The Book itself tells a still more remarkable story by which Mormons identify with Israel's lost tribes and seek to build in the United States a more perfect society, Zion. On this doctrine, Smith built one of the most durable of the new denominations, the LDS.

Mormonism raises the truth vs. myth issue more bluntly than any major faith. By insisting that miraculous events took place in your great-granddaddy's day, it forces you to look on back at the biblical accounts in terms of sweating, sandal-wearing men who did, or did not, see bushes burn. You feel less protected by the thick wall of history that separates us

---

[1] Smith's story has, of course, been attacked many times. It creates an instant credibility gap. One skeptical Mormon, well-read in LDS history, compares Joseph Smith's life to *The Passover Plot,* a New Testament scholar's effort to report Christ as a hip young revolutionary. To the outsider, the primary assertions of any religion, even the secular brands, seem quite incredible, though less so than the universe all seek to explain.

from poetic reports on the Moses tablets and the first Easter. The difference is strong enough so that you can just about smell it among the well-scrubbed, very ordinary people at LDS meeting houses. A Gentile like me looks nervously around the room when a C.P.A. speaks of Brother Jesus as casually as he speaks to Brother Jones. They resent sanctimony, and pray matter-of-factly without Thees or Thous. Romney says grace sort of man-to-man as if he were talking to a business partner, albeit a senior one, on the telephone.

In the spring of 1927, the young missionary was moved to Edinburgh. He was doing better now, though he had a rough time against hecklers when he delivered pat little talks from The Mound, the public soapbox below Edinburgh Castle. One kindly listener stepped up, not to be converted but to offer George a set of golf clubs on loan. The restive athlete, gratefully accepting diversion, went early to a public course and played the first 18 holes of his life—130 strokes. "Not so bad!" he noted hopefully in his diary. This was better than tracting. Two days later, he got down to 116 strokes. On the fourth day, he played 54 holes: 109, 105, 105. (Sweat breaks his hang-ups. Or, as Mrs. Romney says of his early-morning workouts, "it gets his connections working.") With his muscles loose and working again, he bicycled from Aberdeen to Inverness, and pushed his bike 12 miles up Glencoe Pass in a pouring rain.

The new head of the European missions, Dr. John A. Widtsoe, spotted "the gleam in his eye" the first time he shook hands with Romney. A chemist who later served as president of the University of Utah, Widtsoe did not believe in walking on the drab side. "Live mightily today," he urged his missionaries. "The greatest day of all time is today. It is the product of all past and the portent of all the future." He moved George down to London, had him keep track of mission finances and learn a little about living mightily.

George headed for rugby matches, soccer games, Epsom Downs Derby and the Oxford-Cambridge boat race. He tried his hand at oars. Students and titled types of the Oxford Movement (MRA), thinking they heard a kindred spirit, invited him to parties. He touristed hard. He found Windsor Castle "prodigious waste! . . . beautiful? yes." He looked on Eton students as "unfortunates," victims of "fossilized education." After viewing a royal reception for the King and Queen of Afghanistan, he noted, "The ceremony of ceremonies in a land of ceremony adoration."

But he was pushing below the surface. He rummaged into the British Museum for histories of England and Scotland. The distressing thing, he decided, was not the fossilized mythology but the contemporary cynicism that had naturally followed it. He had landed during the General Strike, moved among coal miners during those days of near-revolution and seen the abrupt rise of the first Labour Government. A great nation, he felt, had reduced its principles to mere ceremony and was floundering. "It gave me a greater appreciation of my own country," he says, "and made me feel the danger of going the way England had gone." His exhortations about the United States Constitution are not so much Mormon doctrine as a demand that the document's promises not be treated as finished fact, wrapped in empty ceremony.

Having climbed the hump of belief, he did better on the soapbox—actually a speaking ladder—at Hyde Park and Tower Hill Square. Here, a red-bearded Socialist taught him the educational value of conflict. "Sonny," said the nonbeliever, waving at George's puny crowd, "I don't agree with anything you've got to say, but I think you have a right to get your message across. The best way to draw crowds around here is to have a bit of heckling. Suppose, when I see you ain't doing too well, I come over and heckle you. Then you can heckle me when I need it." George refused the deal, would not heckle. But red-beard read the Book of Mormon anyway and tried to keep George off balance when the clerks from the financial district strolled over to eat their lunch. Sometimes, George had to admit that he couldn't answer the Socialist's questions, but would dig in the library for an answer to stand on next day.

The crowds strengthened on the struggle, and so did the speaker. Though always thin-skinned, the boy learned a campaign lesson. He would one day win labor-management battles, car-sale campaigns and the governor's chair because his outsized opponents, less witty than red-beard, could be counted on to slug back wildly, and thereby help him put his message across. His earnest crusades would drive the other side into such snorting rages that he would generally end up like St. George the dragon-slayer battling bravely through the flames.

Widtsoe picked Romney to head the mission in Scotland. Things were heating up. A newspaper published an anti-Mormon series, and theaters promoted a wild movie titled *Through Death Valley, or the Mormon Peril*. Worried, the church sent over a high-school friend of George's with a counter-movie on the delights of Utah life, *The History of Mormonism*. In setting up showings, Romney invented a new style of LDS missioneering. He called in his two-man teams from their scattered tracting, mustered them all into the area where he would next show the movie.

Scotland's sidewalks mysteriously blossomed with chalk signs: "Stop! Look! Come find out what Mormons are really like!" Instead of staying out of sight, he led his timid forces to see local officials and surprised newspaper editors. The Perthshire *Constitutional & Journal* broke out a story, "Mormonism Exposed." At Saltcoats on the River Clyde, a Romney saturation bombing made London's *Sunday Mail*: "As a result of the visit of seven Mormon missionaries to Saltcoats, the Clydeside

80

town is at present in the throes of a religious war. . . . A local gentleman . . . has taken up the cudgels against Mormonism, and has held a series of open-air meetings. . . . It has been many years since such lively interest has been aroused in a religious campaign in Saltcoats."

The tide began to turn. Hit by the polygamy charge in a Glasgow meeting, George whipped out a portrait of Lenore La Fount. "We do not come to this country with any idea of decoying young girls away to Salt Lake City," he shouted. "You will agree with me that there is nothing wrong with our girls out there." London's *Daily Express* reported: "It was easy to agree with him in the face of such conclusive evidence." The Mormons picked up several hundred recruits in Scotland that year, and Widtsoe had Romney write down his methods so that they could be "used in other places." They would be—in Michigan. In 1967, Romney called up 500 GOP volunteers from all over the state to keep a heavily favored young Jimmy Hoffa from winning a decisive seat in the legislature.

With his two-year hitch over, George still had not decided what he would do for a living. He took a trip to London for Dr. Widtsoe's advice. "If you will keep the spirit that you have had in the last few months in your heart," the chemist had written him, "the doors of this earth will open to you everywhere, and ultimately the doors of heaven. . . . You cannot do better than to go through life with the true missionary spirit actuating you always." Having decided against medicine, Romney had to pick between law and business. Widtsoe argued that the law was more confining and, echoing George's father, said he could break new ground in business. That's the way the boy was leaning anyway.

Back home in Utah, he found the local culture confining. When he talked to his father about a B.A. at George Washington University, and a Master's at Harvard Business School, the bishop made a surprising comment. "I'm glad you are going away to study. I've lived so close to the religious persecution of our people that even though I know that other people are as good as we are, I can't get over a certain feeling. You won't have this handicap."

The shot hit home. In years of struggle along the line between the right and the self-righteous, Romney became acutely conscious of the hidden tax on the persecuted. He felt among Negro friends the familiar sense of the stomped-on who expect nothing but injustice. "We don't realize how long it's going to take for Negroes to get rid of the emotional response built by the centuries," he told me. He was not surprised when I, coming back from a couple of months in the major United States ghettoes, argued that the nonviolent advocates of Black Power represent majority sentiment. Only if that energy could be given a creative channel, a chance to build community institutions, would it ever be turned from a destructive course. I stole some of his insights to reinforce a *Look* article.

Romney never went back to Salt Lake to live, but he gave up none of his Mormon identity. Wherever he went, he and his family would be drawn into the instant brotherhood of a mission branch or ward, with its complex organization, a job for everybody and generally a basketball court to keep trim on. Church was never a dour place to him. "Man is that he might have joy," he said. "When we serve our fellow men, we serve our God." He resisted the elaborations of dogma that please many Mormons. I saw him just about break up a Sunday School class in which the teacher, a converted Baptist minister, diagrammed the routes to heaven. "We don't know that much," he said hotly. "All we know is that nobody is sent to hell, as that word is commonly used, and that what happens to us depends upon how we use our opportunities."

His peculiar underwear, then, asserts the right of a man to

82

be as he believes. That right does not depend upon what others think, much as he frets about that, but upon certainty that each man has to answer for his own actions any day of the week. His God, neither a distant symbol nor dead, is a neighborly being able and ready to take a hand in human affairs. This belief puts him into direct conflict with the main line of recent theology: new theologians, notably Harvey Cox, author of *The Secular City*, hold that God is teaching men to live without Him. The issue is clear. In a recent church service, Romney said, "To me it is inconsistent to think that God would reveal truth to men at one time in history and then quit at a time when truth is so needed."

# CHAPTER SEVEN

# DIALOGUE INSIDE
# THE NEW DEAL

---

"The New Deal reforms were needed for balance," believes Romney. "But the Great Society is the New Deal carried to excess."

The Minority Caucus Room of the Old Senate Office Building was an awesome hall. Built in the ornamental years of government, its decorative interior led the eyes up to a pair of crystal chandeliers that hung formidably from the ceiling. Though the room has long since been chopped down to make office space, George Romney can close his eyes and still see every filigree. He started his Washington worklife there as an inept, 22-year-old stenographer. "The regular offices were full, so they put me at a big old rolltop desk in the Caucus Room," he says. "I was just a kid sitting over in the corner by myself."

He took his seat in early September 1929, less than two months before the stock market crash ended a burnt-out era, more than two years before Franklin D. Roosevelt invented a brand-new era. Romney was working his way through college but would never earn his degree. (He has the course equivalent of two and a half years.) He would instead spend most of the next ten years being a lobbyist and middleman at a point of ideological friction: between the hard-cast beliefs of Pittsburgh's Alcoa and the ambitious improvisations of Washington's New Deal reformers.

He had not heard about the 35- or 40-year cycle which, some political scientists now say, marks the ebb and flow of United States politics. But he would be fully, often painfully, embroiled in the course-setting phase of a new Federal direction that would, if cycles hold, run until the late Sixties or early Seventies.

Politician Romney now makes occasional reference in speeches to his years as a Washington lobbyist. He does little more than suggest that he, too, has been around national government—a not-very-successful response to the popular myth that experience is measured by time on the Federal payroll. I was surprised, then, to discover that he had thought out a provocative analysis of the similarities between the excesses that brought on the reforms of the New Deal and the developing crisis of today. After two or three hours of talk on this subject, I typed out the main ideas he had developed and handed them back for him to rewrite. Here is the result:

> The New Deal reforms were needed for balance. Business, labor, agriculture—the whole nation—had rolled into the industrial age of the auto and of mass production, as well as of rising social expectations, but government had responded very little. The idea of the Wagner Act was sound; it gave the laboring man the power to organize his own force to bargain with the rising power of management. We settled at the bargaining table many matters that would in other countries have been left to government.
>
> The New Deal laws were open-ended, however, without restraint against future abuse. They also became a standard pattern. The nation got into a political habit of handing out the same federal pills for all ills. We have long since passed the point where the reforms need reforming.

85

So, once again, we must deal with the tendency to continue that which produced success until it is excessive. One of the real questions is whether a free society can make corrections without inflation, a depression or some other violent crisis.[1] In a sense, the issue today is whether we can organize community and state forces strong enough to hold their own with Federal power. We have to right the balance and regain responsibility over decisions that affect our daily lives.

If we fail, we not only give up control over government but we also lose the capacity to solve most of the new public problems. Take an urgent one. It is superficial, even cruel, to hope that racial injustice can be wiped out by nothing more than Federal weapons—the Welfare trap and the urban renewal bulldozers. Negro families are being herded into government reservations downtown by special legislation that actually discriminates against them in the name of charity. It cuts off their hope for home ownership and for the other opportunities that the rest of us take for granted. I believe there is a better way.

No such dangers were bothering young Romney when he first came East to Washington in the rumble seat of brother Mike's flashy new roadster. George had watched England's despair for two years, but the U.S. was wallowing in a "normalcy" spirit not unlike what we now call "affluence." The flapper skirt never rose to the inspiring heights of the best micro-minis, but the late Twenties were the swingiest thing yet seen. On the road, the Romney boys swapped off between the wheel and sleep in the rumble seat to save time and hotel bills, but they treated themselves to a tour up into Detroit and across to Windsor, Canada. "I had a beer," says Mike, "and George had a ginger ale." When they reached Washington, they booked into a boardinghouse for a while, but later moved to the Dodge Hotel down near the Senate Office Building.

[1] Democracy's tendency to follow one course all the way to the brink is a flaw that has troubled many men, among them Abraham Lincoln and Winston Churchill. Since worry loves company, Romney has for several years quoted both men on this point, especially Lincoln in the House-divided address.

Both registered for courses at George Washington University. Mike picked up a good job as a construction foreman. Full of the era's bubbly confidence, with money in the bank, he would soon start his own business—and sink with thousands of other small companies in the Depression slump.

George's first businesslike move was to check in with Sen. Reed Smoot, Utah Republican and chairman of the powerful Senate Finance Committee. "I went to get his help on a job," says Romney. Smoot's influence on government opened up the first jobs for dozens of the sober Latter-day Saints who have long been reliable busy-bees of the Civil Service system. The Senator's position looked permanent. The Mormons, once bloc-voting Democrats, had turned hard-rock Republican, and Smoot had built up seniority like a Southern Democrat until he became one of the half-dozen Senate inner-clubbers. He was a symbol, the first Mormon ever seated (1903) in the Congress after the bitter years of the polygamy scandal.[1] George found the Senator at work on the calamitous monument to his convictions, the Hawley-Smoot Tariff Act. More than any other single piece of legislation, this high-duty bill marked the last push of Republican normalcy over the brink of absurdity.

George ended up working on the Smoot bill but not for Smoot. Answering a Washington *Post* want ad for stenographer, he joined a line of about 115 applicants for one job at the office of Sen. David I. Walsh, ranking Democrat on Smoot's committee. The fresh-faced Mormon got the nod—

[1] After Utah became a state in 1896, Congress refused to seat their elected representatives because of the polygamy issue. Smoot, though a one-wife man, was subjected to a two-year committee grilling. Pennsylvania's Senator Boise Penrose finally broke up the silly show by a classic call to common sense. Romney, in a humorous talk, explained what happened: "When asked how he was going to vote, Senator Penrose said: 'I'd rather vote for a polyg who monogs than for a monog who polygs.'"

without Smoot's help, he thought—but quickly proved that he wasn't qualified for the $120-a-month job. The Speedwriting course he had taken that summer in Salt Lake had been a bust because he had been too busy courting Lenore La Fount. With a good memory, he could bluff his way through two days of letter dictation, but the system broke down when Walsh, the first Irishman elected senator from Massachusetts, let his eloquence roll into a dictated speech. Romney worriedly took his scribbles back to the typewriter for two pointless hours. "Oh, my God, he's not a stenographer," said Walsh, viewing the results.[1] He switched Romney to research on the tariff bill.

From September 1929 until June 1930, the non-stenographer did case studies of industries eager to be walled off by the new high level of protectionism. The *Congressional Record* for the period printed pages of the data he provided for Walsh to argue over import duties on items that ranged from the substantial to the ridiculous. Among them: raw aluminum, pig iron, pipe organs, potatoes, sponges, artificial abrasives, ribbon flypaper, valentines, beeswax, blackstrap, agate buttons and mustard seed. This picayune activity of the mighty Senate, as much as the distortion of economics, pushed Romney toward the free-trade side. "As the world's great creditor nation," he said later, "we couldn't precipitate a protectionist policy without hurting ourselves as well as

[1] The stenography flop has been one of the stock stories repeated, with variations, about Romney. In 1959, a newspaper columnist slicked up the incident under a trick title: "The Turning Point, For Romney, Shorthand Fib." The future governor, ever sensitive to the press, drafted a two-page letter and sent his company press agent to deny that he had fibbed his way into the Walsh job. "As a job applicant, I was simply asked if I could take shorthand and type. This I could do and so stated," read the none-too-convincing letter. "I have enough handicaps without the idea spreading that my good fortune was sparked by a deliberate falsehood."

others." He soon cheered the reciprocal trade program with which Roosevelt's Secretary of State, Cordell Hull, cut into Smoot's high facade. Today, he believes in steady steps toward freer world trade but is cautious about sudden spurts that disrupt long-term progress.

He learned the hard way. As generally happened to him, he was caught between two opposing economic philosophies, in this case between the protectionism of Chairman Smoot and the watered-down free tradery of Democrat Walsh. He prepared for the work by reading piles of Walsh speeches on economic problems. He inserted his own views in his research memos explaining the level of United States production on an item, the impact of foreign competition and the likely effect of a duty change on specific jobs.

What shocked him, then as now, was the gap he found between principle and practice. Senators on both sides of the tariff argument acted pretty much the same way: "They responded to regional economic interests," says Romney. "Walsh was for protection on those things manufactured in Massachusetts and for free trade on those things manufactured somewhere else. He was for low tariffs on wool and high tariffs on finished textiles; he was low on leather, high on shoes." Having pushed up the rates on New England products, Walsh then voted with the Democratic minority against the bill.

Romney, an idealistic ex-missionary, turned sensitive to what he calls "ambiguity," that clash in a man between what he believes and what he does. He found abundant examples not only in the tariff debate but among the mayors, businessmen and labor groups who came to beg Federal favors at the expense of the consumer. For Walsh, he had to placate the delegations and answer the petitions. No cynic about people, Romney studied instead the flaw that turns political parties into the tools of specific economic interests, labor or management, regional or national. He later preached as a businessman that corporate officers ought to participate in politics as con-cerned citizens rather than industry advocates angling for breaks. "You're selling out your birthright," he said.

While Hawley-Smoot slowly ground through the Senate, the American economy rapidly fell apart. Since the Govern-ment had few statistics, Walsh sent questionnaires to New England mayors asking for data on how many plants had shut down and how many people had been thrown out of work. He used the answers to back a pre-Roosevelt bill for emer-gency Federal payments to offset half the cost of local relief; the ardent protectionists, still on the normalcy kick, used the crisis to put urgency into their drive to build higher walls around domestic jobs. Senator Smoot believed that what was good for business was good for everybody. He openly cham-pioned Alcoa, which had already become the pet whipping boy of the Democrats and the classic horror for Nebraska's fighting liberal, Senator George Norris. Alcoa was then the ultimate in monopolies—and, to make the politics more bind-ing, it had been part-owned by Andrew Mellon, then Secre-tary of the Treasury for his third GOP President in a row. Alcoa, doing fine in competition with other metals, wanted its share of protection. Without help, Smoot said on the floor, Alcoa would build its future plants near Canada's cheap waterpower or in European countries.

The aluminum lobbyists naturally came to see Walsh's man Romney. He gave them efficient treatment, answered their re-quests for economic data. He had recently studied in a chem-istry course at George Washington the electrolytic process by which bauxite is made into aluminum. "I guess they thought I was smarter than I was," says Romney. When aluminum be-came a critical issue in the Senate-House conference over two versions of the bill, Romney helped two Alcoa executives lo-cate three conference committee members. This was a risky act at the peak of anti-business fury; one senator had been scorched on the floor for innocently talking with Alcoa's president in a corridor. Unaware that Romney was doing his committee job as he saw it, the aluminum men did a double take when he refused their automatic attempt to pay him. They were so amazed, in fact, that they asked him to meet their boss, Alcoa vice-president Safford K. Colby.

Colby was not the gray-flannel type. He wanted his epitaph to read, he said, "Here lies a guy who never missed much." He more or less adopted George as a rough-cut son. They actually became in-laws. But first Romney must work for Alcoa, as Colby's own boy did. Romney says, "Colby argued that after the company training course, I would start about where I would if I went on to Harvard Business School." He would be a $125-a-month trainee for three to six months, then double his pay. Romney pondered the job as an opportunity—until, all of a sudden, it became a necessity: Lenore La Fount had been offered a Hollywood contract. But would he work for a monopoly? "My economic thought hadn't developed that much," he says. "I was thinking mainly of opportunity for personal advancement." And of Lenore.

The tariff job was done. The bill went to the White House for President Hoover's signature five days after Romney, in mid-June of 1930, left for Alcoa's school in the Pittsburgh suburb of New Kensington. He had to scrounge on his pay as usual; he was sending every available dollar back to brother Mike for their joint venture. It was an early drive-in business. Impressed at the success of the Hot Shoppe drive-in chain founded by another Utah Mormon, J. Willard Marriott, Mike had built an ice-cream counter across the Francis Scott Key Bridge in a Virginia suburb, Rosslyn. George helped carpenter the place. It looked like a silo-sized old-time ice-cream freezer with a giant crank hanging down the side. "The most uneconomic building you can imagine," says George. "The whole top was waste space." They quickly expanded into a

91

second creamer only to find that each turn of the Depression crank was congealing their investment. No hope. After George moved to Los Angeles for his final stage of training, this time in aluminum salesmanship, Mike shut down the drive-ins and headed back to Utah broke.

George super-sold aluminum paints and foil in Los Angeles, married starlet La Fount, and moved back to Washington in short order. Colby crossed channels in Alcoa's bureaucracy to make the trainee his No. 2 lobbyist in Washington, slated to be No. 1. Colby, like Lenore's father, was one of several older men who bet on Romney under the protégé system that operates unnoticed throughout the business world.

"It always amazed me," says Mrs. George Romney, "that these very important—I guess wealthy—men have been such real friends with my husband. He had a casual relationship with them that didn't overpower either one of us." The man overpowered was Colby's son, a gentle soul not cut out of his father's bauxite. As the Romney-Colby relationship grew close, young Colby married Lenore's sister Ruth and the two couples took vacations together in the Berkshires. But Ruth's marriage broke up. Though everybody tries not to say so out loud, family candor leaves little doubt that Colby's son tried to be like George to please his father and Alcoa, but to George's dismay gave up the strenuous effort.

The 1932 campaign was about to close the Republican era. George and Lenore, just settled in the newly built Kennedy-Warren Apartments ($90 a month) out on Connecticut Avenue, went home to Salt Lake for a summer vacation—and to defend Republicans. George's father, a commissioner of Salt Lake County, was fighting for reelection on the GOP ticket. Senator Smoot, incredible to tell, was running behind the Democratic nominee, a professor named Elbert D. Thomas. George, queasy about protection but a born Republican, campaigned for Smoot across southern Utah, the Dixie homeland of his grandparents. His conservatism came out strong when he advised his father on a radio speech for Hoover. "I said that under Hoover we'd spent about all we could afford to, and we shouldn't elect somebody who'd be more carefree with the public's money," he recalls. The voters disagreed. Even in Utah, where the church had its own welfare system (later expanded) to help Depression-hit Saints, people had no patience left for stand-pat arguments. Smoot and a county commissioner named Gaskell Romney disappeared with Hoover under the Roosevelt avalanche.

Back in Washington again, the newlyweds had to find their way around a new political landscape. George's job demanded that he get to know as many key New Dealers as possible. But the couple had a social handicap: They did not drink or serve liquor.[1] Playing it straight and open, they plowed happily into the party circuit five or six nights a week and invited people to their own dry feasts. "He has a capacity for friendship, and he pursued friends," says a friend. "He worked at it."

Things went fine until experienced guests learned to prepare for Romney parties in advance—and arrived half stoned. This belly-bootlegging abolished prohibition forever in the Romney home. Once they stocked a few bottles, Lenore noticed, the place became wet but more sober.[2] George and

[1] Romney had tried coffee, tea, tobacco and wine as a youth, "just enough to know what they tasted like."

[2] The Romney determination not to impose liquid restrictions on their house guests insures that you find fresh, hot coffee always in reach. But the whiskey situation is less promising unless you make a to-do about it. At two annual pre-Christmas parties for the press, however, drinks have always been served in the game room downstairs, from a bar that the Governor doesn't ever seem to look toward. A state staffer, summoned in to organize one of the parties when the regular press secretary got snowbound, called his boss to ask where the booze was. There was plenty, replied the chief executive, in a file

Lenore stuck to ginger ale, and kept the talk busy on the fascinating revolution in government. The newspapermen, Democrats and Republicans who lounged around their living room, often on the floor, tended to sip slow so as to talk fast. "Nobody ever abused our hospitality by getting drunk," says Mrs. Romney.

As a social grace, golf was essential, and George went at it like killing snakes. Although he had tried the game on the mission in Scotland, he now read an instruction book and took two lessons. He joined the Congressional Country Club—and later the Burning Tree Club that Ike put on the map—but played mostly with Utah friends on the public courses until he could make his game presentable. He worked at it. On the Congressional course early one morning, New York *Herald Tribune* correspondent Albert L. Warner and United Press writer Raymond Clapper stared into an adjacent fairway at a blocky figure hacking and running to waste not a second. "There goes a young man in a hurry," said Warner. "And with a purpose," added Clapper. Back in the clubhouse, Warner and Clapper shook hands with the young man and to their surprise soon added themselves to George Romney's ever-spreading circle. When club wives organized a dancing class to learn the newest rage, Latin America's rhumba, the Warners teased George because, unlike most husbands, he danced as hard as he golfed.

The Romneys moved into the expensive Westchester Apartments, and when their second daughter was born built a house nearby. By adapting plans from a model house in a magazine, and by working as his own contractor, the ex-carpenter put up a four-bedroom brick for $26,000—using some of Alcoa's first aluminum doors, floor-length windows and foil insulation. In-

---

drawer downstairs. The aide found a year-old gift, one bottle of blend, for 40-odd thirsty reporters and wives.

side, he installed a set of circular stairs rather like those his great-grandfather used to build, and updated the spiral with a gold-color aluminum banister.

He was working and living to the limit. In a locker-room talk with Gerald Smith of Utah, now manager of Salt Lake's ZCMI department store, Romney said, "Gerry, in order to succeed and get ahead, you've got to bet every last dollar on yourself, everything you're making." Adds Smith: "I haven't any doubt that, conservative though he is in money, he lived up to his means and maybe beyond, betting every dollar on himself." Romney never could see money as an end in itself, only as a means to do what he wanted to do.

Lenore directed student plays at George Washington University and read poetry fifteen minutes a week over station WRC. The announcer for her "Poetical Hitchhiking" program was a redhead named Arthur Godfrey. The Romneys, fresh and vivacious, were drawn into older groups. Louis B. Caldwell, Chicago lawyer and general counsel for the Federal Communications Commission, included George among the few regulars in his Inquirindo, one of those all-male, off-record seminars that flourished in New Deal years and reappeared briefly in the intellectual excitement of the Kennedy Administration. At Inquirindo, he met Jesse Jones, Stephen Early, Merle Thorpe, George (crony of presidents) Allen and others excited by the rebuilding of a nation with alphabet agencies. He studied his first Keynesian economics here under Marriner Eccles, Roosevelt's Federal Reserve Board chairman. Reading up, he recognized that stimulative fiscal and monetary policy would work, but developed a lifelong caution about the dangers of over-stimulation. He argued with Eccles that the political problem of managed money would be the failure of most presidents to tighten down during prosperity.

On this point, he feels some pride as a forecaster. "The spending policy of the last few years results in deficits during boom times—the opposite of what Keynes urged, and of the New Economics." However, he misjudged badly, he now admits, on how long it would take for deficits to weaken United States credit abroad. "Our credit turned out to be stronger than I knew," he says, but argues that the test is now excessive. For his general foreign policy education, Romney leaned heavily, as Washington has for generations, upon the articulate British, mainly on London *Times* correspondent Sir Willmott Lewis.

Still shy and impressed by names, the Utah boy played a kind of hurry-up golf with his mind. Though he took over all of Alcoa's lobby work, he did not give up the urgent business of hunting answers to his personal questions. One teacher he kept going back to see was Utah's Democratic Sen. Elbert D. Thomas, under whom he had taken a history of the Far East course ("Because I was interested.") at the University of Utah. Now the student wanted the advice of the teacher—against whom he had campaigned—on the consequences of the Wagner Act for factory workers. Wouldn't a side effect of union power mean that individual workers would be intimidated, knocked around by their new bosses inside the labor movement? Shouldn't their rights be protected? Senator Thomas assured but did not persuade his student that local statutes and authorities would prevent coercion and violence. Only later did he see the more subtle problem of a labor movement that went stale at the top.

New Deal programs shoved a radical question mark into every sector of life. The breakdown of the old economic order forced men into conscious invention of the new. In those exciting years before Washington grew certain it had all the answers, men of various political persuasions carried on bracing dialogues with each other. And the ladies cheered. The brighter hostesses singled out the comers and flattered them with self-appointed fan clubs. The head of George's fan club was Mrs. Louis Caldwell, who unsettled him by publicly predicting Romney-for-President. Asked about it years later, the lady matter-of-factly said she knew all along that he had a special stability, outspoken honesty and a clear understanding of what he ought to be finding out. That ended the question. Also, George and Lenore were never touched by gossip. Alice Roosevelt Longworth, Teddy Roosevelt's daughter and one of the group, carried over her memory of the Thirties into a 1967 announcement boosting George for GOP nominee.

Mrs. Caldwell did her bit at the time. She invited the Romneys to her finest parties, which were an education in themselves. When Donald Richberg, one of several men called "Assistant President," was named chairman of the National Recovery Administration (the Blue Eagle), she honored him with an elaborate satire on NRA regulations. In 1939, when Michigan's Senator Arthur H. Vandenberg looked like a dark-horse GOP candidate, she turned her home at 2900 Cleveland Avenue into the Dark Horse Inn to honor "Sir Arthur and his Round Table." The Romneys were about the youngest couple invited. At another party, they arrived as damsel and knight, a setup for today's political attacks on him as Mr. Clean. George bulged inside the chain mail that Lenore fashioned by dipping dishrags in aluminum paint.

In spite of such delightful sponsorship, Romney was but a minor figure with a student-like freedom to study government at work and play. "We were invited to places," he says, "to which we were not by social and other forms of status entitled to attend."

He kept up his daily reading of the *Congressional Record,* a discipline that inspires compassion for the frailties of the mighty. Alcoa's international empire was interested in a sizable part of what the Government did, or might do. New dams generated cheap power and thus changed the economics of aluminum production. Interior Department activity in mining areas affected bauxite and competitive copper ores. And business lobbies swarmed around the alphabet agencies, especially around the NRA during its attempt to limit competition. When the copper lobby persuaded NRA to lump aluminum and copper together under its regulations, Romney realized that aluminum, a relatively new metal, was about to be stopped from competing with copper, which it had begun to replace in REA power lines and other uses. He fought for, and won, a separate regulation. Since Alcoa had, as he said, "taken a precious metal and found a way to produce it cheaply enough for everybody to use it," he could fight with pride for his company's product.

But there was that monopoly problem. Much as he admired his bosses, Romney began to think of them as prisoners of their own success. Unless they would spin off some of their best talent into new companies, and license competitors, they would never have the daily competitive pressure to do their best. Getting nowhere on this line, he took to Pittsburgh a proposal that Alcoa conduct its business in a fishbowl, like a public utility. "Our rate of return is not excessive," he said, in deliberate understatement. "At about six percent a year, it compares with a public utility." Having served as legman for Dr. Edwin G. Nourse on a Brookings Institution study of aluminum pricing, he also knew that the company had not tried to bilk the public. "We have nothing to hide," he insisted.

Pushing against a blank wall, Romney began to realize that the rigidities had already set in. He got further proof in a very personal form. Alcoa combined the two branches of its Washington office, sales office and lobby, under a single boss. It was not conceit for Romney to know that he was right for the top job. But the company, married to the nepotism and seniority that thrives in noncompetitive areas, brought in a veteran Texas executive, Edward Bell Wilbur. Wilbur's promotion was galling, but not half as much as his accommodating philosophy of doing only what the company expected. The final trap of monopoly, then, was what it did to people. Romney told his friend Colby that he would not while away the years waiting for a vice-presidency at 55 or 60. This represented a considerable change in heart from his boyhood remark to his mother: "I want to arrive and then coast." He now wanted to reach the stage where he "would not have to work for economic reasons," and would be able to take on a public-service job.

Meanwhile, the Department of Justice had brought its landmark case against Alcoa, the longest antitrust case ever. The real payoff did not come until war mobilization, when the Government subsidized three other companies into competitive production of aluminum. Romney was later to admire the way the industry, especially Alcoa, took to its new role, but he still argued that a prudent spin-off could have saved millions for both the company and the taxpayers.

Shortly before the war, he threw away lifelong security at Alcoa to take an uncertain job in the auto industry. Not many people ever expected to find utopia in "The American Siberia of Detroit," but he had studied the ten car manufacturers. They made up an open industry, he hoped, where a man could not be boxed in for long. He was about to discover, however, that competitive freedom had some hidden correlaries.

# CHAPTER EIGHT

# FROM RIOT TO
# CIVIC CIRCUS

---

"The paradox is that it's individualism that makes cooperation worthwhile," Romney discovered, "and it's cooperation that makes individualism possible."

In Detroit, a bristling educator named William Stirton grabbed his phone one morning early in World War II to hear the sad complaint of a burlesque theater manager. An entire troupe of stripping beauties had been induced as one body into coveralls and enticed into a welding class. Stirton, a Methodist minister's son ramrodding a monster program called Vocational Training for War Production (337,000 trainees), had set up special instruction for the girls. He pointed out to the manager that they would make a sight more money welding than stripping. Besides, the whole city was mobilized for production; "Rosie the Riveter," or welder, as a pop tune soon preached, had the right to dress and do her bit alongside everybody else.

Stirton, on loan from a local high school, belonged to a cadre of activists who emerged during the war. His labor-union counterpart was Victor Reuther, brother of United Auto Worker vice-president Walter Reuther. His business counterpart was an auto industry agent named George Romney. One of the informal group's higher-ranked leaders, its man in government, was young Dr. Edward L. Cushman, a cigar-loving Latin scholar who became state manpower czar.

Except for Cushman, few of these activists were considered important. The aging Henry Ford, pacifist, frowned at first on the upstarts. Michigan's CIO president August Scholle, a proud trade unionist of the John L. Lewis school, thought Romney a fink for General Motors and beneath his concern. "It was his bosses I talked to," says Gus.

But Stirton, Romney and friends proved a gift for levering their bosses into unaccustomed collaboration. Nothing between strippers and bombers was too small or too big for them to tamper with. Here are a few events that might not have happened, or not so soon, but for their manipulations of the power structure:

> Bitterly competitive auto giants swapped production secrets, patents, machinery and talent on a daily basis to rush war contracts.
>
> Barbers stretched their nine-to-five clipping into the night to serve the swing shift.
>
> Unions loosened hard-won rules to let men jump jobs without losing seniority, setting a pattern that the whole labor movement followed.
>
> Lily-white FHA housing projects, few but full of precedent, opened to Negro families.
>
> A weird shortage of alarm clocks, which made hundreds late at the gates, became a broken bottleneck when the Detroiters pushed Washington to release critical materials to clockmakers.
>
> Protestant ministers backed Sunday training and work,

101

provided the men had time off to hit one worship hour a week.

Catholic priests okayed working mothers in plants; a lasting day-care center movement sprang up for worker's children.

An ugly race riot was turned into a warning, and a drive started to make Detroit the national leader, for a decade or more, in interracial advance. Romney's work after the 1943 riot made the 1967 riot especially tragic to him.

The city, hoping to mobilize war-type energy for peace, staged a postwar pair of civic celebrations that stirred up the Community Chest movement and produced plans for Cobo Hall convention center, Ford Auditorium, the Community Arts Building, riverfront renewal and a shopping list of public facilities.

Planes, tanks and mobile troops won history's first industrial war. After the victory, General of the Army George C. Marshall, U.S. Chief of Staff, wrote that Detroit's production feats "contributed in large measure to the success of the American forces." Since the auto industry provided a fifth of all the war goods, a decisive margin beyond its share of the economy, the letter was no overstatement. Marshall directed his comment at a peculiar institution called the Automotive Council on War Production. It was neither an arm of government nor a profit-making company. It became, twenty years later, a prototype studied by conservative writers, and one of several models on which politician George Romney began to build his power alternative to centralized government.

Romney had come to the auto industry fresh from Washington in 1939. He was 32. Through former sportswriter Pyke Johnson, lobbyist for the AMA, he had come to admire some of the auto-makers. They seemed to cultivate the discipline of competition. For instance, unwilling to be at the mercy of an uncompetitive interest, all had refused to build mass-production engines out of Alcoa's aluminum. They had stuck with steel because they could buy it from several suppliers. For a reason that Romney did not yet comprehend, the ten independent car firms then in battle also had a record of legitimate cooperation. Through the Association, they had pretested the United States highway network, especially transcontinental Route 66, in part by raising private donations to lay stretches of public road. Donors were honored with roadside markers. AMA had operated a cross-license system in patents that the New Deal's antitrust investigators had considered a handsome exception to the general rule of monopoly patent exploitation. It had pushed safety hard enough to head off for a couple of decades the anger against blood on the highways. But it had become, Bill Stirton complained, "a milquetoast kind of thing." Pyke Johnson, soon to move over to the Automotive Safety Foundation, picked Romney to put muscle into the Detroit office of the Automobile Manufacturers Association and eventually take charge of the whole trade association.

Romney came ready to be impressed by the auto barons, and was. Taken to General Motors' legendary boss William S. Knudsen, whom he had met briefly in Washington, he had a look of awe that provoked the rawboned old mechanic into a quick cure. As Lenore remembers what George told her, things happened fast: "Mr. Knudsen threw his wallet at my husband—'look at my [immigrant] family pictures'—and told how he arrived in New York with ten dollars in his pocket. He talked like that until every barrier was down. My husband told me what a great man Mr. Knudsen was because he never tried to be better than anyone else."

Knudsen had a more powerful admirer: the President of the United States. Franklin Roosevelt drafted Knudsen in May 1940 to be the production pusher on the National Defense

Advisory Council. He was to wear many hats, among them a lieutenant general's, as the trusted industrial genius of the war. While Hitler mopped up Western Europe and bombed England, Knudsen needed all his persuasive prestige to stop the car-makers from grabbing up the short supply of machine tools for new models. The United States was then nervously committed to peace. On the conservative side, the America Firsters were raging against United States involvement in Europe; on the liberal side, Roosevelt was clobbering Wendell L. Willkie with the antiwar plank.

Before the November election, Knudsen opened a major war production drive on personal orders of the President. On October 15, he interrupted a morning session of the Automobile Manufacturers Association board of directors at New York's Waldorf-Astoria. The auto men were trying to present Knudsen with an autographed set of Carl Sandburg's *Abraham Lincoln* to honor his AMA years and his move to Washington. Knudsen abruptly cut off the ceremonies, pledged every Republican in the room to secrecy and said that the President needed their help "as an industry." Blitzed Britain was more desperate than the public knew, Knudsen revealed, and the war would be won by the side with the most bombers. "It has been a bitter, bloody experience," he went on. "Bombers, big bombers, are needed sooner than we dare hope to get them under present circumstances. We must build them at once. You've GOT to help."[1]

Here was an invitation to self-torture, so far as the car chiefs could see, and it came down from the hated FDR. They were already loaded with orders for tanks, trucks and other war materiel in their line of rolling stock. They were being asked in time of peace to put on the "merchants of death" tag, cut off their customers and build parts for the booming

[1] *Freedom's Arsenal*, (Detroit, Michigan: Automobile Manufacturers Association, 1950), p. 2ff.

aircraft companies—which demanded and got promises that the car men would give up the airplane business at war's end. Knudsen could appeal only to patriotism. He had plenty of that. As executives called out, "We're with you, Bill," green AMA staffer Romney felt a chill of pride. He was about to be tied into a job that seemed more urgent from day to day than any he might do in a uniform. Soon beyond draft age, he never went into the Army.

Romney and three more staffers holed up through lunch hour drafting a formal board resolution backing Knudsen, and more. Quick to expand on the idea, Romney persuaded his seniors to enlarge the plan to include not only the car companies but the whole fantastic complex of 654 parts suppliers, body firms, tool and die makers. The board agreed. It released an announcement that read like a promissory note and drew little press play. The hot news was the unveiling of the '41 car models at New York's Grand Central Palace. That gaudy display, while Europe suffered, struck Romney as tasteless. Within two months, he managed to get cancellation of the '42 model show.

Heading back to Detroit, Romney carefully cleared his plans with Packard boss Alvan C. Macauley, who had been the gentlemanly president of AMA since 1928. Things now moved faster. Romney rented an abandoned meat market on the ground floor of the New Center Building, below his AMA office, blacked out the windows and rented chairs from an undertaker. Ten days later, 85 chief executives and production experts met there with Knudsen and his Army bomber officers. Bounding among them was a flying major named Jimmy Doolittle, who had surveyed the German bomb damage in England and the overloaded aircraft plants at home.

Studebaker's Paul Hoffman chaired the morning session. A thoughtful man who stayed at Romney's home each time he went to Detroit, Hoffman had a belief, then rare, in the broader role that businessmen could serve. This conviction drove him to found the durable Committee for Economic Development (CED), the liberal arm of big business, then to serve as chief of foreign aid and take his present job as Administrator of the United Nations Development Programme. Often guided by Hoffman, Romney used the results of the meat-market meeting to give Detroit businessmen a job they had not tried before.

Taking $100,000 out of the AMA kitty, he set up the Automotive Committee on Air Defense (ACAD), scheduled auto company engineers to fly to aircraft plants to study techniques, and rented 27,000 feet of floor space. Here, Romney's workers helped the Army Air Corps spread out several thousand sample plane parts. In a few days, they had a supermarket operation. Slide-rule men from the car complex swarmed into the restricted room to pick out the strange new widgets they could manufacture best. Most were pieces of the new B-25 bomber (also the B-24), then in final test flights. The worst bottleneck for several months was the shortage of sample parts to study and copy. Many of those scavenged were stamped defective; often the blueprints and specs arrived late. Doolittle kept badgering the Air Corps for a whole B-25 so that engineers could see what the parts did.

The details sketch a broader reality. The enlistment of the manufacturers, against their immediate self-interest, gave them an initiative they never lost after the United States went to war. They were not draftees. Because they went all out, and had an effective common instrument in ACAD, they generally had the next bottleneck unplugged before they could be hit with a rigid order on how to do it. Without violating their profit discipline, they were able to deploy their men and machines as only they knew how best to do, many times faster than the smartest procurement officers could have hunted down each talent and written an order. Detroit's money brains slapped together the financial structure for the new RFC-backed plants; its purchasing agents, using their generation of practice on new-model changes, rigged dozens of subcontractor nets to make subassemblies. Government inspectors watched out for cheaters, though not as jealously as the competitive companies themselves. The War Production Board's Donald Nelson later explained that he did not tell Detroit how to do a job. He only told them what needed to be done, he said, and tried to help them get the material and labor to do it. Today, it has become politically popular to suggest a similar approach to the war on poverty by calling upon private industry to cure the slums. But few of these orators understand how to mobilize joint industry efforts or, even more difficult, how to leave the ultimate decisions in the hands of slum residents.

The industry's sudden ardor would have cooled too soon but for Walter Reuther. He was the inspirational cattle prod. In December 1940, he proposed an alternative mobilization scheme that New Dealers would have gladly adopted—they almost did—if industry had slipped or slowed for as much as a week. The Reuther Plan for "500 Planes a Day" was to draft the auto industry's unused capacity for war production under the control of a nine-man, tripartite board: three from labor, three from government, three from management. "With government and labor voting together," Romney warned, "the industry will be taken over and run from Washington." The French, after mobilizing their aircraft plants under a similar control, had managed to produce only 12 new planes before the Luftwaffe smashed them. But the Reuther approach looked efficient.

"Reuther lays out the most revolutionary scheme you can imagine and makes it sound reasonable," Romney griped to his wife. "He is the most dangerous man in America." Lenore smiled at the memory of these remarks a few years later when she served lunches at home for Reuther and Romney, a pair of teetotaling idealists who could agree on many

107

things, but never on the question of concentrated power, public or private.

Though the Romney of the early war was unimportant compared to Reuther, his ACAD mobilization drive headed off Reuther's plan until December 8, 1941. With total war, CIO chief Phillip Murray, an FDR intimate, picked up Reuther's proposal and backed it in full-page advertisements. The industry barely moved fast enough to get results before it got a new set of bosses. AMA president Macauley turned Romney loose on a bigger job. Using the kind of structure tested in the Air Defense committee, AMA set up a new alphabet agency, ACWP, the Automotive Council on War Production. Its first meeting on a murky December day ended with an ambitious public pledge from Detroit's business hierarchy. By "a cooperative spirit in a common task," the statement said, the industry would see to it that "the nation will not lack for one gun, one tank, one engine, that the capacity and ingenuity of this industry's producers can add to the forces of our nation and its friends on all the fighting fronts." The words were windy, but the pledge was kept.

"Cooperative effort"—Romney was barking the phrase into every ear he could reach. He talked like a man who had come across a new word and wanted to try it out once a sentence. Part of the repetition was calculated salesmanship. He has since exasperated business and political foes by repeating, repeating to drive home a theme to the public. Taking a line from newsman Raymond Clapper, his friend of Washington days, he says, "Never underestimate people's intelligence, or overestimate their information." Michigan's Democratic National Committeeman, Neil Staebler, feels that his party "ought to take a lesson from Mr. Romney's boring method."

Romney's harping on cooperation was also part of his own grappling with a basic idea. The language of business had long since stalled in a rut marked "competition." But here he was, an executive hired hand, finagling the world's most Darwinian tycoons into a joint activity that was not, somehow, a contradiction. Romney could never toy with ideas out in limbo any more than he could be serious about a God who wasn't there. His down-to-earth instincts made him itch to smash a paradox and pull the pieces into the system he lived on. He began to feel that the contradiction between competition and cooperation was more intellectual than human. A social system that allows men to be themselves, and to use their capacities to the competitive limit, also invites them to act together as equals, to cooperate rather than toady to each other as masters and slaves. Perhaps there was a necessity about working together. Without a common concern for the welfare of the society, he saw, individualism could never be more than dog-eat-dog.

"The paradox is that it's individualism that makes cooperation worth while," he eventually decided, adapting a remark of the original Henry Ford. "And it's cooperation that makes individualism possible." He was also realizing that the voluntarism that conservatives had lip-serviced for years could not be left to social chance. People have to see the dangers of inaction—the Reuther Plan had made them real to manufacturers—and invent machinery (like ACWP) through which to organize their joint efforts in a practical way.

He now had what he always went after: enough input of data to work out his own way of seeing things, and the "principles," as he tirelessly says, to let him act with confidence. The difference showed, more in his steady, sure work than in the speech he delivered at ACWP's second meeting in January 1942. To his surprise, the auto bosses smelled the change and elected him to run this cooperative thing he'd been preaching. From then until about 1948, when he added a new insight, "consumerism," he pounded at one of the clumsiest phrases yet to enter public debate: "Competitive cooperative capitalism." To leave out any part of the phrase, he believed, was to distort the picture of this vital force that we had some of and ought to invent more of.

Not everybody shared his enthusiasm. The antitrust branch of the Justice Department jolted ACWP with a threatening wire. The mere gathering of such a group, said Justice, would be criminal restraint of trade. After checking with their lawyers, the industrialists went ahead with their most ambitious scheme: machine-tool swapping. They had stopped all auto lines and thrown their plants into mass production of war goods. But you can't simply roll a General Sherman tank off the end of a Plymouth line. The tools had to be shuffled, and in the process, one company would be shut down for lack of tools that were standing idle in another company's plant.

So Romney built a second supermarket, this one on file cards. AMA's staff worked day and night indexing the industry's idle machine tools by function and model, tried to keep track of the fast shuffling. The AMA board laid down anti-hoarding rules. "George kept saying that the auto industry had an opportunity to face some almost impossible problems," recalls AMA staffer Harlan V. Hadley with the exasperated air of those who try to explain why they bet their souls on Romney. "He could use words like patriotism and love of country in a way that wasn't corny. If I said them, people might giggle. We worked twelve and fourteen hours a day, six and seven days a week, because George was an inspiring man. I just haven't met anybody else who never showed any faint symptom of insincerity."

It paid. As war production doubled and doubled again, 90 percent of the auto industry's existing tools went back to work somewhere in the United States within a year. ACWP's survey put 198,000 machines up for swaps, sent tons of the obsolete into badly needed scrap. Overall cost figures measured the efficient use of critical equipment: For every dollar of war

110

goods the Army bought, the average machine tool cost was 19 cents. For Detroit alone, the tool cost was little more than half that, a dime.

A fanatic on building structures that leave nobody out, Romney pushed for seven ACWP product divisions: aircraft engines, ammunition, airframes, armored cars, propellers, tanks, artillery. Each had its own governing board,[1] which devised whatever command system it needed to parcel out the work. Meanwhile, Romney beefed up staff services to cover general needs of the product divisions: the tool pool, a survey of tool needs, a Washington group to scout contracts, manpower and morale experts, public relations via a morale-booster magazine called *Automotive War Production*, a research staff on statistics, and a traffic division to push the weapons toward the ports in flexible, voluntary support of Pentagon priorities. As the war fronts changed military needs, he started a contract-termination division to chop red tape, hurry shutdowns on obsolete equipment and shift to the next job.

That much administrative machinery could have kept everybody immobilized in constant meetings. One day, Romney invited Chrysler's K. T. Keller to a working lunch. "Luncheon!" hollered Keller. "That's the trouble with this country—too many people think they're going to win this war with their teeth." Romney felt the same way: "All right, we'll get together on ice water." So doing, he used Keller's quote to save much of the dawdle time and money wasted on restau-

[1] His Mormonism was showing. The LDS church has mobilized its 2.6 million members into such a complex inner structure of clubs, priesthoods, age classes and self-service welfare units that everybody has a job, or several jobs if he is the busy bee he's supposed to be. Grant W. Heath of the Church Information Service in Salt Lake did a survey for me on the number of Saints who are called "president" of something or other inside a ward, stake or the home office. Total: 22,182 plus President, Prophet and Revelator David O. McKay.

rant sessions; by the time he rose to governor, he could realize his dream of having nearly all of his noon meals while working at his desk alone, or sharing a sandwich with a visitor.[1]

There was a distinctly political notion behind the committee systems of the war years, a belief that Romney elaborated over the years. He hates unilateral decisions, which affect lesser parties without their participation in the process. Stirton kidded him about his auto committees, insisting that GM was all he really had to please, but Romney was literally trying to give even the smallest company a say in the action. Using a concept of procedure that is a kissing cousin to his notion of constitutional process—you treat people as ends, not instruments—he struggled to make his clumsy committees legit, not rubber stamps for the big boys. Each company paid its share of ACWP costs, not out of cost-plus contracts but out of the corporate till.

It was also a time of invention on the workers' side. Since we think of existing institutions as eternal, we forget that real union power was a brand-new thing when World War II broke out. The auto sit-downers of 1937 had made good on the Wagner Act's promise to organizers. It took time to consolidate, and UAW did not crack Ford until after Pearl Harbor. If the New Deal had been an exciting and unsettling thing for the country, the labor union follow-up was still more revolutionary in the hometown of mass production.

"Every lodge and union hall set up debates on what labor

[1] Mrs. Romney or the cook, Mrs. Elizabeth Boyd, fixes him a roast beef sandwich, an apple or banana, a hunk of cake and a thermos of skim milk. The state troopers who drive him take the lunch into the office in a leather shaving kit. They presented him with the kit one Christmas so as to save themselves the indignity of toting the Governor's paper lunch bags. However, one visitor, hostile to Romney's no-smoke and no-drink austerity, resented being sent off with the staffers to eat. "Don't you do that either?" he blurted.

and management should do about the war effort," remembers educator Stirton, who chaired many of the debates. The two contending champs in the early phase were Victor Reuther for labor and one John Lovett for management. Lovett, a former union man, had been hired up to lobby for the Michigan Manufacturers Association, the state arm of NAM. "Lovett was the hardnosed, profit-sheet type," says Stirton. "He spoke ruthlessly, positively for Michigan manufacturers."

Lovett and Romney represented two opposed views of business. "He's a paid mercenary," Romney said. "That's redundant," joked Ed Cushman. "Lovett had been in Lansing as a lobbyist thwarting the programs that were needed," Romney said later. "He hadn't been dealing with industry's effort to meet public responsibility." Lovett returned the hostility with dividends. He found his chance after the war when B. E. Hutchinson, Chrysler treasurer, pushed Romney for president of the National Association of Manufacturers. Lovett realized that Romney would cut down on the NAM's right-wing politicking, start work on public problems, as he was doing at ACWP. "He'd run NAM right into the ground," Lovett told Hutchinson, and managed to nix the Romney appointment. As a result, the NAM floundered deeper into "coal-black reaction," as one blue-chip chief said, until it made an unexpected turn-around in 1964 by starting its own anti-poverty program.

As the war went on, the local debates moved from class-conflict ideology into more realistic concerns about the urgent union-management actions of the time. Romney replaced Lovett as the management champ. The terms and spirit of the debate changed a bit. "Victor Reuther was an entirely different man when debating Lovett from what he was when debating George," says Stirton.

In fighting each other on the platform, Reuther and Romney admitted areas of agreement. And made common cause. The Manpower Board in Washington prepared an order that would freeze all Detroit workers where they were and make job placements under the United States Employment Service mandatory. Reuther and Romney went to Washington with Cushman to win a stay of the decision. They came home to set up the Detroit Victory Council, a civic action force that would help, they hoped, to use manpower so efficiently that they could head off controls.

"It was perfectly apparent that the total community environment was playing an important part in what people were doing and how well they worked," says Romney. "The ultimate limit on war production was people."

Under the school superintendent, a neutral figure, with Bill Stirton as full-time mobilizer, Romney and Reuther paired off on the working level as co-chiefs. Victory Council dabbled into everything, from bus schedules to kiddie-care centers, that would make the general public-private system serve workers better. In a sense, they were trying to turn Detroit into a cohesive community. Nobody could tell how much, or how little, good they did; the urgencies of war brought on many such efforts that seem naive in the cynicism of peace. At Packard, labor-relations director Clyde Vandeburg had set up union-management councils that tried to turn each day's work into a sort of barn-raising. With substantial payoffs for workers who shortcut production delays, the Packard system was franchised through Romney's ACWP to the rest of the industry and passed on around the country to 6,000 defense plants.

The Victory Council had to face up to the racial crisis. On June 20, 1943, a fight on Belle Isle bridge became a forecast of what would happen to many cities, including Detroit, again in the Sixties. From this spark, the flash of violence killed 34 people in a few hours, wounded 700 and sent 1,300 to jail. City leaders knew even less about what to do than they do today. The most abrasive issue, as ever, was housing. George Romney, on the board of the Council's housing committee, took the lead. He delivered a formal protest to the Federal Housing Administration, and helped break loose housing that had been held back from Negroes near Ford's Willow Run plant. "George was the most active one in pushing us into the fight," says Stirton. "If he had leaned the other way, it wouldn't have been done." Others joined the fight. Reuther's UAW, initially reluctant, took up the cause of integration and with the Democratic party helped keep Detroit a jump ahead of serious violence until 1967.

Near the end of the war, the hope of peace became a threat to the existing way of life. Economists speculated that World War I's aftermath would be repeated on a monster scale. Millions, maybe eight millions, would be unemployed while the economy lost its momentum in the gap between war and peace. Fifteen million servicemen would come home to hunt jobs. Reuther came up with his tripartite plan again, strongly supported in Washington agencies, to control the conversion to peace. General Motors president C. E. Wilson called Ed Cushman to his summer home to suggest that a restricted number of engineers be released from war manpower control to plan postwar production. "He sold me on it," says Cushman, who had stood against Wilson on other issues. Heading for Washington, Cushman could not even get a hearing until he worked his way up to Paul V. McNutt, War Labor Board boss. It sounded selfish to plan for future business while men died in battle. Romney, running hard with the idea, was blasted by a bitter general: "The blood of thousands of American soldiers will be on your head."

Bloody or not, Romney reversed gears in his mobilizer staff, expanded the contract-termination operation and plunged into peace planning. (In 1967, he had his Presidential campaign staff at work on contingency plans for what the United States should do if peace came to Vietnam.) McNutt backed the Detroit cadre. So did Commerce Secretary Jesse Jones, who picked up auto industry plans for demobilization, fought inside government for less restrictive rules on reconversion. Paul Hoffman retailed the Detroit system nationwide. Drawing other businessmen into a new organization called CED, he promoted research to prove that the postwar slump could be headed off. The studies helped restore business confidence to bet on peacetime prosperity.

No slump came. But Romney was soon fighting the auto industry's back-to-normalcy trend. Gone, he discovered, was the cooperative impulse that could mobilize a city to a common purpose. The race riot still blighted the city's reputation. Like Dallas after the assassination, Detroit bore a stigma, then a unique one. Romney hunted a way to erase it, found an odd hope in the idea of civic circuses.

It first came from Christy Borth, an auto industry writer who had worked for AMA through the end of the war "because of George. . . . I could always get some of these offbeat things through him." One March day in 1946, Borth was plowing among old automobile documents at the public library, when he happened to notice that "a lot of significant dates were coming up all at once." In autoland, that meant the 50th anniversary of Henry Ford's first Tin Lizzie and the first car on Detroit's streets. Christy hustled his dates over to Romney's office.

"We could have a hell of a birthday party," said Christy.

"Good idea," said Romney. "Why don't you do it?" Yes, he would put the AMA staff behind Christy on a ten-week crash program to meet the date.

So the ex-war mobilizers lined up the usual committee dozens, lured Henry Ford out of seclusion and brought in the other figures of wheel legend. Even Barney Oldfield. They painted Woodward Avenue gold, and the hooves of police horses to match. The city's biggest crowd ever, a million strong, turned out to watch a four-hour parade of floats, relic cars, bands, fresh-minted beauty queens of all nationalities and movie stars lured by the promise of a hard-to-get car. One auto baron arranged a Cadillac for Negro soprano Dorothy Maynor, and Frank Sinatra refused to sing for a mere Nash. "It was," says Borth, "the ten maddest weeks of my life." In its brighter mood, Detroit revived its United Foundation and led the drive to set up community chests in many other cities. Romney carried the word.

There was premeditation in the circus madness. As many race-torn cities have since discovered, one essential element of the fight against violence is to try and stir a little joy into a sullen community, teach it to play again. Even the Fun-City campaign of New York's Mayor John Lindsay makes more sense than the grumbling of critics—provided it is tied to serious moves toward solid improvement. The Detroit cadre eventually found a way to tie civic circuses to solid action. They happened on the solution a few years after the Automotive Golden Jubilee, when the city historian pointed out that Detroit's 150th birthday was coming up in 1950. This time they had a theme: "Bring a birthday present to your city." Romney and the regulars pitched in again, making up a list of civic needs—downtown renewal, convention hall, art center, more parks—and raising private donations for down payments to get them started.

"Things that shape human conduct are very subtle," Romney said one morning years later. "You start with an idea and only gain force as it is reflected by action in a material world." He is fairly certain that the race crisis will get worse until all forces of the society, much more than Government, can be mobilized into a total effort. And he knows that the new solutions will tax our ingenuity even more than our pocketbook.

117

# CHAPTER NINE

# TO BUILD A
# FOREIGN POLICY

———————

". . . everywhere I went I found the most urgent problem was to avert starvation and freezing for millions of people in Europe this winter."—George Romney, first business witness for the start of the Marshall Plan, United States Senate hearings, November 14, 1947.

On foreign policy, especially the Vietnam war, George Romney managed to start his Presidential campaign looking just plain clumsy. At the end of the five-state Western tour in early '67, a frowning Washington correspondent unloaded his fears to me in the bar of Detroit's Sheraton-Cadillac Hotel: "George, this man would be a disaster!"

The young reporter's syndicated reports on the Western trip had not been quite that candid, but in handling Romney's comments on Vietnam, he had taken pains to pass a case of nerves on to his readers. What bothered this honest newsman —and most others on the trip, for as usual the Washington corps pooled its brains—was the candidate's refusal to make himself a hawk or a dove under the definitions in vogue at the moment. He never did. There was also the aggravating Romney insistence that we ought not leave out of our calculations the question of what the South Vietnamese people are willing to fight and work for. The Asia experts of CIA were still hung up on the same worry, I discovered a few days later, but Romney's doubts did not wear the cloak of secrecy.

The most savage, and off-the-point, criticism soon came from Romney's professional foe, AFL-CIO state president August Scholle. Gus improved a bit on the tactics used by the Democratic ad agency in 1964 to pin the bomb-thrower tag on Barry Goldwater. "It would be the greatest tragedy that ever befell this country if that guy [Romney] is sitting beside the button," declared Scholle in an interview. "I'm afraid he wouldn't be fully cognizant that he couldn't go out after the holocaust and say, 'that's not really what I meant; I only pushed the thing a wee bit.' "

The scare-mongering might be worth weighing if you could find a precipitous act anywhere in Romney's adult life. I have yet to dig up one, and I've looked hard. Temper is the opposite of panic. As President, Dwight D. Eisenhower was known to show temper, but he never put his thumb near the panic button. Romney has lost his temper in political hassles—been "intense" as he says, sharing the Lansing joke—but on substantial moves, let alone irrevocable ones, he refuses to let any situation push him beyond prudence. In fact, he openly argues contradictory courses until he finds where data and principle come together. He then cools the result in a fail-safe system of prayer. Though it sounds to moderns like a resort to witchcraft, he prays each issue in specific terms, clearing his mind of extraneous pressures and the ego's distractions.

The press suffered through this process with him on Vietnam. Rather than take the easy way and agree that President Johnson had pushed the right buttons on escalation, he weathered months of blistering criticism for "wavering." He was charged with political opportunism, and put down as a dangerous dove by the hawk majority in his own party. "They think that because I didn't satisfy them on Vietnam policy," he said, "that I'm not smart enough to do anything." He would not tie himself down, however, until he became convinced that further delay might cause the Communists to refuse to negotiate—out of the hope that he, if elected, would make a soft settlement. "Ho Chi Minh is running on the Romney ticket," argued a veteran expert on Indochina.

Romney doubted the premise—and Ho's intransigence later confirmed the doubt—but he knew he must prevent the possibility. So, without waiting to tell his staff, he announced from Washington that he would make a Vietnam statement in Hartford, Connecticut, on April 7. One staffer, hearing the news over a car radio, ran off a Michigan highway.

The Hartford statement, then, was a careful stopgap. The Washington *Post* called it "a model of restraint and balance. . . . It will reassure his friends and give no comfort to his country's enemies." But it did comfort President Johnson. The White House instantly put out a press release thanking Romney for "strong endorsement of the fundamentals of the Administration position. . . ."[1] Pleased that Walter Lippmann and a few others had read him more clearly, Romney had to keep quiet while the Hartford position sank in. He believed that the United States failure in Vietnam was part of a larger failure in foreign policy. "Vietnam does not stand by itself in

[1] The release itself was interesting. In the part-sentence that the White House quoted from the Hartford talk, a deft little edit improved the Romney version into a testimonial for LBJ sincerity. Romney had pledged neither to "give encouragement to Hanoi's aggressive course nor undermine our President in sincere efforts. . . ." The White House went to the trouble to insert a "his" and make the quote read, "our President in his sincere efforts. . . ."

international affairs," he said. So he needed to argue fundamentals rather than battlefield tactics.

Romney's concept of the role of the United States in the world, which emerged in later speeches, came directly from his view of the United States at home. What we do wrong at home, we match that wrong abroad. The domestic policies that trap people in ghetto squalor, ready to riot, have a counterpart in foreign policies that replace the American sense of practical service with the cruder uses of power. The idea was hardly new. But his specific applications of it were based on experiences that began at the end of World War II.

In 1946, Detroit's Dr. Ed Cushman headed the Government section of the three-part American delegation (Government, union, employer) to the metal trades division of the International Labor Organization (ILO). Cushman's friend Romney served as employer delegate from the auto industry. Held that year in Toledo, Ohio, the ILO session got off to as noisy a start as any since its founding under the old League of Nations. Reason: Romney did a Daniel in the lion's den. He called upon the anticapitalist majority to join him in a world crusade for the liberating joys of "cooperative competitive capitalism."

Australia's labor delegate acidly retorted, "That's what we're of a mind to get rid of down under." Cushman recalls with a smile that "they laid into George for the rest of the meeting." He set his jaw and happily slugged it out. He had been bush-leagued in Detroit without the chance to sharpen his style in the outer world. His two years as a missionary in Britain had given him the kind of continuing interest in foreign affairs now seen in Peace Corps vets, and his education had improved on the New Deal dialogues of the Thirties. But he now came on proud from the years of war mobilization, and sounded to Social Democrats like a resurrected Robber Baron. His "cooperative" principle sounded like window dressing.

The employer delegates from eighteen nations elected him to lead their team to the 1947 session, at Stockholm. Through the year, he studied for the job, drafted a resolution on economic development by "free, competitive enterprise" and called the management delegates to Stockholm a day early. "We ought to know what principles we stand for," he said, "so we can stand together." Now he found that he was a minority of one. "George, we don't mind that 'free enterprise' in the resolution," said Sir John Forbes Watson, of the British Federation of Industries (a sort of NAM), "but you've got to take that 'competitive' out of there, or it will embarrass us at home."

Romney was slowly comprehending the depth of European commitment to cartels, the noncompetitive division of business among established firms. He argued bluntly: "You are saying that both industry and labor can organize their power to the nth degree; so long as government doesn't step in it's okay, still free enterprise." His Teddy Roosevelt nerve began to throb. "We'd have gone the same way in our country," he said later, "if Roosevelt hadn't fought the trusts, and other people had not fought to decentralize economic power." Back in his room, he dug out the new one-volume edition of Arnold Toynbee's *A Study of History* which he had read coming over on the *Queen Mary*. Yes, there on page 396, he had marked the passage that would serve as English ammunition to fire at Sir John. "Toynbee says without reservation that the main thing that led up to Hitler and Mussolini," he opened up when he got back to Forbes, "was the fact that industry and labor became so highly organized, so powerful, that the average man had no protection against their exercise of monopoly power."[1]

[1] He handed Watson the exact Toynbee text: "The demoniac driving force which carried Mussolini and Hitler to power was generated out of this intellectual proletariat's exasperation at finding that its painful efforts at self-improvement were not sufficient in themselves

He kept pushing. Sir John did not know that Romney had once made the high school football team by driving so hard that his big nose scraped itself raw in the turf.

Next day at the general sessions, the leader of the union delegates, a Swiss, took Romney aside for an earnest pitch about the rise of communism in trade unions. He had a plan. Europe, he said, could no longer compete with the productive efficiency of the United States, and unless world trade were controlled, would soon collapse. The disaster would give the Communists all they needed to take over. The only way out, the Swiss felt, was to urge member nations to divide up world markets so as to maintain existing production levels. Here was the cartel case again, now from labor in the name of anti-communism, for a sort of world NRA of protectionism.

Romney liked the union man and sensed that his quick mind would see what was wrong with the idea of limiting production. According to notes dictated soon after, Romney argued this way: "Look, if we're going to tell the impoverished people of the earth that they have all the goods they are entitled to—that they'll never get any more—we'll play right into the hands of the Communists. Contrary to what you think about how rich we are, we don't have enough at home. There is a great deal of truth in the statement [by FDR] that one-third of Americans are ill-housed and ill-fed. The problem is to expand output by and for everybody."

The argument may not have sold the union man. Not many ever catch on to capitalism's loaves-and-fishes trick. But the American's startling sincerity piqued the Swiss' curiosity. The two joined forces behind a resolution to throw the ILO staff into a major study of the economic and political principles of the countries that had excelled, namely the United States.

---

to save it from being crushed between the upper and nether millstones of Organized Capital and Organized Labour." *A Study of History* (Oxford: Oxford University Press, 1947).

Romney is not an America-right-or-wrong type. But he believes that when we are true to our own way, we are true to the nature of man and ought not keep it to ourselves.

He was trying to turn the ILO from a limited debate about government programs to a broader study of development economics. But at the next ILO conference two years later in Geneva, he decided that the organization was doing more harm than good. "It was encouraging undeveloped nations to build up the public sector before they had a private sector to support them," he said. Like his friend Paul Hoffman of the U.N., he is impressed by the fact that the welfare state is an invention of industrial nations. To teach thatch-roof nations how to set up elaborate public services before they lay an industrial foundation, he feels, is to deny them their chance ever to have a stable society.

George and Mrs. Romney turned their 1947 Stockholm trip into a two-months' vacation. He had long ago promised Lenore every luxury she wanted, so he made a down payment. In Paris, at Jean Patou's, he grandly urged her to buy a full wardrobe. "I picked one dress; he wanted me to take eight, and I think we settled for four," notes Mrs. Romney. But everywhere they went in eight countries, the combination of war ravages and extended drought struck them, if not around the luxury hotels then in the slums where Mormon missionaries operated. In England, the dreary food persuaded them to eat the canned ham and chicken they had packed for London friends.

Romney came back to do something about those hungry people. He threw his energy into the Detroit Citizens Food Committee, part of European relief, and joined the little movement pushing for foreign aid, the buildup to the Marshall Plan. His talks, reported in the newspapers, hit hard enough to get him called before Sen. Arthur H. Vandenberg's Foreign

Relations Committee as the third public witness, after John Foster Dulles, on the bill for interim aid to Europe.

"The destructiveness of the war and its disruptive effect on European economies was something I expected to see," Romney testified. "But everywhere I went I found the most urgent problem was to avert starvation and freezing for millions of people in Europe this winter." He stomped down the popular dodge that these foreigners had brought the troubles on themselves with unsound monetary policies. He made his pitch on pure humanitarian grounds, certain that the United States would respond to the full facts, but added: ". . . unless America does help to the full limit of her capacity, human want and suffering could destroy any effective resistance to totalitarianism. . . ."

Taking up the data on food production, he urged that fat America deliberately diet so as to share the too-short supply with others.[1] He was working toward his usual cooperative premise, convinced that no program can be effective for long unless it involves the voters in a direct way. Citing the voluntary successes of the war mobilization program, and quoting a wartime report by the Senate's Truman Committee, he argued that foreign aid must not be locked into a government-to-government formula. Though the urgency of hunger meant that official agencies ought to handle the winter's food shipments, he hoped that much of the future food relief would be handled by CARE, the churches and other independent agencies here and over there. Such diffuse efforts, adding up to much, avoid the pressure tactics of a single agency.

[1] Mormonism again. The Governor of Michigan and his family dutifully fast for two meals on the first Sunday of each month and contribute the savings to the LDS Relief Society. It's not part of the tithe. "It's not a gift, because you don't really spend anything on it," Mrs. Romney explains in her plausible manner. "You just take the food that you were going to put in your stomach and put it in somebody else's stomach."

He wanted a different but related policy for long-term economic development. Government insuring of private recovery loans, plus a variety of other efforts, would diversify an all-public subsidy program. (He later argued for multinational development funds, and considered international COMSAT corporations. "If the assistance is rendered primarily by our government to their governments," he said, anticipating the affluent nationalism that peaked in the Sixties, "the charge will be made that their governments have become satellites of America."

He read one sentence twice for emphasis: "Most certainly we must not retard their economic reconstruction to settle differences of economic principles." But we must struggle to shake the reliance on cartels. "The difference between such private cartels and governmentally nationalized industries is slight indeed," he testified. "Loans made [post-World War I] actually became outright grants but European industry remained monopolistic, producing high-priced products for the few and low wages for all."

After the testimony, he followed up with public talks on other ideas, some of them for a United States role in the underdeveloped world. He was intrigued by the thought that, like Mormon missionaries, other young people might be sent abroad for two-year hitches of helping people. "But I gave it up after a couple of speeches," he admits.

His was the simple language of the economic moralist. Daily, in battle along the interface between industry and government, he was struggling to make human sense out of an era when knowledge itself has been compartmentalized in a thousand jargons. He fumbled, often said complex things in simplistic language. Reading notes and speeches he made during the late Forties and early Fifties, I could never get far away from his hidden religious assumptions. He could not view mankind as anything but a brotherhood, perhaps all saints here or later. Foreign and domestic problems were a piece of the same one-earth reality. Acutely aware of the unrest his country's productive skill had let loose upon the world, he knew that we couldn't keep our goodies if we tried to keep them all to ourselves. He had been driven out of Mexico as a child because of the envy of the Mexican people. He now worked for the industry that made the four-wheel symbol of the planet's rising expectations. In the consequent boiling of revolutions, he hunted for a doctrine that would not be a fraud. The effort produced acres of the most turgid prose since Karl Marx, though of course it went the other way.

He found one breakthrough in a little book, now lost, of essays on "consumerism."[1] He took the word and built his own ideas around it. He had learned at ILO that to most of the world "capitalism" meant, in one dictionary's definition, "The concentration of capital, as when in the hands of a few." That's what many capitalists wanted, he knew, but he wanted to fight for a world in which the many, the worker-voter-consumer millions, would be the busy sovereigns in both the political and economic order. To make use of either the vote or the money ballot, you had to have two systems that would respond to both. "We buried capitalism long ago," he proudly told Latin American businessmen.

He sounded as if he were glorifying the act of consumption. But he pointed out that just as the voter's right is a sort of veto, the minimum act of the citizen, so the consumer's right of choice is the negative on which a just economy must be built.

[1] His reading in this period seems to have been gulps from whatever came to hand. He took in anything from literature to uplift trash, from Sunday supplements to *The Federalist Papers*. When a friend demanded return of Bernard Iddings Bell's *Crowd Culture,* Romney sheepishly erased pages of underscoring. His reading habits made him a traffic menace. When his staff learned that he kept a book open on the seat beside him while driving, he reassured them that he read only at stoplights.

"The only reason for having power reside in the individual," he argued, "is to keep it from being held somewhere else."

The consumerism ideal made him more critical of flaws in the homefront economy. If he'd had a motto, it would have been, "Consumers of the world, Revolt!" After he moved out of the auto trade association in 1948 to be an executive of Nash-Kelvinator Company, he whipped up a nationwide protest behind the Rambler compact. It had the political overtones of a rebellion against the Big Three's gas-guzzling go-go-go.

On the foreign side of business, he enjoyed the benefits of the rising expectations in other countries. Kelvinator's strong sales of refrigerators and washers in 18 nations around the world kept the rest of his sick company alive long enough to be treated. His English source of appliance parts let him stand off efficient competitors at home. More important, he saw the political sense of Kelvinator's licensing system, which made him a partner with foreign firms, not the owner of an empire holding outposts against hostile natives. Here was a way to head off reenactment of the Robber Baron phase abroad. In 1960, he flew down to Argentina for a look at Edgar Kaiser's unique auto plant out in vaquero country, and came back impressed that Kaiser had made his company a technical servant by leaving owner-control to nationals. Romney sold Rambler-making tools to update Kaiser's car, and took a 15 percent piece of the Argentine operation. "They weren't run out by the revolution, either," he later said with pride.

As usual, he raised the practical situation into a moral crusade. He once set the financial pages ablaze by charging that wholly-owned United States plants abroad are the instruments of "economic imperialism." "We will make a vast mistake in American industrial expansion abroad unless we put our foreign operations on a partnership basis, rather than under the absentee ownership and control of an American board of directors," he argues today. "It is only right and reasonable that other nations consider their markets *theirs*, not ours, and it is time we woke up to the resentment and bitterness we arouse even in Europe when Americans move in and take over."

It was in his international business years that Romney began to demand a change in public policy on foreign investment. Instead of being blind to how differently companies operate overseas, the Government could encourage those that help other nations build a commercial base. He proposed an International Partnership Investment Insurance program for firms that would share the fruits of progress by setting up partnerships with local people. Expanding on a United States-Canadian plan, he urged "international trade bridges" for tariff-free swaps of goods between industries and individual companies. Because government-to-government relations are unstable unless based on a network of private and independent relationships, he felt that aid ought to strengthen, not replace, this base. It had to happen in a hurry.

"We are like billionaires living in a few mansions in the middle of a vast ghetto," he said later. "And too often our actions have tended to belie our words." For example, the United States patiently pushed its foreign aid, which contributed to the balance-of-payments deficit, then clamped down on foreign investment that would, if used right, help other nations more than direct aid. Though no foe of foreign aid, Romney began to suspect that most of it would have to flow through multi-national development funds. As long as it came directly from the United States, little despots could blackmail us—"the Russians are coming!"—rather than compete over how best to develop their nations so as to draw in more public and private capital.

Once he had moved into state government in 1963, however, Romney lost his daily involvement in foreign economic development, aside from Michigan State University's Point

Four activity, plus the state's contract to help British Honduras under the foreign aid law. At national governors' conferences, he told the press that his business was domestic. "They kept trying to get me to commit myself on foreign policy," he says. And, being George Romney, he answered enough to show that he was out of touch.

Worse yet, his approach had not been spelled out, so his comments did not have a context. By his lights, the function of government under law is to protect honest relations between people, at home and across boundaries. The CIA subsidy of student groups and labor unions was to him a corrupt inversion. "It's part of this manipulation system," he said to me. "You use people for anything you can get away with." In a press release, he deplored the failure of business and foundations and churches to finance idealistic students.[1] Even if adults don't agree with their politics, students ought not to be forced into cloaks and daggers. Such thoughts sounded fuddy-duddy to a press corps that later flipped over "brainwashing."

Having not defined his position in terms the press understood, Romney had no place to stand when reporters kept demanding that he make like a hawk or a dove on Vietnam. When he announced the Hartford speech, he was fresh from talks with men like strategist Henry Kissinger, and still reading piles of very different opinion. He set up four separate production lines of ghosts to push speech ideas directly at him, all very different in their emphasis, and had aides flying off to test drafts on Nelson Rockefeller, Dwight Eisenhower and others. Meanwhile, he had to spend a sizable share of his

---

[1] Business does more on this score every year, often taking chances that Government dare not try. Foreign conferences like *Pacem in Terris II,* which the State Department boycotted, was sponsored in part by United States capitalists. A few businessmen even contribute to foreign unionism, to help reduce wage differentials. This is called problem-sharing.

working days in a struggle with the legislature. A bitter tax-reform fight was building up.

On Sunday, five days before the talk, Romney still had not settled on a clear line. He prepared for the big affair by having daughter Jane cut his hair, for a dollar. It was not until Wednesday night that, working at home, he pulled ideas out of the four proposed drafts and in his looping longhand inscribed the Romney version of it all. Next morning, he handed the draft to Peg Little, his secretary. On Friday, with a plane to catch, he called in ghost Al Applegate to order an eight-point summary for the end. Before Applegate got the first five points through his typewriter, Mrs. Little came in with Romney's own eight points, just dictated:

1. It is unthinkable that the United States withdraw from Vietnam.
2. We must not oversimplify this conflict by talking only in terms of bombing or withdrawing.
3. The failure to induce negotiations at this time should not result in massive military escalation. We should continue to seek meaningful negotiations.
4. We must learn from the lessons of this tragic war to avoid similar involvements in the future.
5. We must give our gallant fighting men our full support. We must use military force as necessary to reduce or cut off the flow of men and supplies from North Vietnam, to knock out enemy main forces, to provide a military shield for the south, and to establish military dominance.
6. We should help South Vietnam to get an effective program underway to win the "other war," which because of its inherent nature is primarily their war.
7. At the point of achieving military dominance, we should encourage the Government of South Vietnam to achieve "peace with amnesty" to avoid a very long and brutal "other war."
8. If "peace with amnesty" or some similar negotiated solution fails, we should continue to help the South Vietnamese win their "other war" but keep from Americanizing it as we have done the military conflict.

131

One observer, certain that the text had not come out of Romney, suggested that he step aside and run the ghosts for President. Future foreign policy talks came much easier, in part because Jonathan Moore, his young foreign affairs aide, settled into the Romney Associates staff in Lansing for the kind of constant conversation that both needed. Romney can't use borrowed or rented opinions, so he used Moore as the man on whom to test his own. His way of using advisers was not understood. "The Governor doesn't know what he's doing," decided a Detroit taxidriver. "The paper says he's brought in a Harvard man to tell him what he thinks on Vietnam."

Within the staff, both before and after Hartford, Romney encouraged an unconventional direction of study. It had to do with the connection between domestic and foreign policy, and the trouble areas in each. If the Federal Executive cannot find cures for the core city, it may not do much better in the village economies of Vietnam. Present policies, however productive in the past, seem to have turned counter-productive; the heavier the commitment, the more uncertain the results. To Romney, this was no coincidence. In the underdeveloped areas at home and abroad, solutions imposed from above lessen the capacities of people rather than strengthen them. "Unless you diffuse power you're in trouble," he said. "We have to rebuild our relations all over the world, in ways that prove we don't need to dominate." But the staff was climbing the walls trying to put the point in more sophisticated language. As in the slums, failure in Vietnam was leading to automatic escalation of the unsuccessful.

"Our interest has been defined largely by the commitment," Romney said, "rather than the commitment by the interest."

The outcome of the Arab-Israeli war, he said when the news came of Israel's victory, made a telling contrast. "It shows that you can't forget people, and the question of what they can do for themselves." Russia's unsuccessful trouble-making in the Middle East, he felt, underscored the difficulty of any great power that tries to dabble too much. The world troublemaker has no less of a problem than the world peace-maker (the United States).

"We are slipping too far into the role of trying to solve all problems," he said later. "We are tending to preempt the responsibility of other nations more directly involved, and we are in danger of spreading our resources too thin." He argued that the original policy of containment, at first limited to meet-ing major Communist thrusts, had been turned into a rigid formula. "Containment by itself is a policy of mere reaction, which surrenders the initiative to others," he said. Anti-Com-munist preoccupation, he feared, often makes the United States a foil for Communist leaders.

He was working toward a more flexible policy to buy the advantage of time. The United States must maintain the most powerful military force and provide basic international sta-bility, but neither force nor peace must be considered as ends. Given time, our best offering, to be proved again at home and shared abroad, must be an economic and social order by which all those worker-voter-consumers of the world could climb out of hunger and helplessness. On how to do this, he had a life-time of experience and ideas, and he didn't care if some thought him a chauvinistic American. He was, he admitted, operating on a premise that might seem quaint: The United States must learn to respect other people as if they, too, were possessed of the natural rights of man so vehemently stated in a revolutionary document called The Declaration of In-dependence.

"We are not," he said, "filling the footprints of our history."

# CHAPTER TEN

# SELF-TRUST
# IN A JAM

---

"It's management's fault," Romney told the American Motors executives. "We have a responsibility to tell these people the facts and see if they can help us save their jobs."

It happened to him in the winter of 1955–56, but he's not sure exactly when, or even that it was much of a turn. George Romney was 48. He remembers "my back was against the wall." By the rules of the business game, he was already shot down. Then he slowly got hold of the inner reliance most men never find.

"I didn't have any choice," he admits. The caution of his advisers, he saw, would only slow the fall that was killing jobs for 21,000 men and women. "You follow the beaten paths, and you lose," he said. So he pushed out on his own ideas, though friends warned him, and day by day he found that they worked. The pieces inside him were slipping into place. His taciturn secretary, Mrs. Margaret Little, studied the shakedown: "After that, he was more compact, all of a piece."

Romney could have ended up just one more ambitious

134

businessman who talked ideas on the side but walked lock-step up the standard ladders. Because his ladder broke, he became one of the set-apart sort who, win or lose, never again stop short for fear of personal failure. If he loses on the bid for President, he will, he says when asked, be on the golf course at six the next morning staying in shape for the next job, whatever it is.

You see this thing happen now and then to strong people in business or science or politics, and sometimes to writers. For the leadership trades, it generally comes late in life, and may be part of the calm that comes from knowing you won't live forever. Perhaps it happened to young John Kennedy on the wreck of the *PT-109*, though his *Profiles of Courage* hunted the event in older men.

Romney's situation at American Motors was almost a business soap opera. He had been president since late 1954, when his mentor George Mason suddenly died and left him alone in the front seat of a rattletrap outfit skidding for a crash. It was worse than anybody knew. AM had just been invented by Mason, who wired the worn parts of Hudson Motors into the battered frame of Nash-Kelvinator but had not made a permanent weld of the two organizations. The banks were ready to foreclose. Debt: $90 million. Of the 27 bankers whose loans soon had to be renewed, a majority guessed that they would be lucky to salvage 50 cents on each dollar. Nash and Hudson cars were lemons on the market, where Ford and Chevrolet were forcing their own dealers to dump juicy bargains in a price war for first place. The smaller company, squeezed between the wrestling giants, had bled losses until it had a $33 million income tax credit on its books—fresh bait for corporate raiders. Even then, Louis Wolfson, whose raid on Montgomery Ward scared hundreds of executives, was secretly sniffing, though he did not pounce for several months. And for a clincher, American Motors was ailing inside from a high-cost labor infection that had been spreading since World War II. Compared to the Big Three (GM, Ford, Chrysler), it was paying higher wages for less work and some highly institutionalized loafing. One enterprising lady had even set up an in-plant restaurant to sell meals to fellow workers on company time.

One of Romney's prayerful decisions had put him into this mess. It came about when he had to make a choice between dazzling propositions put to him by the two auto barons who knew him best. One was Alvan Macauley, Packard senior man for whom Romney worked during the war mobilization years. The other was Nash-Kelvinator chief George Mason, under whom Romney had staged the Automobile Golden Jubilee to put Detroit in a mood to mobilize for peace. But General Motors, Big Daddy of the trade, wanted to go back to normalcy, away from the cooperative frontier. By 1948—after his first two slugfests as employer delegate to the ILO—Romney knew that his Automobile Manufacturers Association would now stand pat. Word went out that he was restless, and back came feelers from other trade associations, among them the whiskey lobby. Teetotaler Romney didn't even pick up the phone. Then, plop, over the transom came such a handsome offer that Romney had to pray mightily before he found the strength to resist it.

Macauley of Packard had a lawyer draft the offer into a firm contract. All Romney needed to do was to sign; he would become Packard executive vice-president at $50,000 a year, with a clause raising him to president and higher pay in two years. It was a bold bet on a man with no production experience. The company was fat and elderly. Still considered the quality car of all time ("Ask the man who owns one"), Packard then had the highest percentage of total car sales in its history and the biggest profits since 1929. Its upper echelons of executives were at retirement age, so the new boss would be able to build a full new team without cutting throats. "I assumed he'd take it," says Mrs. Romney.

He came very close before he called George Mason to talk about quitting as managing director of the AMA. "Wait until I get back," spluttered Mason from his vacation home in Bermuda. "Promise me you won't make any decision." He, too, needed new blood. His creditors were pushing him to pick up a younger man to be his successor in Nash-Kelvinator. But his offer came down to one of those come-try-us apprenticeships: Romney would be Mason's assistant at $30,000 a year, a second-stringer and not even a vice-president among the veteran executives still strong in the company. Mason made no firm promise about the future, nor did his quixotic bossing style offer clear hope. An Episcopal philanthropist who could not stand the emotional strain of weddings and funerals, this auto baron was a tubby sentimentalist who loved good food and wine, lobbed fancy cigar butts into a corner wastebasket and refused even to go look at the unpleasant labor mess on his production lines. He was the last of the entrepreneur-inventors. His dream was to sell tiny cars against the road hogs.

"I knew I should take the least flattering offer," George decided. So he took Mason's. His reason came from unflattering self-appraisal, which prayer reinforced. He needed time to learn the inside of the business under Mason and his seasoned vice-presidents. By then, he understood himself well enough to hunt the chance to take in data and absorb it, so that he would not have to act on borrowed opinions.

Romney trained the way he plays golf. He started, as usual, with what he calls "the fundamentals," in this case the guts of a car. The Nash service department was in its Milwaukee plant, so he checked into the Milwaukee Athletic Club, a leather-upholstered businessman's establishment not generally inhabited by student mechanics. He piled his room with engineering manuals to pore over at night. To learn blueprints, he took a night course. He carted paper piles home to Detroit for family weekends. Late one Friday he bounded into the kitchen, grabbed Lenore in grease-streaked arms and gleefully invited her out to the garage to admire his triumph. "He said he could take the car apart and put it together again with his hands," she says. "I didn't go because I didn't want to spend all night out there watching him prove it." He was no more a natural mechanic than he had been a natural athlete back when he made three varsity teams in high school. He gritted himself into both skills. He was not even a natural driver. As a teenager, he got teased by Lenore's sisters each time he put another dent in his father's fenders. Deputy Sheriff Occi Evans of Salt Lake, with whom George had double-dated, says, "We laughed when the worst driver in the world became the president of American Motors. I'm glad that he now has a job (governor) where somebody else does the driving. It's safer for everybody." Fellow executives at the company remember how a ride with Romney, speeding and brainstorming, inspired them to a lively interest in alternate means of transport.

But Mrs. Romney still stands loyally by her man. "I think my husband drives like a professional, like a trooper," she says, "fast but efficiently." She has a point. As a passenger on his 5:30 A.M. sprints to a Lansing golf course, I found my head efficiently cleared of all lingering sleep.

In spite of later press-agentry, Romney had not exactly melted into a class of student mechanics. The company grapevine had announced his arrival. Because a new rug had been laid on his floor in the walnut-paneled executive suite of the home office, the gossip tagged him to be Mason's heir apparent. He was in the spotlight. So, when not taking a crankcase apart, he used each spare minute to roam the plant's production lines, and sat down for a talk with each foreman. Since

the men constantly put the new boy to the test, he watched for
tests he could pass. When he saw the champion upholsterer
spitting tacks out of his mouth, George called up the talents
of his carpenter years. He casually stuffed his mouth full of
tacks, fed them out point-first with his educated tongue and
hammered the champ into a narrow defense of his crown.

After one year of methodical moves through Nash-Kelvinator's business—day shift and night shift, shop and office,
domestic and foreign, appliance division and car division—
Romney resolved never again to start a new career. "You have
to learn too much from the bottom up," he said. Gearing himself for the long, hard pull,[1] he realized that sheer physical
stamina might make the difference. On the wall of the Milwaukee Athletic Club gym, he grokked a sign about the
benefits of exercise. "The sign," he remembers, "said that it's
not the amount that counts, it's the regularity." (Milwaukee
Athletic Club can't find the sign anymore.) From that day on,
he never missed a day's workout if he could help it, or rode if
he could walk.

That's when he started the habit of getting up at 5:30 for a
round of "compact golf." Playing alone, he could chase three
balls at once—two years ago, he added a fourth—and run
with the golf cart so as to be dripping with sweat by the fourth
tee. Contrary to press rumor, he always kept strict score—"I'm
usually somewhere between bogey and birdie"—but never
exasperated himself sinking putts of less than two feet. "I'm so
bad that I just play for exercise and humility," he says.

[1] His son Scott diligently quotes a Cal Coolidge paragraph his
father recited to him often: "Nothing in the world can take the place
of persistence. Talent will not; the world is full of unsuccessful men
with talent. Genius will not; unrewarded genius is almost a proverb.
Education will not; nothing is so common as an educated derelict.
Persistence alone is omnipotent. The slogan 'press on' has solved and
will solve the problems of the human race."

Romney was bracing himself against the nightmare he was finding in the plants. Older executives, gentlemen closeted in walnut, could not believe what bizarre things were going on. In the labor-short war years under the new unionism, Mason's management had given up production discipline. He was holding his profits down during the war anyway. The car plants in Milwaukee and Kenosha, which had been UAW's first organizing victory, were bad enough, but they were efficiency models compared to the old Kelvinator refrigerator shop at Detroit. It was dominated by an acerbic Cockney, the late Matthew Smith, through an independent union called the Mechanics Educational Society of America (MESA).

Matt Smith billed himself an "alien, atheist and Socialist." When Romney talked about productivity, Smith laughed and pointed out that Romney was helpless. "Look, I've got your workers, your foremen and your plant protection people," said he, ticking off MESA's cover-all membership. "What are you going to do?"

He didn't know for sure. Established, floating crap and poker games ran on regular schedules in the rest rooms; if a foolishly diligent foreman approached, he would be bodily ejected by lookout bouncers. New workers were hazed, threatened into slowdowns. Getting comfortable, men installed Kelvinator stove and refrigerator units for in-plant use, and working wives cooked family dinners in the shop to save time at home. A hunter brought in a bear carcass too big to fit his kitchen oven, basted it in the shop's compressor-dryers. And one man on the line made double pay by barbering on the side.

MESA's Smith did not encourage the loafing, or like it, but his total control of the plant headed off reform efforts. There hadn't been many. Nash-Kelvinator's manufacturing vice-president refused as a matter of policy to let his foremen handle grievances and responded only to gripes sent up by the union. The foremen had joined MESA, Romney believed, "because management wouldn't back them up."

A small, secret chapter in Romney's past made his union battle a time of personal drama. Only a few years earlier, he had almost joined the labor movement. Around the end of the war, when the productivity lag began to trouble many companies, he learned that many workers who wanted to produce were forcibly discouraged by union machinery. That meant that people were being pushed around by brute power, his pet hate. He told Lenore to get ready to move the kids into a cheap house in a working district. She swallowed, said fine. He would take a plant job, join a union and see what he could do about reform from within, or start another union. "Workers ought to have the option to be with a union that has a social principle," he said. "Instead of a sheer power struggle, it could be related to the progress of the enterprise."

But he always seeks advice from whichever one of several dozen friends seems likely to understand a problem best. This time he went to the late Blair Moody, Washington correspondent for the Detroit *News* and later Democratic United States Senator. Moody, by then not startled at Romney's willingness to act on the logic of belief, talked him out of the scheme on grounds that his kind was rarer in management.

At Kelvinator, then, he sounded at times like a rival unionist, rocking established types on both sides of the table. He argued in AM's Policy Committee that the workers must be freed from the trap between a union that usurped power and a management that did not manage. The elders ignored him. In a few months, when competitors priced appliance parts cheaper than the disorderly shop could make them, the Nash-Kelvinator manufacturing vice-president decided to shut down the plant. Romney could not accept that. He laid out a new industrial relations program by which he hoped to raise productivity 20 percent. "It is management's fault for letting the situation get this bad," he insisted. "We have a responsibility to tell these men and women the facts and see if they can help us save their jobs." Overruled again. But Mason heard of the blowup, and that afternoon promoted Romney to executive vice-president. Though Mason hated tension, Romney now had a clear go-ahead signal.

Shutting down the shop, he called a mass meeting of the workers. "I am no college man," he preached in shirtsleeves. "I've laid floors, I've done lathing. I've thinned beets and shocked wheat." He showed them on charts what had happened to competitive costs, and why their jobs would die. Betting that they resented being trapped in the labor-management stalemate, he believed that most of them would welcome the chance to do an honest day's work. He got through. Matt Smith, who tagged him "Lochinvar" and "Romeo Romney," sent word that if there were another meeting, MESA would strike. Romney stuck to his plan for another meeting. Smith struck. Romney wrote to each worker by name, and Smith retaliated. They swapped about 67 missiles apiece in a literary war. Smith, the more eloquent, lost by attacking Romney's Mormonism. "People showed that thing to me, and some of Smith's stewards refused to pass it out," Romney remembers.

His clutch luck also paid off another way. With Romney behind them, the foremen were about to pull out of MESA. To head them off, Smith came up with a tactic that would let MESA represent both a foreman and a worker in a discipline issue, and thereby prove that management could not even referee a fight. So a union steward came back late from chow and slugged the foreman who griped. The foreman had been carefully selected—a high-tempered Dutchman who would hit back. "But he had a bridgework, and the blow knocked it down his throat," says Romney. "While he was gagging and

142

getting the teeth out, somebody stepped in and broke up the fight." The foreman moved over to management's side, and washroom lookouts soon vanished. Smith, no little man, took his defeats and worked closely with Romney.

While the labor struggle was still undecided, Mason worked out his 1954 merger with Hudson Motors, and had Romney draft a secret proposal of a second marriage, to Packard. The postwar car boom was over; the smaller companies were trying to huddle together to stay alive. Mason was the one man trusted to plot survival strategy for several companies. But the good life had worn out his pancreas. On Friday, October 8, 1954, at 11:45 in the morning, Mason died. At Mrs. Mason's request, a Mormon priest named Romney stood in an Episcopal pulpit to deliver the funeral tribute to "a great man with human frailties overbalanced by his good and noble qualities." Next day, the AM board elected Romney president, chairman and chief executive. It was like being commissioned captain and first mate of the *Titanic* a minute after it hit the iceberg.

To keep the company afloat, he had first to fight the spreading panic over word that it was sinking. People do not like to buy new cars that soon will be orphans, low in resale value. No, he told his first press conference, he was not about to add American Motors to the recent merger of Studebaker and Packard. He explained that he had a "product reciprocity" contract under which his Hudson plants would sell bodies to Studebaker-Packard, and in return he was buying S-P's V-8 engines. He made the same case to his chief money source, the Prudential Life Insurance Company, and hit the sawdust trail preaching the hope gospel to the Eastern financial press and analysts. Then came more trouble. Studebaker-Packard president James Nance, suddenly Romney's chief rival, did not read the reciprocity contract the same way. American Motors had to hold fire sales for the Hudson plants, and invest $10 million to develop its own V-8. Cooperation apparently had crisis limits.[1]

Inside AM, Romney had a mixture of breaks and heartbreaks. He brought off what would normally be considered a total reorganization. However, the immediate shake-ups turned out to be only first moves toward the revolutionary tactics he would have to try over the years before the old company was alive to his idea of "cooperative competitive consumerism." He sounded the general note of improvisation in his new ad policy and applied it throughout the company: ". . . kill the tired clichés. . . . We can screen out the completely crazy ideas . . . but we can't screen out no ideas."

Taking aim on the smaller-car market, he seemed at first to want only what was left over from the Big Three's drive into longer, lower, more powerful tailfins. He bet on the narrow advantage of sincerity. You had to believe in what you were doing, he said, before you could do it right. Sales boss Clay Doss did not believe in small cars, so Romney replaced him with Roy Abernathy, a small-car man out of Kaiser-Willys. He streamlined the top echelon, much as he would later do Michigan's state government, and passed authority down the line toward the foremen. He took his money worries straight to the workers in mass meetings, went off-the-record to tell them plans before he unveiled them to the trade press. To prove how serious things were, he cut his own salary 40 percent; three other top executives, inspired by his rate-busting example, took voluntary cuts, too. Yet, no top man bugged out during the dark years.

Comforts vanished. On the way to another employee meeting to preach paper-clip economy, he suddenly stopped, said, "I've got it—the airplanes!"

[1] The cooperative theory, however, gained a certain negative validation at Studebaker-Packard. Its $20 million V-8 plant eventually had to be sold for scrap.

"What about them?" inquired a vice-president. It was a foolish question; he knew in a flash that Romney was going to announce the sale of the two hard-flying executive aircraft to encourage economy all the way down the line. Perhaps a more constant reminder appeared in the rest rooms, where the luxury of toilet rolls gave way to cheap paper sheets. Costs came down fast enough to make survival possible and inspire many a ribald joke.

During that critical winter of 1955–56, he still had little to show for the complex ideas that were coming together into a single, unorthodox structure. The company was still on a disaster trend, though compact-car sales were turning up. He had only aggravated the Big Three with that pitch against their "gas-guzzling dinosaurs." So far as they knew, he did not become a true rebel until after he got a phone call from Washington early in 1956.

Over the line came the Oklahoma accent of square-faced David Busby, counsel for a Senate subcommittee investigating auto marketing practices. Calling from subcommittee chairman A. S. Monroney's office, Busby explained that he was following up evidence that Detroit was jamming its hapless dealers with car inventories. American Motors had just announced a new deal policy that seemed to correct the injustice of the system.

"Mr. Romney, we want you to be our lead-off witness," concluded Busby.

"I'll call you back in ten minutes," said Romney. He checked executive suite, found no convincing arguments against what he had in mind. He called back: "I'll be there."

On January 19, 1956, he told the senators: "I think the marketing practices . . . have reached the point where men in this industry are no longer proud, as proud as they were, of being associated. . . . I certainly am not here taking the position that the . . . deterioration in the marketplace is solely the

145

responsibility of my competitors. I think my own company has been responsible to a degree for this situation. . . ."[1]

He spelled out his reform plan for American Motors. With the help of the Senate spotlight, he believed that competition would cure the abuses, without regulatory legislation. GM's Alfred P. Sloan, Jr., had cleaned up a similar scandal after a 1938 Federal Trade Commission investigation, he said. "In my book, if the industry will go at this problem intelligently, we can stop from going down the political road." His eight-point program turned his weak dealer councils into strong dealer boards with grievance procedures built in. Local businessmen holding franchises to sell cars would always be captive outlets, unless they stood together and elected representatives who could fight down Detroit's impulse to use its muscle carelessly.[2] Romney never loses track of his belief that men work well together only if each can tell the other off.

Busby had known that Romney felt strongly about the dealer crisis, but had not expected such tough testimony. It headed off regulatory legislation. But it also made Romney a pariah back home. General Motors President Harlow Curtice sent word he wanted to talk to the American Motors president. In his anger, "Red" Curtice spelled out exactly what he was going to spend making up to his dealers. Romney felt that he was again using the raw muscle of money, not redressing the imbalance to give dealers greater independence. Maybe

[1] Automobile Marketing Practices Hearings before a subcommittee of the Committee on Interstate and Foreign Commerce, United States Senate, Eighty-fourth Congress, second session [Washington, D.C., 1956] Part 1, pp. 7–89.

[2] As the hearings rolled on, Chairman Monroney accidentally uncovered some political by-products of the economic imbalance between the big manufacturers and their dealers. At least one giant had forced its local outlets to contribute to a favorite Presidential candidate, Dwight Eisenhower.

the habit becomes ingrained. For the first time, Romney blurted out a belief that he would one day turn into a legislative proposal. On his fundamental insights, he tends toward a blunt candor that can be embarrassing.

"If you want to be a real industrial statesman, you have a great opportunity," he said while Curtice turned sideways to stare out his office window. "You could voluntarily spin off GM divisions into separate competitors."

"Who the hell would that benefit?" demanded Curtice, whirling around.

"It would benefit your shareholders, the workers, the customers, the executives and the general public," shot back Romney. "It would benefit just about everybody but you."

Having privately nailed his heretical views on the industry's front door, Romney now acted with the calm assurance of a man who could do no other than follow where belief led. His small-car conviction—plus his remarkable cost-cutting—carried along the bankers who gathered in July to consider renewal of his credit line, though it took all day to make the conversion. The same group had just refused to renew Studebaker-Packard's credit. They cut him down from $75 million in operating capital to a starvation diet of $43 million and appointed a watchdog committee. But he was alive. "He sold it," says Roy D. Chapin, Jr., then AM finance man and now its boss. "Believe me, it was blue sky, too, because we didn't have a thing in the book to justify it."[1]

Next, on July 16, in that same 1956, Louis Wolfson broke cover by firing in his first warning letter. Much has been made of the Wolfson battle because of his reputation as the

---

[1] Bankers do not wear their villain's moustaches every day. In this case, I happened to watch one of the key bankers, a friend, sweat out the thought of chopping Romney off without a chance. Though his mind told him that even the reduced loan was money down the drain, he simply could not do in a man who was trying so hard.

big bad wolf who would blow your house down.[1] Romney has been painted as little St. George holding the wolf at bay. This cliché does not capture the full flavor of the facts. If anybody was had, it was Wolfson; impressed by his own previous ability to inspire foolish hostility and panic, he had never run up against a genially unafraid man who, as Mrs. Romney once said without blushing, "wears an armor of righteousness." The result was rather comic. Wolfson not only ended up in Federal court under SEC charges, but he out-smarted himself when he could easily have multiplied his fortune. Made the butt of Wall Street jokes, he never re-covered his ominous image, and has been slipping deeper into trouble ever since.

The first Romney tactic was the stall. "We were bidding for time," he says. If he could get his company on the upturn, Wolfson could never win a proxy battle. He did have plenty to do besides talk to stockholders, and it is not surprising that duty took him clear out of the country, to England. All told, he managed to delay the requested meeting three and a half months. He did not circle back to New York to see Wolfson until Halloween.

It was a good day for scares. Saturnine and handsome, in a continental suit and with suave Southern manners, the raider plied his magic against a bouncy fellow who came in wearing a double-breasted blue suit and pleated pants off the rack.[2]

[1] John Thomas Mahoney, *The Story of George Romney, Builder, Salesman, Crusader* (New York: Harper & Brothers, 1960) pp. 28–47.

[2] By then, American Motors press agent Howard Hallas had maneuvered Romney out of tattered white shirts that tended to be grayed with age. "George, there must be something in the water," said Howard. "Had you noticed what it does to shirts?" To get him out of double-breasted suits, however, the staff eventually had to col-laborate with Mrs. Romney. "My husband sent them all to the little tailor down the street and had them cut down to single-breasted, for

"Before I leave this hotel room," Wolfson announced, "I am going to decide whether to have Buddy Gilbert here buy through A. M. Kidder and Company one million shares of American Motors stock up to eight dollars a share." Since the stock had plunged to six bucks, he was threatening go-for-broke to grab control. He already had 200,000 shares and, he said, $8 million cash on hand for more. "I had more than $100 million behind me in the Montgomery Ward fight." He was not alone this time, he added. Discontented shareholders had written begging him to "move in or take over." He had found two banks willing to sell him their American Motors debts at half price, if he could talk the other banks into a general sellout. He also criticized a high consultant's fee that American Motors was paying—the kind of item that, right or wrong, can be played up big in proxy propaganda.

The fellow in the double-breasted suit did not take offense. He worked it around to "Lou" and "George," and at the first opportunity delivered his enthusiastic spiel about his plans for the company's future. That would read fine on proxies, too. When pressed to accept a Wolfson man on his board and consider mergers with Wolfson properties, Romney readily agreed to take it all under consideration. He meant it.

Wolfson was like a man playing patty-cake with a tar baby. "Buddy, I've made up my mind," he told Gilbert. "I'm going to back Romney. You take that eight million and go off on the other deal."

Lou and George had many more chats, of course, because this was only the warmup. But George kept Lou off balance by embracing his claim to have the company's best interest at heart; he accepted suggestions on merit, and turned down merger proposals on the same ground—though he once more

---

$10 apiece," she says. "He hadn't noticed that suits had changed." The cut-down suits embarrassed Romney; while in them, he was listed among the best-dressed men of the year.

had to risk a proxy threat. Meanwhile, he was shaping up the company faster than Wolfson could credit. Wolfson's holdings rose to 415,200 shares or higher, so Romney opened two places on the board for men of his choice. He also honored his biggest shareholder at a 1958 dinner for crack salesmen— for buying Rambler fleets in companies he controlled. The ultimate irony soon came clear. At the time of the dinner, Wolfson's brokers were dumping his stock at $10 to $12 a share and moving toward a short position so as to clean up if, as they expected, the stock fell. It did slip a bit after newspapers quoted Wolfson, presumably still the biggest shareholder, on the view that AM was seriously overpriced. In spite of all this, the stock took off so fast that he had to scramble to cover his 137,400 shorts, some as high as $28 a share. He was left with little more than a million profit. If he had held on until the man in the double-breasted suit started to sell, he would have topped $40 million. George Romney, the financial world discovered, now knew what he wanted to do and how to do it.

# CHAPTER ELEVEN

# THE CHOICE-KILLING
# DINOSAUR

---

"The conspicuous car was the symbol, a symptom, an advertisement of our excesses—of our self-indulgence when good judgment and even some sacrifice were the crying needs."—George Romney in a 1960 Rambler advertisement.

The deadly war between Lilliput and Blefuscu, Jonathan Swift reported, arose from an ideological difference over whether a boiled egg ought to be cracked on the big end or the little end.[1] But liberals and conservatives in America do not waste passion on such trivial matters. Our ideological wars have been raging around the issue raised in the late Fifties by the tailfins of automobiles. The tailfin struggle goes beyond matters of poverty and prosperity at home and abroad. It has to do with the specific question of whether a people rich enough to buy fancy cars become passive masses willing to be manipulated or stiff-necked dignitaries determined to have more say-so in their economic and political system.

[1] Jonathan Swift, *Gulliver's Travels* (Dublin: Faulkner, 1735), Chapter 4.

Two economic moralists brought the tailfin into disrepute: One was John Kenneth Galbraith of Harvard, who was selling a political theory in a book called *The Affluent Society;* the other was George Wilcken Romney of American Motors Corp., who was selling a utility car called the Rambler. Oddly enough, the ideological division between these two men has become about as fundamental as any in U.S. politics.

Though they met only casually, Galbraith and Romney responded to affluence on similar schedules. Galbraith put the final coats of gloss on his magnum opus during the years when Romney was struggling to apply the first coat of acceptability to the near-finless compact. Houghton Mifflin Company published Galbraith's finished product in 1958, the model year when Romney shocked his industry by bringing out his most radical Rambler. The Detroit businessman's efforts were not considered an intellectual event, of course, or even very important. Galbraith will resent any comparison. Romney simply forced his big competitors to trim their fins and offer people a chance to buy sensible cars that saved millions of dollars for other purposes. In the process, he discovered a serious malady inside the country's biggest institutions, and proposed a relatively painless cure.

But the more complicated Galbraithian analysis is the one best understood by intellectuals, so we have to begin with it. His book was welcomed by American reviewers, and even more by the British, as a monumental work to put on the shelf alongside R. H. Tawney's 1920 critique of *The Acquisitive Society* and John Maynard Keynes' 1919 prophecy on *The Economic Consequences of the Peace.* Though more dismal economists put Galbraith down as a pop-culture phenomenon, none ever came close to him in writing influence upon the body politic. His public and private sector concepts, easy codifications of our era's conventional wisdom, quickly became the standard terms of debate on the Right and the Left. He expanded his themes in a 1967 book, *The New Industrial State*.

On *Affluent's* first page, the author announced that rich nations act like rich men:

> The poor man has always a precise view of his problem and its remedy: He hasn't enough and he needs more. The rich man can assume or imagine a much greater variety of ills and he will be correspondingly less certain of their remedy. Also, until he learns to live with his wealth, he will have a well-observed tendency to put it to the wrong purposes and otherwise make himself foolish.

The wrong purposes, he moralized with graceful wit, are brought about by advertisers, who create foolish desires in people for excess consumption of everything from gaudy cosmetics to fancy cars. As the Robber Barons of the past exploited natural resources and workers, corporations in the consumer era exploit the customer. Galbraith naturally viewed the consumer as a helpless, stupid animal who races through life on a squirrel wheel.[1]

Especially in industries dominated by a few giants— monopolies or oligopolies—big labor and big business make deals to administer wages and prices and foist the cost, he argued, upon the ad-hoked public. Galbraith held out no hope for curative antitrust legislation; to the vast relief of businessmen, he had made traditional antitrust positions unfashionable some years earlier by suggesting that "countervailing forces" now replace specific competition.[2] For instance, supermarket

---

[1] John Kenneth Galbraith, *The Affluent Society* (Boston: Houghton Mifflin Company, 1958), p. 159. Galbraith dresses his public sector in the toga of virtue and his private sector in the dirty underwear of sinful desire. The present generation of middle-aged thinkers, perhaps disturbed by Sigmund Freud, hold their inner selves in deep suspicion.

[2] John R. Bunting, *The Hidden Face of Free Enterprise* (New York: McGraw-Hill, 1964).

153

chains had gained the countervailing power to break the price-setting strength of the meatpacker oligopoly. But such accidents cannot be relied upon. So Galbraith generally put his faith in the biggest countervailing power of all, the Federal Government. The main pitch of his book, then, was for bigger public expenditures on unfoolish needs, to be paid for by taxes levied on the private sector's conspicuous consumption. He turned the tailfinned car into the symbol of our synthetic private wants. "To create the demand for new automobiles, we must contrive elaborate and functionless changes each year," he wrote, "and then subject the consumer to ruthless psychological pressures to persuade him of their importance."[1]

"We faced at American Motors the kind of problem that Galbraith talked about," Romney admits. The public did act brainwashed. One solution, then as now, was public preachment, on the theory that people can't be conned once they catch on. Romney identified his economy car with moral revolt. "He always insisted that whatever the company did had to be identified with the public interest," says Howard Hallas, then Romney's speech writer and one of several argumentative alter egos. "It took us out of the drivel category." The public-interest pitch also properly invited suspicion. As patriotism is the last resort of the demagogue, so the claim of public service is the slickest defense of the venal vendor. Ladies in the oldest branch of commerce have for centuries advertised their sincere desire to fulfill an urgent human need. Because old hands in Detroit excused Romney's heresy on just such grounds—he was, they felt, merely trying to stay in business—they were later to feel betrayed when they discovered that he meant that public-interest stuff.

His car notions had been taking shape since he joined the industry in 1939. He had come to the Automobile Manufac-

[1] Galbraith, *Affluent,* p. 308.

154

turers Association in search of a competitive utopia, a free-form contrast to the stodgy bureaucracy of the aluminum monopoly. Soon sold on the workhorse car, he assumed that some sharp competitor would fill the need. He had facts to go on. The United States Bureau of Public Roads had compiled a mountain of surveys on car use, but lacked funds to tabulate them. Romney's staff, doing the numbers for the Government, startled the industry with a statistic: On 85 percent of all auto trips, people drove less than 13 miles. The data showed that the car was becoming more of a daily servant than a Sunday yacht for tours between cities. If so, then big cars were silly and public road strategy was ridiculous; the traffic jams of the future, Romney argued, would come not on interstate routes but within the metropolitan commute. With the postwar flight to the suburbs, the busy-bee life of the typical family required two or three cars to shuttle Dad to work, Ma to the super-market and the kids to school.

Unfortunately, the suburbanite and his car became a liter-ary and political stereotype, and nobody looked behind it. The same liberalism that in its crusading phase had laid the money base for suburban affluence now disposed of its problems the easy way by condemning all suburbia as the wasteland for Jones-chasing. Business seemed bent on confirming the thesis. General Motors had clobbered Ford by making the car a status symbol. Each brand was now carefully styled to mark an in-come step from the Levittown Chevy and the Oak Park Olds, up to the Scarsdale Buick and the Beverly Hills Cadillac. Motivation research, with its boasts of managing the psyche, inspired sexy cars to compensate for the frustrations of other-wise drab lives. By the mid-Fifties, both Ford and Chrysler had capitulated to the GM strategy of ever larger, longer and more powerful models, pulling people by "dynamic obsoles-ence" into annual splurges to keep their status symbols up. Romney called it "the size and power craze."

Semanticist S. I. Hayakawa put the specific issue more clearly than Galbraith. The problem was not that many people bought fancy cars, he said, but that the industry "produced them almost to the exclusion of other kinds." People fresh out of scarcity could apparently be talked into a single scale of superficial values. In *The Hidden Persuaders,* pop sociologist Vance Packard enlarged upon the advertising craft's new boast of being able to put consumers under a psychological spell for the benefit of their corporate accounts. These claims confirmed modern liberalism's anti-business demonology. As the Women's Christian Temperance Union disdains booze, so the puritanical liberal condemns the fruits of commerce.

There was, then, a political issue buried under the vulgar showmanship of the car dealers. At American Motors, Romney's first boss George Mason had experimented with basic transportation since the Thirties. He and engineer Meade F. Moore had shop-tested everything from the two-wheeler to three- and four-wheel midgets. They failed, however, to anticipate today's motorbike boom. In 1950 they had brought out an expensive little Nash Rambler convertible on a 100-inch wheelbase, no longer than Ford's original Model T. Seeking designs that would last more than a year, Romney persuaded Pinin Farina of Italy, Europe's finest auto stylist, to simplify the early-Fifties models of Rambler convertibles, hardtops and station wagons.

But the understated vehicle was crowded aside by the flashy chrome and hot new colors of the Big Three. When Mason died in October 1954, Romney was left with a menagerie of Nashes and Hudsons that looked mangy in every status category. He had no success pattern to copy. European cars like Volkswagen had not yet made a dent. To bet his company's survival on the non-status of the compact was to defy the hard-proven logic of the whole Detroit Club. He didn't even have a car that boldly defined his idea. He was huckstering the too-small 85-inch Metropolitan, made with Austin of England, and a too-big 108-inch Rambler that was not dramatically different from the gas-guzzlers. Twenty-one of his twenty-three zone managers, he discovered, felt that he was being a sales idiot or, worse, a fumbling do-gooder.

The whole company studied "George," as he was known, at fairly close range. Though he had streamlined the chain of command, he refused then, as he did later in Lansing, to hide himself behind a second-in-command. He ran what can only be described as management-in-the-round with himself in the center of a day-and-night seminar. Hallas, Dr. Ed Cushman and others took any wild idea straight to him, and were startled at how quickly he would take it or leave it. "We decided," says Cushman, "that it was because he reasoned from what he called principle, and unless he was troubled by conflicting principles, he could get to the core quicker than any of us." But, to their dismay, his principles did not translate into standard sales jargon. He restudied Henry Ford's equalitarian revolutions, both the $5 wage and the proletarian Model T. Here, he found personal comfort for the unorthodox notion of starting with public service. The whole industry, convinced that the car was for the rich few, had ganged up on Ford. The original auto trade association, AMA's predecessor, had been set up to control all car production through restrictive patent licenses. "They put an absolute limit on how many cars Ford could make, but he fought them and won," said Romney.

Ford also had trouble with the cynical rhetoric of business. Romney likes to quote Ford's testimony in court after shareholders sued him in 1919 for paying an army of men higher wages than he had to and selling cars to millions cheaper than he had to. "If you give all that, the money will fall into your hands; you can't get out of it," Ford said. The court ruled against him, for orthodoxy. He had to buy out the complainants' stock before he could get on with his way of making cars at less than the "awful profits" they expected.[1]

When the Ford comparisons failed to comfort his colleagues, Romney fell back on a more candid argument. This one gave them the heebie-jeebies. AM lawyer Richard Cross, later board chairman, will never quite recover from the day Romney added God to the market surveys. God looks after decent people who try to do the right thing, and they were a company of good people doing their best, he said as if discussing his biggest customer. He admitted to Lenore, however, that his timing was dangerously tight; he could well set off the compact revolution, but go bust before it spread enough to save his company.

He had to hurry it up. With his self-trust toughened by the winter of 1955–56, he quit compromising on compact design. In the winter struggles of 1956–57, he went back to the 100-inch model that had first come out in 1950 and later flopped. To get such a car even to look at, he had to send an official out to a used-car lot, have a secondhand relic rolled into the secret styling shop. Roy D. Chapin, Jr., then vice-president, remembers the whole executive corps trooping down with their shirt-sleeved boss to inspect the dusty heap. Its basic design was still ahead of its time—an all-weld body like an airplane—but its style looked quaint as a buckboard.

"We took a pair of tin snips and cut the fender housing away from the wheels," Chapin says. They then had the snorkel sliced off the hood, the rear window cut bigger and the heavyweight taillight flipped upside down so it looked lighter. "We put in a radiator grille made out of stamped steel like that office radiator covering there," grins Chapin. Hauling old tools and dies out of storage, they spent only $1.1 million —"You can't retool a fender for that today."—to set up pro-

[1] R. L. Bruckberger, *Image of America* (New York: Viking Press, 1963), p. 206.

duction on their basic new model for 1958. Though one toady urged that the reincarnated car be named the Romney, it was dubbed the Rambler American. The little fellow's purpose was not to sell a heavy volume itself but to engineer a reverse twist on the market strategy of the Big Three. Instead of promoting high-status cars and selling the customer more than he could afford, Romney's men used the Rambler American to make their pitch for the low-cost compact—and let the customer hedge upward to the bigger Rambler, the 108-inch Classic (renamed, post-Romney, the Rebel). The strategy saved AMC. It broke open the United States market for Volkswagen, and also drove the Big Three into compact competition to please buyers.

The most aggravating chore, of course, was to ram through the wall of opinion in the ad trade. "We . . . changed our advertising policy, and incidentally that was a tough one," Romney told the Harvard Business School in 1958. "Boy, Madison Avenue has got fixed ideas! You just look at the ads. They're almost stereotyped by industries. . . . It took us three years to get our advertising agency not only to agree that our policy should be different, but also to reach the point where they could reflect accurately our product story in ads that would command attention of the American people." In short, he found that most advertising men had hoisted themselves on the status petard. They were prisoners of their own concepts. This captivity made them public menaces to Galbraith; to Romney, it just made them poor salesmen.

Teamed up with an iconoclastic copywriter, Sam Ballard of the Guyer Agency, Romney now began to throw his pitches in low and hard. He wanted to talk to whole families, urging savings on cars to leave money for education and other needs. So he lured Walt Disney and Davey Crockett into television. He did the commercial spots in person. "It took him a while," says Mrs. Romney, who coached him, "to learn to be himself and talk naturally to the camera." Eventually, he swung away from TV into printed media, a largely instinctive reach for the same kind of news-reading, independent people on whom his political career would later be based. Using words to say something, rather than for misplaced TV blurbs, he spelled out his Rambler beliefs in long, newsy essays. For instance, when John W. Gardner, a close friend now in Johnson's cabinet, published an essay on "The Pursuit of Excellence," Romney quoted its basic theme on "striving for the highest standards in every phase of life." He pledged to drive for the same excellence in the workaday auto: "To avoid fads and extremes, impractical styling. . . . To change the design of our automobiles only when change represents genuine improvement, never to change for the sake of mere change."

The difference was relative, of course, for he made inexpensive changes to mark annual models. But the difference was also real. Though the Rambler tended to drive like a string-halted mule, it built up a faithful and growing force of customers and the trade's highest resale price. He was not undercutting Rambler owners by deliberate obsolescence.

Once his Rambler revolt caught fire, he fed the flames of discontent with any piece of fuel that came to hand. When New York's Mayor Robert F. Wagner, Jr., complained of traffic congestion caused by long cars, Romney quickly offered to supply three compacts so that His Honor could set a civic example by giving up long Cadillacs. Wagner was not *that* concerned, but Mayor Norris Poulson of Los Angeles abandoned his limousine for a compact in the first stages of California's antismog campaign. "If a car uses one-third as much gas there will be one-third as much exhaust fumes in the air," said Poulson.[1] American Motors happily exploited whatever

[1] Romney is still sensitive to dinosaur smog. One warm spring day in 1967, he stomped around midtown Manhattan muttering at the sickly overcast left, at least in part, by the acid breath of dinosaurs.

writers and cartoonists provided by way of satire. Romney had fun with *The Insolent Chariots*, a 1958 book by John Keats and illustrated by Robert Osborn. And as usual, the pop culture people caught the spirit of the thing more precisely than the highbrow writers. Out of the night club circuits, unaided by Romney, came "Beep Beep," a million-record ballad about the Little Nash Rambler that bagged a Cadillac on the road without shifting out of second gear.

Romney saw the broader political implications of his fight, and exploited them. By testifying in January 1956 before Senator A. S. Mike Monroney's special subcommittee, he made himself the leader of the dealers' mutiny against Ford-Chevrolet dumping tactics, and won desperately needed new outlets for the Rambler. He had come home from Washington to be called on the carpet by his old friend, President Harlow Curtice of General Motors. It was in that stormy session that Romney first blurted out his belief that GM ought to spin off its divisions into independent companies. He talked this one over with his vice-president, Ed Cushman, who persuaded him that to say it in public while he was still losing money would only look like a beg for Government help. So he waited—until his first quarter in the black. Then he demanded and got a hearing before the late Sen. Estes Kefauver's antimonopoly subcommittee.

To catch the flavor of this decision, you need to know that the auto industry has become a club. For one of its visible executives to consort voluntarily with Kefauver would hardly be thinkable. A rough comparison would be for a Methodist preacher to announce plans for a still in the parsonage.

Romney tried to prepare his old friends in advance. He sought and got Ford General Counsel William Gossett's help in drafting the proposal, and explained his reasons to other key men in the Big Three. "George's always had this idea that if he can just lock people up in a room and talk to them long enough, he can change their minds," says Semon Emil "Bunky" Knudsen, stolid son of the legendary Bill Knudsen and by then a vice-president of General Motors. As George and Lenore's closest friends since 1939, Bunky and Florence Knudsen were not surprised one February night in 1958 when Romney called to ask if he could drop by late. "He sat over there and told me of this [antitrust] statement he was going to make the next day," recalls Knudsen. "He asked if it would make me mad. I said, 'No, it won't make me mad. But I don't agree with it. And if you feel that way, your timing's wrong. You may not always be in the automobile business. You may be in something else, maybe in politics, and people aren't going to forget it. They have long memories.' "

Knudsen knew his industry, though it took years for his prophecy to prove out. He, Henry Ford II and philanthropist Max M. Fisher raised tens of thousands of dollars at country club dinners for each of Romney's three gubernatorial campaigns, when the choice was between him and a union-minded Democrat. Besides, governors do not make antitrust policy; Presidents do. So the payoff, or lack of it, came early in Romney's bid for the GOP Presidential nomination. A couple of the auto chiefs not only kept their checkbooks shut, setting a strict example for subordinates, but passed the critical word on to friends and suppliers around the country. "I could raise $100,000 for him in two hours when he was running for governor," says one loyal friend, "but right now, I couldn't raise $5,000. My personal check won't do him much good." Though newspapers kept saying that Romney's effort was well financed, reporters were slow to sense that his fund-raisers were throwing themselves against locked doors in executive suites.

No conspiratorial dishonesty is involved. A devoted GM executive, for instance, cannot help but doubt the judgment, if not the sanity, of any man who would subdivide GM, even to preserve private enterprise. The standard argument was that George Romney made a good Michigan governor—the speaker could usually say he contributed to those campaigns—but was not Presidential timber and lacked Richard Nixon's sophistication in foreign policy. Nixon encouraged this view at black-tie stag dinners, where he briefed blue-chips on his travels abroad.

Even so, Knudsen had realized in '57 that hope for the future would not stop Romney from acting. "George has one great trait and attribute. You may not agree with him, but you can't doubt his integrity," says Knudsen. "He's completely open, no scheming, no monkey business or anything. People who are that way, like my father . . . are trusted even when you don't agree with them." From all I can make out, Romney became fairly reluctant in the St. George role this time but felt silence to be wrong. He was by then buried in *The Federalist Papers* and other historical documents published by the University of Chicago in two heavy volumes titled *The People Shall Judge*. With customary enthusiasm, he spent pocket money on four or five dozen of the $9 book sets to give to friends. "He was passing them around like popcorn," remembers Howard Hallas. The founding ideas, if treated as relevant, remind the reader of the slow death to be found in concentrated power.[1] So Romney felt it necessary to report the threat to "fundamental principle" he had run across in the auto trade.

In his testimony before Kefauver, Romney was careful to avoid the sensational simplicities. He was not making the trite

[1] By transferring Romney's annotations into my pair of *The People Shall Judge* volumes, I could follow his tracks at leisure. He had traced two main themes, anti-concentration and the need for moral renewal, down through the years. Even Robert M. Hutchins had linked these two ideas, in his 1947 essay on "The Constitutional Foundations of World Order."

case against bigness; indeed, large-scale operations had long since become an economic necessity. Size itself was irrelevant; control of market was not. American Motors had proved, in an industry characterized by giants, that a company with only a small share of the market, he said, could compete profitably if it had a unique product. He didn't need help, or want it. But he wanted the Senate to consider the situation that was developing in many industries. The effects were hard to spot at first. In autos, ten strong prewar companies had been reduced to five, the Big Three plus AM and ailing Studebaker-Packard. The result was a creeping concentration of power that resulted, first, in a monolithic marketing strategy. Consumers could hear about, and buy, except for Rambler, only the status-step cars. Other rigidities would show up later. Aspiring workers (more than half of them now in white collars) would slowly be trapped in a seniority system that grows rigid from the top down, like civil service. Administered prices and wages become inevitable, and the Government steps in more and more as the public's only referee. Without competitive check, cost-push inflation disrupts the domestic economy and prices the United States out of foreign markets. (This point did not sink in, because the United States had not yet begun to worry about the gold drain.) In short, business was itself destroying the discipline of competition, and thus inviting the only alternative, absolute Governmental control.

In spite of the detail of Romney's statement, the senators could see only the surface of it. They did not know the thought behind the ruddy-faced witness' belief that capitalism of the few must give way everywhere to consumerism for the many. As democracy's ultimate check upon governors is the secret ballot, so consumerism's ultimate check on companies is the purchase. But if the consumer is not presented with real choices, the system becomes a fraud. Companies can then control buyers, not serve them.

The antitrust laws had kept the United States from turning down Europe's cartel route, Romney said, but they were no longer effective. Drawn up in the Robber-Baron era, they required criminal prosecutions against mild executives who won by fair means. And such suits took years in court. He also doubted the wisdom of spending taxpayer money to subsidize competition in monopoly industries, as had been done in aluminum. By the same token, he saw no justice in the Defense Department efforts to salvage individual companies such as Studebaker-Packard.

He had a proposal. Competition properly brings on mergers and other "business deaths." But in mature industries, the high cost of initial investment now prohibits "business births." Existing companies provide the only ready source of talent and plants to start new companies. So what you need is a way to induce new business births out of established companies. Such a method already exists in the spin-off, the financial maneuver by which a corporation issues new stock to its shareholders so that they own a division that has been set apart in a company of its own. Market trading soon wipes out the overlap in owners. Romney's proposal: Once a firm takes 35 percent or more of an established market, say in cars, it would have to spin off part of its operations. Conglomerate corporations would have to spin at 25 percent. For an incentive, he proposed that shareholders be allowed to postpone the capital gains taxes they might have to pay if the spin-off were not ordered under law.[1]

In short, he would induce new business births by a kind of cell-division. The idea had obvious bugs. The parent company would surely pile all its cats and dogs, the least promis-

[1] Hearings, Subcommittee on Antitrust and Monopoly, Committee on the Judiciary, United States Senate, February 7, 1958.

165

ing divisions, into the new company. So be it. In occasional antitrust cases where this scheme had been followed by consent decree, the weaklings generally had grown strong. Lawyers could see other problems, such as the difficulty of defining exactly what constitutes an industry. But few of these uncertainties matched the gossamer chaos of existing antitrust precedents. Never dogmatic on the specifics, Romney invited any other practical, nonpunitive approach to the problem. He hoped that once the spin-off ideal caught on, the wiser kings of corporate empires would take pride in being the daddies of healthy offspring and shareholder capital gains. But the blue-chip chiefs shivered at the thought and hoped nobody noticed. One exception: the late C. E. Wilson, GM's fair-minded Engine Charley, calmly rumbled that the proposal ought to be looked into.

The most sophisticated argument against his proposal has been in terms of research and development. Only the giants, the line goes, can afford to invest in applied science for tomorrow's new products. The case for huge research labs seems especially convincing on defense contracts, which call for the incorporation of exotic technology into entire weapons systems. But, as usual, looks are deceptive. Recent studies of existing research centers have demolished the big-lab-only theory. Monopoly, public or private, chokes applied science quicker than it does routine business. Though some biggies are needed, the creative research complexes of the future, like those of the present, will be large clusters of small lab companies that spontaneously cell-divide like microbes each time a man gets an idea he wants to try on his own.[1]

[1] *Technological Innovation: Its Environment and Management* (Washington: Government Printing Office, 1967). In this study for the Secretary of Commerce, a distinguished panel reported the "unusually consistent" evidence that true innovation comes more often from the loner than from the organization scientist. See also the

This finding, spelled out in 1967 Congressional hearings, came as no surprise to Romney. In his antitrust testimony ten years earlier, he had shown that the smaller car companies of the past had made proportionately greater contributions to auto technology and safety. He also was then dealing with a lightweight jeep, the Mighty Mite, his one serious bid for a major defense contract. Its sad saga was proving how one big bureaucracy embraces another. When the Army and the Marines went hunting for vehicles light enough to drop with air-mobile units, American Motors saw a competitive advantage: Years of research into small cars ought to pay off here. Pulling together the best developments to date, AM engineers designed an entirely new aluminum mouse that would, Romney argued, do all the old quarter-ton could at two-thirds the weight, size and cost. The Marines, then somewhat independent in their decisions, bought $5.5 million worth of Mighty Mites and struggled with the inevitable troubles of untried vehicles. But the Army's cautious brass eventually paid a bigger firm millions more just to work over the parts of the World War II jeep, cutting a pound of weight off here and two pounds there. The Defense Department, of course, standardized on the Army choice.

Back at the shop, Romney kept testing his notion that the affluent society is not passive. Convinced that active consumers could bring the Rambler rebellion to full flower, he hunted a closer tie to his customers. He needed to bring them into financial alliance with the company, sign them up to be his progress-sharing partners along with workers, dealers and other volunteers. The movement needed pay for the unknown troops who helped sell compacts to their neighbors. So, in

testimony of Albert Shapero, University of Texas research professor, before the Subcommittee on Government Research of United States Senate Committee on Government Operations, May 11, 1967.

1961, he set up the consumer bonus plan. Adapted from a scheme once used by Henry Ford, the plan paid back discounts to buyers who helped push each month's sales over the level set a year earlier. If gross sales ran ten percent higher, the new Rambler owner pocketed a $25 savings bond as a rebate. For a 20 percent rise, the rebate was a $50 bond, and so on.

Romney's methods inside and outside his company proved to be sound business, and his antimonopoly crusade put him closer to free enterprise tradition than his critics. It took one man's incredible drive, however, to lead the Rambler movement against overwhelming odds. Within a year after Romney left, the company began to wobble back, as Hallas put it, "to the Right." AM tried to act like a little GM, spent $250 million on new model tooling and went schizophrenic on the compact. Roy Chapin eventually moved up to chief executive and in 1967 bet on a retooled Rambler American to save the company. Though Detroit will argue forever over what would, or would not, have happened if Romney had stayed, the fact remains that he pushed American Motors from a dead 81st to a live 44th on the ranked list of United States corporations. As he says, "I must have been doing something right."

A businessman's experience does not automatically qualify him for political insight. Neither does a scholar's. However, Galbraith and Romney happen to have concentrated, one by word and the other by deed, upon a specific kind of problem that is becoming central to the politics of the future. Galbraith's line of thought, more or less in tune with President Johnson and many others, is for steady escalation of the central government's functions and expenditures. This method gets quick, visible results. For instance, the Federal wage-price guidelines in the early Sixties were based on the fact that a few large companies and unions start the upward

moves. By holding these few down with political pressure—
and in the steel case, Department of Justice intimidation—the
Administration promoted economic growth for a while. "It was
elementary," said Galbraith. But since the basic problem was
not solved, it was only a matter of time before the guidelines
became a general joke.

Out of such struggles, a semiarticulate businessman came
into politics with a quite different answer. Romney wanted to
treat the cause, not the effect. He worried over the memory
of Sir Stafford Cripps' desperate remark that Britain could
choose only between private monopoly and public monopoly,
which is not a choice. Within business tradition, he argued,
the well-proved method of spin-off could loosen the bonds,
let competition hold down prices, and give the whole culture
more choices. His proposal was brushed aside by leaders in
business, labor and government whose careers were based on
the power struggle with each other. But he hung to an unpopular belief during the pressures of his Presidential bid.

"If we don't do something about the situation," he said
grimly, "we'll go the same way Britain did."

To his mind, the theory of advertisers manipulating customers was only a surface sign of the deeper problem. He proved
with a funny little car, sometimes called "the upside-down
bathtub," that consumers will not only exercise choice but
sign up as irregulars in the fight for a chance to choose. He
was later to find the same thing about voters trapped in a two-
party stalemate. "And my faith in the American people was
again confirmed," he said. His experience in both fields suggests, but hardly proves, that in the post-affluent era people
will at least want to rig their own version of Galbraith's
squirrel wheel.

Romney's spin-off concept became but one part of a general,
careful strategy for bringing millions into direct action on the

problems that affect their lives. "It's like trying to stop a run-away team," says Romney. "The Goldwater people wanted to jump in front of the team and stop it cold, push it back. But you've got to run alongside and get hold of the reins, then slowly turn the wagon the way it ought to go."

# CHAPTER TWELVE

# COMMUNITY IN
# THE FACTORY

---

"Mr. Reuther, do you believe in God?" blurted George Romney.

In room 1070 of Detroit's Whittier Hotel on Tuesday, July 21, 1959, four men started an awkward conversation. The four: redheaded Walter P. Reuther, president of the mighty United Automobile Workers; Jack Conway, Reuther's able aide and later president of the AFL-CIO's Industrial Union Department; George W. Romney, president of American Motors; and Ed Cushman, Romney's vice-president and labor negotiator. It was not a bargaining session. Indeed, unless you knew both Reuther and Romney well, you would not have expected this talk to go anywhere, let alone lead to some unusual experiments.

Since the unionist and the industrialist had been heaving brickbats at each other for twenty years, the handshakes revealed a touch of tension. Romney was sitting down with the man he believed to be "the most accomplished economic revolutionary in America." He never got over a suspicion of

Reuther's ideology. But, as he had done with raider Louis Wolfson, he was eager to grant the benefit of the doubt.

Cushman provided the bridge between the two. He was no company flunky. A New Dealer and intellectual prodigy, he had been a prewar pioneer in development of United States employment security programs, vocational training, fair employment and union-management councils. He had belonged to that small cadre of activists, along with Romney and Walter's brother Victor, who had levered Detroit's power structure into mobilization drives and postwar civic projects. Cushman also belonged to a group that is more difficult to categorize: the men of very different persuasions from whom Romney drew ideas and on whom he tested proposed courses of action. Often unknown or hostile to each other, they ranged from the Washington operators Romney had studied as a lobbyist to Chrysler treasurer B. E. Hutchinson, a businessman so conservative that he resigned from the NAM because it refused to hold aloft the gold standard. Among the others added to the Romney list over the years: the Right Rev. Richard S. M. Emrich, Episcopal priest and now Bishop of Detroit;[1] Saul D. Alinsky, organizer of ghetto protest and social jujitsu; Malcolm Moos, the political scientist who wrote President Eisenhower's famous farewell warning against the "military-industrial complex." Not impressed by establishment intellectuals—disgusted, in fact, because they now produce few original ideas—Romney has maintained ties with unlikely outsiders such as French Catholic priest R. L. Bruckberger,[2]

[1] Emrich seldom sees Romney nowadays or mentions him in print, but the Bishop's Detroit *News* column often reads like a private letter to his old friend. With an eerie accuracy, he probes issues like Vietnam in ways that raise the same problems of principle that Romney is wrestling with at the same moment.

[2] After he became governor, Romney's saddened fan club back at American Motors brooded long over what kind of gift he might like. They happily settled on a Bruckberger visit, flew the white-haired

172

the Gaullist author of *Image of America,* and a Chicago lady named Mrs. Jules Lederer, known to millions of advice-to-the-wayward readers under the name Ann Landers.

Cushman, who previously refused to box himself into either union or management, had come over from Wayne University in 1955 to help Romney untangle the bizarre labor mess at American Motors. Moving into management, he had resigned from a panel of well-known economists called in by Reuther to vouch for the feasibility of the UAW's original Guaranteed Annual Wage (GAW) proposal. But panels, it turned out, could be used by both sides. Cushman persuaded the same economists, minus himself, to study the peculiar hardships that GAW would bring to his company, and to look into the premium that UAW had built into AM contracts over the years. Romney's plants had generally been forced to accept the pattern set by the industry's Big Three, plus afterthoughts. The panel did its independent audit. Result: For the first time in UAW history, Reuther made an off-pattern settlement, the first stage in a substantial reduction of AM's serious labor disadvantage.

The union found itself in a strange position. "Usually, when we enter negotiations with the big auto companies, we're the underdog," said a UAW braintruster. "We're David facing Goliath, or, if you will, St. George facing the dragon. We have all the sympathy on our side. But here, something happened. Suddenly, we were made to feel that *we* were the monster—the giant union ganging up on a courageous little company fighting for its life. What could we do in a case like that? We had to make some allowances to help keep St. George in business."

---

priest in from Paris for two days of bobbing pointlessly on the tail of a political schedule. Before he left, Bruckberger told Mrs. Romney that her husband was badly needed in the Presidency but feared that his staff was too weak to get him through to the voters.

There was more to come. Cushman, an active Episcopal layman, next invited a panel of leading ministers to come into the plants, not just to see its wage troubles but to take a step in the church's slow shift toward involvement in an industrial society. Romney and Cushman had long recognized the benefit of a third force to mediate struggles between workers and managers as well as a way to get public insight into their problems. As Romney had stolen Reuther's economist panel, Reuther stole Romney's preacher panel. He signed them up to advise UAW. "It was a fair exchange," said Cushman, puffing his La Corona cigar.

Without such triumphs, Romney would not have won bank refinancing, but these were small comfort to a man who saw that his labor policy was to be run more and more by deals between his competition and the union. From 1955 onward, one auto chief executive tells me, "We have had collaboration on union negotiation." Confronted by the UAW's industry-wide demands, the Three generally settled among themselves on what package they would buy to avoid a strike. Though not yet as formal as the steel industry's bargaining combine, the auto industry's labor policy was becoming as rigid as its marketing. Here was the danger that Romney had been warning against since 1946. A union that negotiated for all the workers in a basic industry, he believed, would kill weaker corporations and push the strong into oligopoly. Their operations would become so standarized that they would act like merged outfits even if they held on to separate letterheads.

"Can employers combine to negotiate with industry-wide or national unions and still remain sufficiently competitive to provide maximum employment?" Romney asked. The coal industry, he felt, had proved otherwise.

The threat of dead conformity on the labor side, as much as on the consumer side, drove Romney to his Senate testimony in 1958. In his 35-page statement to Senator Kefauver's subcommittee on antitrust and monopoly, he had devoted nine pages near the end to the rationale behind Reuther's latest demands, then on the bargaining table. They were aimed at Ford and GM. As usual, the UAW strategy exploited the sensitivity of the giants to public censure. "How many other companies in the land are so vulnerable as General Motors?" demanded Romney. By whipping up public sentiment against the fatcat firm, he said, UAW could win favor for its demands, which would then be imposed on the smaller car companies, aircraft manufacturers, parts suppliers—more than one-seventh of the national economy—and spread to other industries. The members of big unions would thus grab more than their share of the benefits of rising productivity in the whole economy, and effectively penalize all other workers. And the labor movement was becoming an ally of monopoly capitalists.

Most of the penalty, Romney explained, would be passed on through higher prices for cars. He warned that such wage-push inflation would be more damaging than in steel and other raw material industries. Anybody on the road would feel the bite personally. "The direct impact of auto labor costs and prices on the car buyers' pocketbook would almost certainly spark demands that government participate in the bargaining and pricing process to protect the unorganized consumers' interest," he said. His warning was early, but over the next ten years the United States sweated through the guideline era when the White House became a constant arbiter of wage and price decisions. "The President's at the bargaining table again," Romney snapped during Johnson's intervention in the rail crisis.

He spelled out the most reasonable alternative that anybody, as far as I know, has yet put forth: company-by-company bargaining. International unions would retain their central staffs of economic and legal experts to serve the local unions, not boss them. Where the bargaining unit included 10,000 or more men and women, it would work out its own unique settlements with a single company management. Unions representing smaller units of employees would negotiate with several companies but on a regional basis, as the Teamster conferences did before Jimmy Hoffa tried to establish a nation-wide transportation contract. No patterns, no industrywide negotiations. While his analysis reflected the complexity of the problem, Romney's solution had the basic simplicity of his spin-off proposal on the corporate side. He refused to go for shibboleths. To the rage of right-wingers, he would not adopt their union-busting scheme for slapping antitrust statutes on labor. Nor could he jump on the right-to-work bandwagon. He treated these idiocies as symbolic crusades, and opposed right-to-work when the issue was forced on him. He considered himself more aggressively pro-labor than were top union leaders.

So spin-off and unit-bargaining came as two halves of the same whole. He had first raised the union point as hired head of the auto industry's trade association, and later regretted the one-sided prejudice of his move. He had been too worried, he said, about his bosses. Without first reducing industrial concentration, he realized, it would be impossible and unfair to unspin union hierarchies. "The deepest contradiction in our economy," he still believes, "is to have labor law based on the monopoly principle and business organized [in part] on the competitive principle."[1]

Romney confronted Reuther, when they met in the Hotel

[1] The Romney proposals raised hard questions about big industry and big labor. But Washington editors like Stewart Alsop of *The Saturday Evening Post* proved their skill at water-skiing right over the surface of his thought. "Romney's ideas about politics, economics and government are as uncomplicated and easy to grasp as the idea of the compact car," Alsop wrote in a genially patronizing 1962 article.

Whittier's Room 1070, with a considerably more interesting prospect than he faced with the Big Three. Prone to think in social blueprints, the UAW's chief was beginning to discover that neither the labor movement nor government—both less than 30 years old in the modern sense—was entirely immune to arthritis. He was, as usual, hunting new directions. Then near the peak of his power, Reuther had just come back from Berlin where he had made what UAW porkchoppers affectionately call "Walter's speech" to 600,000 people. He was thoroughly convinced, he told friends, that Russia's drive for world dominion had become a more serious menace since Stalin's death. Unless United States labor and industry could find a more cooperative relationship, Khrushchev and others might well bury us.

Romney studied the unionist with that total gaze that makes his hazel eyes look blue. Where could they begin? If Reuther believed that men were only dots on the good society's blueprint, not blessed with divine cussedness, then it was hopeless. Should he ask first about the power dispersion of the Constitution?

Like a man who gets a bad oyster in his mouth at a formal dinner, Romney bowed his neck and swallowed. "Mr. Reuther, do you believe in God?" he blurted.

Reuther, the ascetic Methodist, also a nondrinker and nonsmoker, smoothly answered yes, and in the rush of questions that followed said no, he would not know how to go about improving upon the Declaration of Independence or the Constitution. The problem, the two men agreed, was to make human dignity a domestic and international reality in this complex age.

The talk trotted along briskly, but there was a rough spot that Romney later described to his wife. "Mr. Reuther felt that the tremendous power is all right if exercised by good men," says Mrs. Romney. "But my husband felt that the only hope is diffused power, checks and balances." Reuther was too experienced ever to perch on that slippery a limb, but in terms of emphasis, the diffusion principle was a real division.

Over the months, the two met whenever possible, in hotels or at home. They edged toward bargain-table specifics. Reuther, aware that the public might blame him for rising car prices, had proposed that the industry cut prices at the same time he asked for 1958 wage hikes. He had also asked for, but failed to get, a profit-sharing scheme. Romney believed both in price cuts and profit-sharing. His customer rebates, announced months later, owed as much to Reuther as to Henry Ford's plan of many years earlier. Profit-sharing with workers would take more time to work out and have to go to the bargaining table. Cushman and Romney hinted at a New York meeting with Reuther that they would come up with something new, but avoided specifics. To win acceptance in the plant, the idea would have to be proposed first to local UAW negotiators at the table. "We knew Walter wasn't actor enough not to give himself away," says Cushman.

Once the formalities had been carried out, at the 1961 reopening of contract talks, Reuther coldly demanded assurance that they were serious. Told yes, he set aside Big Three negotiations, locked himself up day and night with American Motors on a five-day deadline. Standing exhausted beside Romney when the job was done, Reuther told reporters the contract was "the most significant and historic collective-bargaining agreement ever signed in the United States."

In principle, and within the context of the trend toward cookie-cutter patterns, Reuther did not overstate his praise. This one could have been the turning point, not just because the workers were getting a bite of the profits. That was not new; the scandal was that it was not more common. What Romney had done was to show that a union and company could go their own way, begin to improvise solutions that fitted them better than prefab contracts. The irony was that Reuther had to use all his political muscle to get the American Motors locals to accept the idea. When they voted down the progress-sharing contract the first time, he had to put it back up and sell the workers on a second vote.

The formula was simple. Beginning with before-tax profits, the management subtracted an amount equal to ten percent of the company's net worth, to cover carrying charges on capital goods. The rest of the profit went into the progress-sharing base. From this, fifteen percent went to the workers in two bundles. The first bundle went to finance health insurance and other fringe benefits that workers had previously paid by deductions. The second bundle, half as big, went to buy company stock for each worker, on a formula weighted both by the number of hours a man worked and his pay level. In return, Romney won clear definition of management authority, by then very cloudy in UAW contracts, and much greater freedom on work rules and in-plant economies.

Over in AM's Wisconsin plants, car-painter Carl Norman caught the main point in a complaint against the new contract: "We are on both sides of the fence." In place of the tidy lines of worker-company warfare, the conflict of interest was partly transferred to the insides of the men. As stockholders, though minor ones, they were no longer invited to sit on the sidelines while the impersonal forces of union and management decided their future. They also turned into a fairly fierce legion of Rambler salesmen—"Let's beat the bushes," said a union official—and encouraged the Kenosha paper to run a feature series on stock investments.

George Romney left the company for politics within months after he signed that contract. Like the Rambler revolt itself, such a precedent-breaking move in labor relations can seldom become an established system for others to copy unless a unique personality pushes it through the test years. Roy

179

Abernathy, Romney's successor, lacked the fierce independence to override orthodoxy for either the compact or progress-sharing. By the time of the new contract negotiations in 1964, the downturn in sales and the consequent fall in stock prices had soured a plan that sprang fresh from the Romney-Reuther talks.

Meanwhile, the unlikely pair had branched out into a new partnership to start, they hoped, a national movement. Romney had worked closely with labor representatives in the late Fifties on a task force that salvaged Detroit's declining public school system. He also accepted Reuther's offer to put two top union reps on the board of Citizens for Michigan, a statewide crusade that brought a new constitution to Michigan. Both realized that when they could agree on a public issue, they could launch a promising reform move. So they teamed up with like-minded men, among them columnist Ralph McGill and IBM's Tom Watson, Jr., in a nationwide thing called ACTING, an acronymn for Americans Cooperating to Implement National Goals. Had it lived beyond two vague organizational meetings, ACTING might have mobilized the kind of forces that have, since the Detroit riot, at last banded together in the Urban Coalition.

This diverse group had a valid impulse. They were reaching for an instrument to cut their way out of the tired polarities that hang men up today. As the hippies would say, they wanted out of their old boxes. The ossified institutions that set labor vs. management, liberal vs. conservative, black vs. white, and even Republican vs. Democrat were shaped by previous struggles. For the most part, they have about as much to do with present conflict, practical or ideological, as my mother's butter molds have to do with margarine.

This Romney-Reuther baby died, but was reborn several times. Romney used the citizen-force idea in his campaigns and in state government, and will expand it if he has the chance in Washington. Reuther founded CCAP, the well-financed Citizens Crusade Against Poverty, a nongovernmental attack on poverty. If CCAP ever gets going on its plans, orthodox liberals will be distressed to learn that Reuther, still thought to be their boy, has left them far behind. In rebellion against the welfare state's traps, CCAP Director Richard Boone is trying to start new industries in Negro communities, induce public-housing victims to buy homes and eventually to find a way for millions more people to own company stocks, as Rambler workers once started to do. Reuther himself, ready to resign from the elderly baron's club at AFL-CIO, is testing a community union in Watts. The Watts experiment, I discovered from a visit in the winter of 1966–67, is beginning to prove that poor people do want the chance to own homes, train for good jobs, run strong community schools, and escape the newest brand of plantation overseer, the welfare system.

Romney won't admit, even when I push him with specific examples, that "the most accomplished economic revolutionary" is moving in his direction. And Reuther, trapped in his own political alliances, is not eager to sound a friendly note about Romney, or to risk another attempt like the discredited progress-sharing plan. Reuther says that Romney, while a good man, thinks that when you oppose him you must be in league with the devil. But the two still share specific goals. Using Federal tax policy, Romney wants to work for a steady expansion of the base of shareholders in the economy, enlarge the number of families able to improve the quality of life on a second income from capital.

He does not go for the capital-diffusion plan set forth some years ago by Louis Kelso and Mortimer Adler in *The Capitalist Manifesto*. Kelso's proposal would involve more, not less, Government control of the stock market. But there is a hidden by-product in the combination of Romney's spin-off and unit-bargaining programs: One would expand the number of stock shares traded, and the other would lead, through union-company cooperation, to new varieties of progress-sharing contracts. The inevitable result would be real worker owner-ship of the means of production, a broad bridge from capitalism of the few to consumerism of the many.

Perhaps the dream is too utopian. But Americans have built the world's biggest, most active generator of talent and capital. In the United States' work force of 73 million men and women, who sweat their brains more than their muscles, the average education is that of a college freshman. Those left out burn to get in. To use and develop their human capital (education, health, skill) to its full potential, they need the freedom provided by a solid financial base. "Each of us has greater opportunity than ever before in history," Romney says, "to develop our innate talents and abilities."

# CHAPTER THIRTEEN

# FAMILY
# FREEDOM FUNDS

---

Radio interviewer: "Mrs. Romney, what do you like best about your husband?"

Governor's wife: "The way he kisses me good-night."

Judged by their Federal Income Tax Form 1040 over the past 12 years, 1955 through 1966, George W. and Lenore L. Romney of East Valley Road, Bloomfield Hills, Michigan, have been able to live high on the hog if they cared to. The chart on page 184 is an abstract of their tax returns. In 1959, Romney's annual pay (Line 5 on the form) hit $200,000, and he began to exercise his stock options as president of American Motors Corp. Because he made the company prosper, the stock made him a millionaire.

The major change in his money supply came in the four years from 1957 through 1960, when his adjusted gross income (Line 9) took off from $92,573 to $661,428. The annual taxes he paid (Line 12) rose from $23,959 to $237,-000. His yearly cash donations to church and charity rose from $25,081 to $172,735.

## ABSTRACT, FORM 1040 U.S. INDIVIDUAL INCOME TAX RETURN
### George W. and Lenore L. Romney, January 1, 1955 to December 31, 1966

| Year | Salary & Bonus* | Deferred Compensation | Dividends, Interest & Taxable Portions of Capital Gains | Adjusted Gross Income | Church Contributions | Other Contributions | Total Deductions | Net Taxable Income | Tax |
|---|---|---|---|---|---|---|---|---|---|
| 1955 | $125,000 | $ | $ 3,541 | $129,674 | $ 23,888 | $ 3,191 | $ 36,119 | $ 89,355 | $ 45,651 |
| 1956 | 125,000 | | 7,032 | 133,763 | 33,154 | 2,262 | 43,370 | 86,193 | 43,172 |
| 1957 | 87,500 | | 3,607 | 92,573 | 22,341 | 2,740 | 32,948 | 56,025 | 23,959 |
| 1958 | 168,750 | | 4,280 | 173,859 | 39,758 | 5,766 | 56,760 | 113,499 | 63,469 |
| 1959 | 200,000 | | 60,452 | 260,802 | 64,027 | 5,591 | 86,761 | 170,441 | 109,150 |
| 1960 | 173,125 | | 487,203 | 661,428 | 156,038 | 16,697 | 181,905 | 476,522 | 237,000 |
| 1961 | 158,083 | | 116,494 | 272,977 | 41,244 | 26,875 | 81,036 | 188,941 | 124,956 |
| 1962 | 75,803 | | 117,117 | 194,920 | 13,404 | 37,150 | 66,062 | 125,858 | 73,173 |
| 1963 | 27,500 | 31,705 | 507,567 | 566,771 | 42,822 | 2,054 | 60,676 | 503,096 | 249,999 |
| 1964 | 27,500 | 31,705 | 211,858 | 271,163 | 78,941 | 3,052 | 97,263 | 170,900 | 80,831 |
| 1965 | 30,000 | 31,705 | 74,804 | 136,509 | 31,034 | 1,363 | 47,232 | 86,277 | 35,214 |
| 1966 | 30,000 | 11,705 | 41,131 | 78,484 | 13,956 | 8,466 | 33,723 | 41,760 | 12,980 |

* All from AMC prior to 1961. All from state of Michigan after 1962. 1961 includes $3,000 in Constitutional Convention salary and 1962 includes $4,500 Con-Con salary.

184

Auditors notice two unusual facts in these returns. First, the Romneys have never made much use of the tax loopholes, such as depletion allowances, that are taken for granted by most people who reach their bracket. Second, over the 12-year period, they have donated an average of 19 percent of each year's adjusted gross income to their church. Only in two years did they contribute less than 15 percent.

What's involved is Old Testament tithing. This double-strength form of tithing means that you are only paying your dues, and haven't started to "give," until after you ante up the first ten percent of your total "increase," your material gains of any kind, not just a tenth of your pay.[1] In 1960, when Romney sold a chunk of stock to pay off bank loans, his charity contributions were only $400 less than his full year's regular income, before taxes, in salary and bonus. He was digging into capital to pay the tithe, not only on income but also on the stock's increase in value. In 1962, when tithing as usual to the church, the Romneys donated another 19 percent of their adjusted gross income to non-church charities. Over the twelve years, their charity donations beyond the church have averaged $9,500.

By big business standards, Romney's pay and capital were solid but still limited, perhaps the beginning of a fortune. He was not, however, counting that way. The returns after 1961 measure another value, the one he put upon going to Michigan's Constitutional Convention and then running for governor. As a Con-Con delegate for two years, he rode back to Detroit at night, generally sacked out in the car bed, so as to be in his office next morning. But he still docked his own salary. These self-administered cuts amounted to several times the $7,500 that Con-Con paid him in per diem. By 1966, on

[1] The Bible (King James Version), Deuteronomy xiv. 22: "Thou shalt truly tithe all the increase of thy seed, that the field bringeth forth year by year."

a governor's salary, his adjusted gross income had moved back down to the $80,000 bracket.

After a study of Romney's income tax figures, I got curious about his habit of consciously holding down his pay scale. He had, I discovered, been at it for several years before he went into politics. The numbers had to be dug out of the accounts at American Motors. During the tight-squeeze year of 1957, he cut his pay nearly in half. Then, when the company boomed and pushed his bonuses to gaudy levels, he elected to turn part of the money back. In fiscal 1959, which began in October 1958, he refused $99,444. The next year he refused $41,646. He kept on cutting, either because the company was doing very well or not well enough. When the sales recession hit cars, he took two progressive reductions, one in October 1960 and the next in March 1961. An auditor, responding to my inquiry, discovered that Romney had refused to accept a total of $268,000 over a five-year period. And each time the board of directors tried to raise his formal pay level toward the standard for a chief executive of a major company, he brushed the proposal aside.

But the success of the Rambler car had given him financial independence, and he promptly used it. He first built Lenore the roomy house that he had promised her in early marriage, then found that public job that he had promised himself.

Being George Romney, he figured that cash success could be a trap. "My mother had always made beans taste pretty good," he said. "As a fellow that came from humble circumstances, I can appreciate the temptations of success. When I first realized I was a millionaire, I had trouble enough keeping my balance, even at my age. . . . The point of victory—that's when most people lose out, when they reach a worldly success."

Mrs. Romney had listened to him hash it out. "The more I discussed it with him, the more I came to feel that to be

186

fulfilled he had to use all of his talents," she says. "His area had to be more than cars and refrigerators."

Romney gave up capital as well as income, because the American Motors stock that he still owned started to lose value after he left the company. As governor, he turned his stock portfolio over to the trust department of a Detroit bank. To avoid conflict of interest, he gave up the right to decide what stocks would be bought and sold with his money. While the bank diversified his holdings in 1963 and 1964, he continued to pay heavy capital gains taxes. He still collected deferred compensation from American Motors, but that was sliding, too.

If he worried, it did not show. Mrs. Margaret Little, his secretary, worked with his auditor to make out his annual tax returns. So far as she could tell, the Governor just signed and did not bother to read. He had settled that part of his life and gone on to the next job.

While getting the money side of life in order, the Romneys had moved through the diapers-to-diapers cycle, children to grandchildren, with more than the usual drama. Mrs. Romney, five feet six inches and slender at 115 pounds, always had more energy than strength. Her physical worries began before the first child in 1935.

"We wanted a baby very badly, and I was getting worried," she says. "I guess you don't feel quite like a woman unless you have children." When Lynn came on July 6, 1935, it was a difficult birth. George brought Lenore home in an ambulance, and settled down to marvel at the baby by the hour. When Lynn started to hiccup, he charged down the hall yelling for the nurse. "But Lynn was a perfect baby," says Mrs. Romney. "When the book said she was supposed to be toilet-trained, she *was* toilet-trained. She did everything she was supposed to do." She later had to be cured of a perfection complex.

Jane was born on March 18, 1936, when her father happened to be locked up in negotiations between Alcoa and TVA officials over the prospects for electric power. George called the hospital every time he could get to the phone. By 2:30 in the afternoon, when he finally broke free for a rush out to the hospital, his lower lip had broken out with a solid row of fever blisters. "But they went away in a few days," says Mrs. Romney, "because they were emotionally induced."

With the two little girls, she followed her husband to Detroit in 1939. They rented a house in Grosse Pointe for two years while house-hunting down closer to George's office. What they settled on was an elderly mansion in the Palmer Woods section near Woodward and Eight Mile Road, five minutes from work. "It was too large, too much running up and down," she remembers. They spent $15,000 for the old place, invested $6,000 to make it habitable and eventually sold it for $35,000. Except for a little pile of stocks that Mrs. Romney inherited from her father, the Romney capital during those years was measured by the difference between what a house was worth and what they owed on it.

When their first son, Scott, was born in 1941, Mrs. Romney was told by her doctors that she could never be pregnant again. She didn't quite buy that. But by 1946, the Romneys were making arrangements to adopt one, maybe two, war orphans. Then, driving west on vacation, she discovered that she was pregnant. Her doctor, on the phone, told her that a miscarriage was inevitable, and on the way back, at Grand Forks, North Dakota, his forecast started to come true. She went to the local hospital and, determined not to lose the child, lay on her back without moving for a full month quoting Emily Dickinson poems at the ceiling. Her husband had administered a Mormon blessing, as he did any time she wasn't well, and sadly loaded the three children into the car to take the Lake Superior ferry route home. The children knew that Mother was better when, after one of his dashes up a dock to the telephone, he broke his fast on the fourth day.

They named the child Mitt, after the Romney first cousin who had made All-America at the University of Chicago and a pro for the Chicago Bears. The doctors now settled the argument about more children; it became necessary to perform a hysterectomy. But over the years, she expanded her brood by taking in any children who needed shelter.

The visitors ranged from her sister Elsie's baby, who demolished things for a year, to two emotionally disturbed teenagers and a volatile Italian student named Tito. Lenore made it a rule to spend an hour a day with each child. When Jane, pretty and independent, developed reading trouble, her mother tore up a book word-by-word until Jane's eyes stabilized the letters. She had been involuntarily reading backwards.

Bursitis, the first of several more physical aggravations, immobilized Mrs. Romney's left arm for five years. So George organized the children to handle as many of the chores as possible. He also, they now tell in high good humor, instructed them in the joys of walking wherever they needed to go. Jane walked a mile and a half, there and back, for each dancing lesson. She became a tournament player at tennis. Fiercely competitive, Jane always hated to play with her less accomplished father, who psyched her with spins and lobs until he could, at times, beat her.

On household duties, recalls Mrs. Romney, "My husband did all the heavies, like the Saturday marketing." The children remember that he tended to roll the supermarket cart along at high speed, and often come home with wilted vegetables. "But he got better at it," says Scott.

Though Lynn felt that her father could do no wrong, the rest of the family kept him on his mettle. Mitt, white teeth flashing, said, "Dad, if LDS is the best church and Rambler is the best car, why don't more people go for both of them?"

Once, told by his mother that they couldn't take a certain route "because we can't drive on water," Mitt shot back: "No, I guess not, since Dad's not with us."

Generous as they were with charity, the family was downright frugal with their own spending money and time. When Romney put Walt Disney on television, he would snap on the set to check the commercials, then turn off his own show and tell the children not to waste time watching. "Get a book," he said.

Family trips were on the budget plan. As far back as he can remember, Scott was always handed a lunch bag to feed him on a trip, even a three-day train trip. Driving West with his father in the Fifties, he remembers being routed out of a cornfield in the dark by a farmer who did not like two strangers using it for a motel. The president of American Motors was sleeping on the car bed, and his son on the camp cot alongside.

Sometimes, when Mrs. Romney was along, they splurged on a motel room or two—and there they charbroiled dinner steaks bought from a supermarket. They bought milk and dry cereal for the next morning's breakfast. Once rolling, they didn't dawdle in restaurants. "We could stop for gas, buy cheese and meat for sandwiches at a store, all go to the bathroom, and be on the road again in five minutes," says Lynn.

They did their touristing at the same speed. All remember a one-day blitz of San Francisco. "Dad said we ought to see it kaleidoscopically," the girls say, bubbling fondly over the way he drove through the scenes from Twin Peaks to Muir Woods as if he were playing a 6 A.M. game of compact golf. On a winter trip to Ogden, Utah, he tried the same method on the ski slopes. Connie Scowcroft, Lenore's sister, remembers that "George had never been on skis in his life, and he decided to go on Wildcat Slope, the biggest hill in Snow Basin." An instructor pleaded with him to take lessons, and he did consent to a few minutes of talk before he took the tow. While Connie,

Lenore and the instructor watched in horror from the ski shack, Romney came tearing at an angle across the slope. He would crash at the side, get up and crash on the other side of the slope. "He must have fallen a hundred times," chuckles Connie, "but the next trip he fell only four times."

In summers, first at Torch Lake in northern Michigan and later at a cottage in Canada, the family could be fairly sedentary until Romney arrived to mobilize.

At his adaptation of paddle tennis, Romney tennis, he generally played until he won, maybe 20 or 25 sets. Or, in one instance, until his toes bled. The children of other summer families christened him "the Brick" because of his blocky shape, and awarded him a brick wrapped in aluminum foil. (Around golf courses, caddies call him "the ghost"; by the time they arrive, the only trace of him is footsteps in the dew.) Romney expected others to share his joy of the workout. When Scott made his first try at water skis, Romney drove the boat. Scott remembers that he finally learned to stand up on the skis because his genial father seemed willing to drag him through the water all day.

At the lake one summer, while making a bed, Mrs. Romney slipped a disc. Nothing moved from the waist down. The local doctor hinted that she would be paralyzed for life. Her husband, roaring up from the office, used a door to hoist her up on the car bed, headed back over the three-hour road to a Detroit hospital. "It was a memorable trip," says Lenore with her dewy look of joy. "We sang at the top of our lungs all the way as if nothing were wrong."

The Romneys possess an innocent earthiness about themselves and about each other. In a radio interview, Mrs. Romney was once asked what she liked best about her husband. She told the folks: "The way he kisses me good-night."

Once the disc got harnessed back into place, she found herself under orders to take a long swim at least once a week. "If

191

you can call it swimming," teases Scott. The forced swimming was eventually to cause her distress as Michigan's first lady; using the state highway troopers' pool in off hours, she was embarrassed to crawl out dripping right into the lens of a news photographer.

The main cause of all her ailments, a specialist found, was her body's failure to absorb enough calcium. So she had to go into a lifelong schedule of taking a heavy calcium shot each week, an elaborate checkup once a year. Coming back from her 1967 checkup, she bounced into her Bloomfield kitchen full of the best news yet. "I guess I'll be around to look after him," she said, looking at her husband. "I was afraid for a while that he'd have to try and find another wife who wouldn't know how."

Healthier than she had been in years, she was left with nothing more aggravating than allergies. She happened to react in a way that handicapped her on the campaign trail. If she ate chicken, a staple of politics, her upper throat would swell so that she could not talk, which is somewhat inconvenient for an after-dinner speaker. She became adept at messing the chicken around on the plate so that it looked eaten-at.

Liquid was another matter. She also reacted to milk. Knowing that Mormons do not drink coffee, her hosts generally provided her with a glass of milk, unaware that it would turn her into a clam. The trouble with a glass of milk, presented as a proof of thoughtfulness, is that there's no way to make it look like it's been drunk. The test of her gallantry was then to charm people so much they didn't notice.

In the summer of 1967, trying to find out what other foods were bothering her, she took a week of allergy tests at Chicago's Swedish Covenant Hospital. Result: She could no longer eat potatoes, which had been campaign sustenance, or peanut butter, the convenient sandwich-maker which had been supplied to her in carton lots by an understanding political ally who owns a peanut-processing plant. To her joy, however, she ate a hospital plateful of 14 pork chops and could still talk to the Governor on the telephone.

Five years of politics, her friends agree, have done wonders for her health. "It really brought her out," says Mrs. Bunky Knudsen. Compared to motherhood, it seems to be sort of restful. But she keeps her hand in on Sundays, when the children come over after church with station wagons full of grandchildren and paraphernalia. Lynn, married to a lawyer, Loren (Larry) G. Keenan, and living nearby, already has seven of the eight children she resolved to have. Grandma would just as soon she stopped now. Jane, married to Dr. Bruce Robinson of Ann Arbor, Michigan, has three children. Scott, married to Ronna Stern, started husbandhood with one child, by Ronna's previous husband. And Mitt, with another year to go on his European stint, took a few hours off from his duty as head of the LDS Paris mission when blonde Anne Davies, from his church, flew over for a visit. Watching Anne deliver a brief talk at the home ward one Sunday, Governor Romney was pleased at the thought that she would, everybody said, join the family Sundays one day. "She has that inner beauty," he said, "close to the way Lenore looked at that age."

The Sundays have been widely reported as a sort of religious withdrawal, one of Mormonism's peculiarities. I found out otherwise when the Governor set aside Sunday working time for our interviews on this book. Tracing back through his life, I discovered that while in Washington he used to play golf each Sunday in the random foursomes at Burning Tree Club. But he has gradually drawn a wall around Sunday, even letting people blame his church, so as to have one day of almost total rest from the incredible intensity of his other six days. He generally goes to Sunday School, but the main LDS service, with its water-and-bread communion, comes Sunday

193

evening. This, too, is part of his resting, and he bellows out the hymns with that off-key baritone.

When the Presidential talk first got serious, Mrs. Romney had several tears and said to a friend, "I'd rather have a live grandfather at home than a dead President in the White House." But the tears dried as she settled down to the political drudgery she does with a flair, because "I really believe in what my husband is doing."

"Politics is like washing diapers," she says with her voice vibrant. "You want the baby so much you don't mind washing his diapers."

# CHAPTER FOURTEEN

# MEXICANS, NEGROES AND MORMONS

"If the Republican Party tries to buy the White House with the rights of others, it will become the greatest white elephant in the history of party politics."—Romney, to Utah's Mormon conservatives, 1964.

Looking at the barriers between him and the White House, George Romney tells himself that what will be, will be. "I think Lincoln was right—a great deal depends on circumstance," he said one morning. I asked if he meant it all depends on being in the right place at the right time. "Well, it's whether you suit the need or not. I can't change myself to fit what people want. I'm not a political animal in that sense. I'm no Lyndon Johnson or Richard Nixon."

His religion, for instance, was not up for a face-lifting. Because Mormonism does not allow Negroes in its priesthood, he had often been under pressure to quit his church. He wouldn't even criticize it. As far as he was concerned, he could no more switch faiths than he could change his place of birth, Colonia Dublan, in Mexico. And both of these implacable facts, Mormonism and birthplace, would figure in the politicking for the nomination.

The Mexican birth has been an embarrassment since boyhood. In Los Angeles when he was six years old, the neighborhood kids called him "Mex." He finally found a retort. "If a kitten is born in a garage, that doesn't make it a car, does it?" he said, yah-yahing back. "I'm as American as you are."

He was on better legal grounds than he knew, perhaps better than he yet knows. The evidence, buried in family journals, involves an old cookstove. When Miles Park Romney, one of George's two polygamous grandfathers, was chased across the border into Mexico by United States marshals in 1885, his first wife, Hannah, followed the next spring with two wagons, farm tools for the first crop and the big cooking range that was her pride and joy. Driving with her through Apache Chief Geronimo's warpath was her fifth child, Gaskell, George's father, who had been born 14 years earlier in St. George, Utah. Near the border at Deming, New Mexico, she spent her last $5 on a pound of sugar and shoes for a barefooted son. So she had no money when she hit Ascension, where Mexican customs officers levied a $25 duty on the stove.

Some of the Mormon colonists avoided paying customs by signing affidavits of intent to live permanently in Mexico. Hannah made no such arrangements. Though it was like losing an arm, she was about to leave the stove at the customs house. She wanted to get away fast because of a smallpox epidemic in Ascension. The officials tried to lift the stove off the wagon, but gave up after breaking two rods and pulling the top loose. Promising to come back with the money in 30 days, Hannah drove with the stove on to her husband's camp, a stockhouse with a dirt floor, and there learned that he hadn't seen as much as $25 since he fled south. "That was a worry to me thinking that I had brought more worry and trouble to him," Hannah recorded. Miles Park got a carpenter's job on a ranch to earn the duty on the stove.

So George Romney was born in 1907 into a family of native-born United States citizens who had never intended to be anything else. Driven back to the States in 1912 by the Mexican Revolution, he grew up in this homeland. He never doubted that he was a natural-born American, but others did. The problem kept coming up because there was always somebody around who thought he ought to be President one day. In high school, where he was the widely-admired student body president, Lenore's sisters remember "the kids saying what a pity George wasn't born in the United States." But it was the late Forties before Lenore's father, Harold La Fount, decided on his own to have lawyers check out the eligibility of the son-in-law he admired so much, enough to imagine him in the White House. Retired from the Federal Communications Commission, La Fount was running a New England network of radio stations that included New York's WNEW when Lenore came from Detroit to visit him one day. As they strolled around the streets, he told her what the lawyers had reported: There was no legal barrier to her husband becoming President of the United States.

But Romney never had a formal brief drawn until February 3, 1967. His friend Eustace Seligman of New York's Sullivan & Cromwell (the Dulles law firm) prepared documents to go with a letter for circulation among leading constitutional lawyers.

The problem begins with Article II, Section 1, Paragraph 4 of the Constitution: "No person except a natural-born citizen, or a citizen of the United States at the time of the adoption of this Constitution, shall be eligible to the office of President. . . ." So what does "natural-born" mean? Seligman, intrigued by the vagaries of words, dryly mentioned that in one colloquial usage it means a child of nature, not of wedlock.[1]

The term had been defined by centuries of English common law before the 13 Colonies adopted the Constitution in 1789. More consistently than in most matters of common law, the citizenship question had been settled by politics rather than geography: The courts decided what king was by nature entitled to a man's loyalty. In 1609, after King James I rose to the English throne, the courts ruled that a man named Calvin, born in Scotland when it was out of England's realm, was a natural-born subject of England. The opinion stated:

> Whosoever are born under one natural ligeance and obedience due by the law of nature to one sovereign are natural-born subjects; But Calvin was born under one natural ligeance and obedience, due by law of nature to one sovereign; *ergo,* he was a natural born subject.[2]

*Blackstone's Commentaries* made "nature" an explicit question of the child's father: ". . . all children, born out of the king's ligeance, whose fathers are natural-born subjects, are now natural-born subjects themselves, to all intents and purposes, without any exception. . . ."[3]

The framers of the Constitution, largely lawyers, were of necessity working within these precedents, and took no exception to them. The next year, in 1790, the First Congress removed any doubt by passing the Nationality Act: "And the children of citizens of the United States, that may be born beyond sea, or out of the limits of the United States, shall be considered as natural born citizens. . . ." One hundred years

[1] But being a no-nonsense lawyer, Mr. Seligman did not speculate on how such a definition would affect the way Americans view their presidents.

[2] *Calvin's Case,* 7 Coke la, 77 Eng. Rep. 377 (1609).

[3] *Blackstone's Commentaries,* Twelfth Edition, Volume I, Chapter 10, p. 373.

later, in the Nationality Act of 1890, which was in effect when Romney was born, Congress used the same definition.

But, on March 28, 1898, the Supreme Court left a small fly in Romney's soup. That's when Justice Horace Gray wrote a majority decision to relieve the troubles of Wong Kim Ark, 23, son of Chinese immigrants and born in San Francisco. After a steamship visit back to see relatives, Wong Kim Ark had been refused permission to land again on these shores. Locked up, he was charged by the United States Attorney under the Chinese exclusion acts with having been "at all times, by reason of his race, language, color, and dress, Chinese person, and now is, and for some time past has been, a laborer by occupation." By extension of that doctrine, you'd become an alien by wearing a shamrock. The narrow passion of the charge was countered by the breadth of the Court's decision, a 19-page document full of *obiter dicta*. In his legal over-kill, Justice Gray sought to wipe out any trace of racist taint, or, as he wrote, "the theory that a general rule of citizenship by blood or descent has displaced in this country the fundamental rule of citizenship by birth within its sovereignty."[1]

The Court was not dealing with the question of children born to United States citizens abroad. But to make his point, Justice Gray chose to show that the statutes conferring citizenship on such children did not upset his place-of-birth theory. In dealing with these exceptions, Gray at one point spoke of them as "naturalized," notwithstanding the fact that they became citizens at birth and went through no naturalization process.

Because the extra passages in the 1898 decision have never been taken seriously, they have never been cleared away by court test. The foreign-born children of Americans have been

[1] United States v. Wong Kim Ark, 169 U.S. 649, (1898) p. 909.

considered natural-born. To get his first passport, Romney, like hundreds before and since, merely submitted affidavits on the circumstances of his birth and went abroad in 1926 as a natural-born citizen, U.S.A. Both the Republicans and the Democrats have considered as potential Presidential or Vice-Presidential nominees men who were born abroad—Franklin Roosevelt, Jr., and Christian Herter—and both parties have more or less assumed, after checking, that the birthplace issue is a phony.

But Presidential campaigns are high-pressure affairs, full of rumor and the opportunity for legal maneuver. Among 300,000 lawyers in the United States, there must be several hundred eager for an inexpensive bit of excitement, with or without a secret client in higher politics. So, sometime in the primaries, the papers will blossom with headlines about a suit that cites Wong Kim Ark's story to charge that Romney is not natural-born.

And there's not a thing Romney can do about it. He will have to wait until the first case hits him, and hope that some judge doesn't sit on it long enough to create confusion that might cost him a primary.

If the birthplace question is legalistic flim-flam, the Mormon church's treatment of Negroes is more important to Romney than his critics have yet discovered. The reason has to do with political philosophy, not religious belief. Romney once said that his church "has taught me . . . to accept truth wherever I find it." The same church now holds a sort of idiot's question mark over his political belief that government is not the society's sole repository of virtue, or the only public-service institution. He grabs for any evidence that fellow Mormons are not bigots, but has to watch other churches lead the fight for racial justice. With a spirit big enough to enjoy most political knuckle-dusting, and give as good as he gets, Romney is often driven to stare at the ground in silence on this subject.

200

Michigan Democrats, sensing his agony, have come up with elaborate psycho-political explanations. "We've got it figured out that he's going to blow it [the campaign] on the race issue," says Zolton Ferency, Democratic state chairman who lost to Romney in 1966. "Race issues are very bad issues, because there *is* a backlash. We know it, and so do the Republicans. There has, in fact, been a tacit agreement among politicians not to bring this up. They say, 'O.K., baby, we don't know which way this one cuts the most, and it cuts both ways.' But he's the only Republican that has in his background anything indicating bias, so it will keep coming up. In his mind, he relates it to his religion. When anyone disagrees with him on civil rights, that is an attack on his religion. So he's going to overcompensate, and get into trouble with the suburbs, with the nationalities, with the Southerners and with the Conservatives. Each time the question is raised, it costs him Negro votes; each time he answers, it costs him white votes."

Maybe so, but for a less imaginative description of what's going on in Romney, we can go back to the facts. First off, there is the crisis in his church. Mormonism was founded on a liberal doctrine of man, be he pale or vivid. The Lord, said The Book of Mormon, loves us all: ". . . and he denieth none that come unto him, black and white, bond and free, male and female; and he remembereth the heathen; and all are alike unto God, both Jew and Gentile."[1] In Missouri, their first Zion, antislavery Mormons found slaveowners hostile. From this difference of opinion, the hostilities flared into general war, and the Saints were shot, burned out and chased out of the state. Adaptable LDS President Joseph Smith's next book, *A Pearl of Great Price*, contained three passages indicating that the dark Mark of Cain, killer brother of Abel,

[1] The Book of Mormon, 2 Nephi, 26:33.

had been passed down as a curse "pertaining to the Priesthood." With a few thin sentences, the central authorities of LDS built a picket fence around themselves. Negroes could join the church if they insisted, but they were excluded from the inner organizations of laymen (called priests) who ran the churches, married white girls and were promised the higher joys of heaven. It was openly avowed racism—rather like that practiced if not preached by most of white Christendom until the civil rights movement started Sunday tokenism a few years ago.

Mormon racism always had a demonic quality. Brigham Young, Joseph Smith's successor, affirmed it with the vehemence of a man paying his debt to the devil. Negro exclusion not only denied the central Mormon tenets on the dignity of man, but perverted the social values cherished even by the "Jack Mormons" who drink, smoke or drift away. The values were built into a brother-keeper system. Unlike the lonely-cowboy camps in most of the West, the Mormon colonies in the desert were scale-model experiments in decent urbanism,[1] and the cities that grew out of them retained the warm fabric of recreational groups, welfare societies, child-training classes and social action organizations of the young marrieds. To exclude anybody was to weaken the system. However, under LDS doctrine and church organization, to invite Negroes into the priesthood would amount to active promotion of racial intermarriage. Mormonism was not the only denomination that moved slowly on this front.

In late 1961, Romney knew that if he went into politics, he would draw a harsh spotlight on his church's Negro doctrine. He was not isolated in an executive suite. Having

[1] Evon Z. Vogt and Thomas F. O'Dea, "A Comparative Study of the Role of Values in Social Action in Two Southwest Communities," *American Sociological Review*, Vol. 18, No. 6, December 1953, pp. 645–654.

led a fight for open housing in World War II, he had for years been involved with Detroit's Round Table of Catholics, Jews and Protestants, which included clergymen moving into civil rights. The Anti-Defamation League gave him its 1959 Action for Democratic Living Award. Through men and women who were then Detroit's Negro leadership, among them a judge, he had a fair idea of how black people felt about segregation anywhere.

So he made an airplane flight that he could not talk about. Around Christmas of 1961, he strode into Mormonism's Salt Lake headquarters, a heavy Romanesque bulk just up the street from the Hotel Utah. With its dark, quiet corridors, the building where the Council of Twelve keep office (Monday is the day off) was like the Federal Reserve Board building when the governors happen to be at lunch. Closeted with President David O. McKay and a group of his advisers, Romney went straight to the point.

"I want to know if there is any *religious* reason why I should not run for governor," he said. "I will make my own decision, but if there are any religious [he came down hard on the word again] objections, I ought to hear them now."

President McKay, then 88, twinkled and understood instantly. Romney was serving notice on his church: Don't dabble.

Though only a moderately important official, one of 345 stake presidents, Romney was holding a position of trust. So he owed them the right to argue within the terms of that job, a religious one. Not everybody in the room got the message. Romney found it necessary to repeat, though not to McKay, that he was not asking for their political advice. Quite the opposite. That question about *religious* reasons was to be sure that nobody in the hierarchy would ever be confused about the separation of Church and State. He would, if he became a candidate, resign from the stake presidency. He would manage his business; they would manage theirs. He ran, and that's the way it went.

The correlary later became obvious: He would not criticize them—that would be dabbling—and they would try to be charitable about the troubles that his public life would stir up for LDS. It was still possible in Salt Lake to believe that civil rights, if let alone, would not be much more than a matter of answering all those unpleasant letters from Gentiles.

The illusion didn't last long after Romney got going. As the press moved in, Joseph Fielding Smith, an apostle and the church authority on doctrine, published a defense. The criticisms, he charged, were due to inexcusable "ignorance on the part of writers who do not belong to the Church. . . ." Mormons knew better. From the ranks of the Utah priesthood, young Jeff Nye wrote a response: "The Negro is a junior partner in my Church." Nye mailed his simple, clear statement to *Look* Magazine, and managing editor William B. Arthur promptly flew out to be sure that Nye was genuine. Then, checking the facts of Mormon practice, Arthur took down these comments from doctrinarian Smith:

". . . a change can come about only through divine revelation, and no one can predict when a divine revelation will occur.

"I would not want you to believe that we bear any animosity toward the Negro. 'Darkies' are wonderful people, and they have their place in our Church."[1]

The revelation business had been in a slump for many years. President McKay, a shy gentleman who dedicated himself to building up education services, seemed to enjoy more private forms of religious communication. So LDS tended to hold with previous doctrine and practice. Unlike other faiths, Romney told the press, Mormonism could not change direction to follow new opinions expressed by members and clergy.

[1] Jeff Nye, "Memo from a Mormon," *Look*, October 22, 1963.

It could not ease into the era of racial freedom a little at a time. In fact, the Mormon Church had become a bit of a dinosaur, though Romney would burn at the stake rather than say so. Talking privately with a University of Utah president, now retired, he once joked about the difficulties of running a school so close to church power. "That's *your* General Motors," he said.

If he couldn't change his church, he might be able to change its environment. Because of his work while still a Michigan businessman, Michigan had been the first state to write a civil rights clause into its fundamental law, the new constitution. As governor, he kept raising the enforcement budget, later asked for additional enforcement units run by local government. In June 1963, he led an NAACP march for open housing, not downtown but into rich Grosse Pointe. When slum organizer Saul Alinsky, with the West Side Organization's militant Negroes and clerics, wanted to meet the white Detroit rulers, Romney indirectly arranged the meeting, and attended. Democratic Mayor Jerome Cavanaugh avoided the rough company. "I think you ought to listen to Alinsky," Romney told his reluctant white friends. "It seems to me that we are always talking to the same people. Maybe the time has come to hear new voices." Said an Episcopal Bishop, "He made Alinsky sound like a Republican." The only out-of-state Republican leader he ever invited to help him campaign was Edward W. Brooke, then Attorney General of Massachusetts. In return, Romney spoke at Brooke's birthday party.

When Mrs. Viola Liuzzo was murdered by racists in Alabama, Romney rushed to the family's home, took a weeping child in his arms and told the story of Joan of Arc. "Some people die for a cause, as Joan of Arc did," he said. "So did your mother." The closer you get to Romney and Mrs. Romney, the more strongly you feel their aversion to racism. He

refuses even to exploit Negro "experts," but has outdone
Mennen Williams in appointing Negroes to higher offices.
His passion infects many. Covering a GOP state convention,
I was once cornered by a forcible Negro matron, a Catholic,
who believes that Romney was put on earth to bring the races
together.

A completely orthodox Mormon, Romney accepted without
argument the doctrine that it would take revelation to open
his church to Negroes. He stuck to his political idiom. For
instance, in January 1964 he spoke within sight of the Salt
Lake Temple. Not until he got there, and was briefed by
Mike and Janice Romney, his kin, did he realize that he was
slated for as conservative an audience as could be recruited in
Birch-bound Utah. Shifting his text to ram the Birchers
head-on, he lectured that to be anti-Communist was not
enough. And he still got in his civil rights licks:

"If the Republican Party tries to buy the White House
with the rights of others, it will become the greatest white
elephant in the history of politics," he said, and endorsed the
rights bill then before Congress. To exploit racism would be,
he concluded, "to renounce the spiritual heritage of the Judeo-
Christian world." He could not help it if his politics sounded
more religious than the average Mormon sermon.

Three years later, starting to run for President, he again
picked the shadow of Mormonism's home temple as the place
to talk about race, and be questioned by Negro and white
ministers on his religion. His answer:

> If my church prevented me from working to eliminate social
> injustice and racial discrimination, as I have worked for 25
> years, I would not belong. But that is not the case. . . . I think
> that I'm entitled to the same right that any other American
> citizen is entitled to—namely, to be judged on the basis of my
> record and the actions that speak louder than words.

That is his position, and he will stick by it. But his political philosophy warns him of a flaw that he can do nothing about, at least nothing direct. Because he knows that a society is more than government and business, and that cities cannot be communities without churches and other organizations taking a hand in the major problems, he also knows, but refuses to say, that the church he loves is not facing up to the crisis of the time. Mrs. Romney, talking more of what ought to be than what is, goes the next step: "The Negro is going to have every opportunity I have. He has full citizenship, he has full fellowship [in Mormonism], and priesthood, too, will be his one day. I hope very soon."

If so, say many young Mormons, it will be because their church has been pushed out of the persecution complex that hangs it up. That old minority feeling is hard to maintain once you have a member running for President. In this way, John Kennedy inadvertently turned loose a surge of energy inside Catholicism. "George Romney has precipitated a crisis in the Mormon Church that may well rank with the plague of the locusts," says a delighted Arizona State University professor and Mormon, L. Mayland Parker. Along with other young LDS thinkers, Parker has carefully demolished most of the theology behind Negro exclusion, including the passages in *A Pearl of Great Price*. He believes that his church is stuck with a practice, not a doctrine and, like other churches, can now change without revelation. But LDS conservatives, sensing that the Negro issue is the first stage of a general de-mythology drive, resist the young men rising to demand reform.

As in other churches, change is apt to come by stages. Something like that may be going on now. For instance, missionaries in Hawaii and the Fiji Islands have been converting Polynesians into the priesthood for many years, and the effort is escalating. The theory is that, not being of African descent, they are not banned. Such work picked up a few months ago on the island of Tahiti when a new man arrived to head the mission. His name is Carl Richards, a retired Detroit executive, the friend and brother-in-law of Michigan's governor. Some of Richards' new priests, a church leader says proudly, "are as black as night." Romney insists that he had nothing to do with Richards' choice of mission.

Mormonism's leading citizen maintains as unusual a position in his church as he does in politics. If his one purpose in life were to be removal of the LDS racial barrier, he could not have improved upon his moves to date. By being as faithful and orthodox as any conservative, and refusing to save himself politically by blasting the church, he has forced Mormons themselves to face the squalor of their built-in bias against black people.

# CHAPTER FIFTEEN

# HOW TO BACK
# INTO POLITICS

---

"Calm down, now, Gus," soothed the new politician with the terrible temper.

The more engaging literature of our time, highbrow and pop, suggests that man is as helpless inside his institutions as he would be if nailed in a barrel drifting over Niagara. The writer or artist lives on a Hobson's choice. He can strive for the blind courage of the existentialist, who admits with the late Albert Camus to the absurdity of all human action. Or he can cop out with the escapists, who are only half kidding about the enviable doings of Batman, Napoleon Solo, Marshal Dillon, Travis McGhee and several equally unreal James Bonds. The superhero is an elaborate spoof of human dignity.

Sensitive young people search for ways out of the trap. The miniskirt culture puts a heavy premium on sex, Mrs. Romney says, simply because "it seems to be all there is." Since to act is only to have a transitory happening, a few million of the young have learned to turn themselves off with LSD and "grass." Others rebel without showing it. The pied piper of

209

the campus, Paul Goodman, moved from his *Growing Up Absurd* book into a radical attack upon the adult power structure that is, he says, so bound up in its own muscle that everybody is helpless from the bottom to the top.[1] Executive vice-president Ed Cushman of Wayne State University, close to the student leaders who half-rioted in 1967, believes that if the society does not start to change now it will be torn by revolution when the college masses move out into politics.

Such unhappy thoughts are seldom mentioned by politicians. Under the rules jointly enforced by the press and the parties, a candidate must have slick answers ready for every question, and show no symptom of the doubts we feel deep within ourselves. He and his party must claim to own the Superman suit. They can do anything for us if we won't listen to the critics, certainly not to those "cussers and doubters" that Lyndon Johnson lumps with anybody who's not all-the-way. To break the rules is to look stupid or self-centered. For a man to suggest that his own political party is less than perfect, and that the voters might have the gall to clean it up, is to ruin everybody's institutional front. George Romney has committed this cardinal sin.

"We have a Democratic party increasingly dominated by union leaders and a Republican party importantly dominated by business leaders," Romney said in the summer of 1959. "Many union members are defaulting on their political citizenship and relinquishing it to unions for the economic benefits of union membership. Too many corporate executives and white-collar employees have become political eunuchs who have substituted corporate citizenship and the hope of economic advancement for their priceless heritage of independent political action." In other words, the man in gray flannel, like the one in the blue shirt, is finking out.

[1] Paul Goodman, "The Psychology of Being Powerless," *New York Review of Books,* November 3, 1966.

In Michigan, the result was a stalemate in which men could no longer even pretend to be in control of their institutions. Nobody ran the government in Lansing. The Democrats used union money and numbers to secure a long-term lease on the statewide offices of the executive branch (G. Mennen Williams, prop., 1949–61). The Republicans used mal-apportionment and lobby finances to hold a grandfather title to both houses of the legislature. With these official monopolies under a moribund constitution,[1] each party had perfected a cynical game of blaming the other for the mutual irresponsibility that pushed the state to the border of bankruptcy. "People say the Democrats are bums and the Republicans are bums," admitted a GOP state chairman.

So it went until the businessman in holy underwear stepped between the parties. Romney couldn't even cuss very well. He talked like a schoolboy about how the people ought to run government, and looked like an innocent who wanted to play poker with the card sharks. As if to prove his naiveté, he organized a citizens' crusade in 1959 to break the two-party stalemate. And it worked. Then he pitched his crusade above both parties, convinced against shrewd advice that the voters would rise up to save the state from financial disaster. And that worked. When it became clear that a new constitution would have to be drafted, he turned even more antipartisan. Constitutions, to him, are not political toys. He seemed to keep winning until October 1961, when freshly elected GOP delegates to the Constitutional Convention, Con-Con, met in caucus at the Elks Hall in Lansing.

Then it happened. Party elders, hardly eager for constitutional reform, not only blocked Romney's antipartisan bid to be Con-Con president but began to organize the GOP

[1] Drawn up in 1850, the Michigan constitution had been patched by amendments in 1909 A.D.

211

delegates, as labor leaders were doing in the Democratic caucus, for a return to the familiar politics of stalemate.

Romney blew his stack. He marched off the Elks Hall floor with two aides trailing in his wake, and disappeared into a back room. He didn't go there to pray. He ripped off his suit coat, grabbed it by the collar, twisted into a pitcher's motion; with all the force in his well-tuned body he slapped the coat-tail against the floor. He never felt right in a coat anyway, being a shirtsleeves man. Three minutes and a bit of pacing later, he put the coat back on and resumed the patient years of struggle that eventually gave Michigan four things: (1) a model constitution, (2) state government that did more work and paid its bills, (3) a responsible Republican majority and (4) its most promising prospect for the Presidential nomination since Sen. Arthur H. Vandenberg.

"I don't think my husband gets angry," said Mrs. Romney, "but he does tend to be intense."

Romney had backed into politics. He had started with work on public problems and ended up running for office, not the other way around. The real beginning came in '57 and '58, when Detroit's public schools were going to pot. The Board of Commerce, the alliance of business powers, had organized opposition to the Board of Education's pleas for higher taxes. Since the public didn't know much about its teaching empire, many believed the rumors that administrators were frittering away the cash on swimming pools and frills. Superintendent Sam Brownell, former United States Commissioner of Education, needed an ally who knew the whole community and would not be afraid to step on large toes. After culling 3,000 names, he settled on Romney.

It was hardly an obvious choice. Romney was not only in battle with unions but also openly attacking Big Three cars and management. He was not widely expected to keep his company alive much longer. When Brownell led a delegation

out to the Moorish-towered company offices at 1400 Plymouth
Road, he found a man with all he could cheerfully do. "You
couldn't have come to me at a worse time," Romney said.
"American Motors needs to make some money." Brownell
insisted, though he wondered at times over the next few
months if he had made a mistake. "The people out at American Motors think George Romney is God," he said, dissenting
from that view.

As usual, Romney did not seem to have the answers ready
in advance. He refused to box himself in by prejudging the
need for a tax boost. He hedged while he recruited 270 volunteers from labor, business, the police, education, nationality
groups, government and civic organizations. They formed the
Citizens Advisory Committee on School Needs, CAC, one of
the most irregular bodies since Coxey's Army.

Romney worked his forces hard, and not on abstract debate. With a tiny staff of full-timers, he deployed squads of
committees to inspect all 336 school facilities. By sending
regional subcommittees to study local schools, he found a way
to help decentralize the board of education's authority, a way
that might someday lead to neighborhood-run schools served,
rather than bossed, by the superintendent's staff. Private
specialists dug into school management and money use. They
spaced their final reports to give the newspapers one shocker
every day or so, and brought photographers in to see children
in firetrap classrooms. The monster project, which took nearly
two years, gave Detroit its first close look at its educators'
problems.

Strict as ever about procedures, so as to prevent charges of
railroading proposals, Romney spread the credit and applied
his "substantial majority" doctrine. That meant hash over each
proposal until only an odd few opposed what everybody else
wanted. Romney's own ideas had to be kept in check. Because
of his high regard for the institutions people build for them-

213

selves, he wanted to encourage Catholic parochial schools, by a tax credit or any appropriate device. When he surprised his committee with that suggestion, the shocked silence and whispered warnings did not quickly persuade him that the parochial issue would deadlock action forever. "We'd still be there fighting," says one CAC veteran.

Out of its labors, the committee brought 182 unanimous recommendations for school reform, and prepared Detroit to vote resoundingly for both a bond issue and a tax boost. The decisive turn came when Romney took his report before the Detroit Economic Club, the business forum. At the end, questioned about the pools and frills charge, he threw up his arms and reacted with such furious intensity as to override most doubts.

The success of the school committee, he now admits, convinced him that citizen action might work better than he had thought. It set him up for the state job a few months later. On a foggy day in the East when planes were grounded, he and Mrs. Romney took a New York–Boston train with company vice-president Ed Cushman. Both American Motors executives happened to be lecturing on Harvard's campus the same day. They chatted about their state's money troubles. Gov. Soapy Williams had just appointed a study committee headed by a utility company executive. Romney snorted that a utility man, under the thumb of political regulators, could never be independent enough to deal with the real issues. A thought hit Cushman and Romney at the same instant: Why didn't they take on the job?

Back in Detroit, Cushman talked it over with two other people: Ford's Robert S. McNamara and editor Martin Hayden of the Detroit *News*. On April 28, 1959, seven such citizens had dinner in a private room at the Sheraton-Cadillac Hotel. Out of the meeting came Citizens for Michigan, soon to be a broad-based organization designed to give state government the kind of total checkup that the education committee had given Detroit schools. All knew that the job depended on Romney, with Cushman for deputy.

McNamara wondered on the way down in the elevator that night just what Romney had in mind for himself. Hayden, who dropped out of CFM to retain editorial independence, argued that Romney would have to plunge right into party politics to have much effect. So did quick-witted Charles Moore, Ford's public relations vice-president and Romney adviser through the 1962 campaign. Romney said no. McNamara thought it over. When another executive asked suspiciously if Romney were using CFM to make himself governor, McNamara said, "This state could do a lot worse."

CFM spread like Asian flu to 5,000 members, many of them educators and civic leaders around the state. The financial mess in Lansing had become a national joke, in part because of a Democratic ploy to embarrass the Republican legislature for failing to act on taxes. The flap was typical of stalemate gestures. Since the state was delaying on its bills, it would be officially broke any day it tried to catch up. After checking with Neil Staebler, Democratic national committeeman, a state official suddenly paid a pile of back bills—so that he could honestly announce that he could not send out bimonthly paychecks to the lawmakers and several thousand state employees. The ploy boomeranged. Payless payday inspired grim humor about a new drink, Michigan-on-the-rocks, which has since been hemlock to Democrats.

CFM now had the crisis pressure it needed. McNamara, though not a patient man, sat through wrangling months on the tax study committee that eventually proposed the inevitable, a state income tax. And Romney learned that the tangled administrative system could never be straightened out without a new constitution. It wouldn't be easy. The League of Women Voters and the Jaycees were out chasing 300,000 signatures to be sure of 210,000 valid ones on a constitutional convention call. They reported trouble: only 85,000 names. Unless CFM could put up money to print and distribute thousands more petitions, the drive would fail.

As often happened, Romney had to pay for his purity concepts. He had insisted, as he did later to campaign fund-raisers, that CFM raise its money from the many rather than the few. He set the single contribution limit at $100, later $500.[1] You could be a CFM member for a dollar. Result: no money for petitions. There were other money troubles. When CFM persuaded the University of Michigan's famous Survey Center to set up a controlled experiment on how to involve people in either politics or community projects, the Ford Foundation turned down the request for funds. But the petitions had to go out. Cushman and Romney personally anted up $10,800 to be sure there would be a Con-Con. Technically, CFM provided the funds, but when they folded their organization years later, Cushman and Romney each paid $7,500 to cover the leftover debts.

The election of Con-Con delegates in August 1961 brought a Republican harvest, a two-to-one majority (99–45) that included many a CFMer like George Romney of Oakland County. With labor suspicious of the convention, Democrats discovered that their voters did not turn out to help write pieces of paper. But if Democrats were unhappy, they had company among the Republicans in the house and senate. Con-Con's commanding GOP majority meant that, for once, the party would be held responsible for what happened or did not happen. But convention reapportionment of the legislature, even on a compromise with the one-man, one-vote idea,

[1] He set the same $500 ceiling on contributions to his first gubernatorial campaign. But as the bills piled up, a money-chaser noticed, "he got over that."

would break the party's absolute control and force some senate
lords to fight to retain their seats. There was also cause to
wonder if some of these earnest Republican delegates who
came to work on the constitution could be kept out of politics
later on. They couldn't; they were to become the first wave of
Romney's assault and a permanent addition to party activists.
It should have been no surprise, then, that veteran party men
among the Con-Con delegates swore to stop Romney. They
succeeded only in keeping him out of the convention presidency.

It was a favor. Soothed by friends into accepting a vice-
presidency after the coat-slamming, he remained the central
figure of the convention but, not being president, was free to
announce for governor long before Con-Con adjourned.
When other chores, like running a car company and planning
his campaign, kept him away from committee meetings, the
press editorialized him back to the job. He worked out the
critical compromises—on apportionment, flat-rate income tax
and short-ballot—that produced a majority document, perhaps
a sounder one than the idealistic paper he envisioned.[1] The
political solution, for which union chiefs never forgave him,
came when he turned his back on the Democrats and led his
moderate Republicans into bargaining with the conservatives.
He was learning, in spite of his antipartisan stand, that the
GOP division need not make the party helpless. Mrs. Romney, gifted in basic English, explains it this way: "Just when

[1] Gus Scholle charged that the voters-vs.-area compromise on the
legislative districts made one citizen equal to fifteen acres. By taking
the reapportionment case to United States courts, Scholle eventually
got one-man, one-vote reapportionment. His original suit in Michigan
provided the legal brief for the Tennessee case on reapportionment
that, decided by the Supreme Court first, brought the one-man, one-
vote rule to the fifty states and inspired the Dirksen Amendment
counterattack.

the Reactionaries were going to form a coalition with the Democrats and sweep out all the reforms, he was able to form a coalition with the Reactionaries."

"I'd rather have ninety percent of something," Romney said, "than a hundred percent of nothing."

As the storm center of basic political change, Romney had been talked about as a prospective candidate all along. In 1960, Richard Nixon had pleaded with him to run against Democratic Sen. Pat McNamara (not related to Robert). The incumbent's stock was low enough that few professionals in either party doubted that Romney would win. He did not say yes, but GOP national committeeman John Martin, who led a delegation to urge him into the race, came away feeling that "we had him." However, he would have to resign from CFM, leaving it in the lurch and undercutting its nonpartisanship. "I thought it was all set up for George to resign at a meeting of the CFM board called for that purpose," says editor Hayden. But Democratic leader Staebler smelled the move coming, alerted Walter Reuther's labor members on the board to build up opposition. They were ready at the January 30, 1960, CFM board meeting when chairman Romney brought up the question of his resignation. Before the labor men spoke, an ex-president of the League of Women Voters, Mrs. Berrien Ketchum of Flint, tore into Romney for backing down from his antipartisan stand. Here was a voice he had to respect. He quietly stepped out in the hall with Cushman and another American Motors man, neither of whom wanted to lose him from the company. He stayed with CFM.

"If I had known he was going to change his mind, I would have gone out into the hall myself," said Robert McNamara, who had not yet become a Democratic cabinet officer.

"The smart people said that nobody turns down a sure seat in the United States Senate," says Cushman. "But I knew one man who would." The biggest loser was Richard Nixon. With Romney on the 1960 ticket, he would easily have picked up the miniscule margin of 67,000 votes he needed election night to carry Michigan.

As the governor's race of 1962 came closer, however, all the reasons for not running in 1960 had been turned around. He was an executive, not a Senate debater. This time he would not be undercutting the constitutional drive; in fact, only as governor would he have half a chance to get it ratified in the referendum of 1963, and to reorganize state government under its authority. Democratic Governor John Swainson, who later attacked the document as "defective," would have been able, if he chose, to use the governor's office to rap it with the cautious voters. The stakes were fairly high. Con-Con study of state administrative machinery had added a thousand specifics to Romney's conservative belief that sheer ineptitude made the states shift responsibility on to Washington. "Michigan's administrative structure is like a 20-mule team hitched up in the dark by a blind man," he said. Former President Eisenhower had complained to Romney that "he had to sign bills [preempting state power] primarily because the state and local levels were not stepping up to their responsibility." Ike's point was almost pathetic. Hard as he begged, he had not even been able to stir states and cities to act on their own in obvious areas, not even in sewage disposal.

It all fitted together now. Having shown a skill at mobilizing voters to shake their state out of stalemate, Romney would see if the states could rise up and have a say on the Federal level. His timing was better than anybody could guess from the evidence available. The Michigan governor's office would become a sort of standard reference source for many of the states soon to follow suit, work over their constitutions on the way back to a stronger role in the Federal system. Romney, to whom an idea is less a mental game than a physical command, sensed that the time was ripe, much as he had sensed that people were ready to revolt against big cars.

He set January 10, 1962, as the deadline by which he must decide whether to run or not. The self-forcing deadline, which he also used to make himself work out a Vietnam position (by April 7, 1967), is a standard management procedure. But in politics, and blended with the story of his fasting and praying, it made for breath-holding. The press conference was a mob scene. He came on camera full of bounce wearing not a Republican symbol but the Romney-blue (intense) tie designed for him by Dewitt Wallace, *Reader's Digest* editor-owner; it featured dinosaurs, the gas-guzzlers he had been dethroning in this previous career. Declaring that his first job was to help finish the constitution, he stubbornly berated both parties for "acting like narrow partisans first, and citizens of Michigan last." He had found another pair of dinosaurs.

Incumbent Governor Swainson, an attractive young veteran, derided it all as a "publicity countdown." Gus Scholle called Romney a religious clown. The attacks burned his thin skin. And his private polls soon showed that he had troubles. MORC, Detroit's Market Opinion Research Company, had him trailing Swainson by 41.9 percent to 50.7 percent.

Then came the stab from Senator Barry Goldwater. Five days after Romney's announcement, the chairman of the GOP Senatorial Campaign committee entertained a sellout crowd of 5,000 at a party rally in Detroit's Masonic Temple. "This myth that business dominates the Republican party of Michigan should be exposed for the fraud it is," said the visitor from Arizona. Having gone out of his way to tag Romney a perpetrator of fraud, without calling his name, Goldwater stirred giggles among the Grosse Pointe Republican ladies, hostesses of the affair, by expressing sardonic pleasure that their gubernatorial candidate had finally "decided to join the Republican party." Getting still more personal and derisive, he told reporters after the rally that Romney's appeals for broader citizen action in the GOP were "standard fare for politicians, like mother love, free beer and wide roads." Goldwater is a sportsman with a strong sense for taking as much as you dish out; two years later, when running for the Presidency, he showed little inclination to beg peace from the man he had kicked in the face at the previous scrimmage.

Romney bled without squealing. He hung to his rule—don't attack a man personally—and came down harder on the citizen-first theme.[1] He now called the GOP "the one party that has an opportunity to become a genuine citizens' party, responsive to citizen control."

After the Goldwater statements, Romney did not find it easy to draw support from conservatives in the party machinery. He didn't make it any easier by looking for, and finding, a chance to attack the Birch Society as a conspiracy trying to infiltrate the GOP.

It was just as well. The party had little machinery worth leaning on, and to the Michigan majority the elephant label looked a bit like the skull and crossbones on a medicine bottle. Romney won the August primary without opposition, and the state convention endorsed his slate of candidates for the "ad board," the administrative board made up of the Attorney General, Secretary of State and four other executive posts

[1] The glaring exception came in 1967 when Detroit *Free Press* reporter Robert Popa, quoting a remark that other reporters understood to be off the record, published Romney's view that Sen. Charles Percy of Illinois was an "opportunist." As irony would have it, the quote was published the morning the Romneys were entertaining the Percys at home at breakfast. Percy was keynoting the Michigan State Republican Convention that day. When reporters asked about it at a joint Percy-Romney press conference, Romney apologized in public as he had in private. Trapped by a deft followup question, he swallowed and said, yes, he was himself an opportunist by the dictionary definition of one who "takes advantage of opportunity."

(cut by the new constitution to two). He recruited what old hands he could into this 100-man Steering Committee, but none of the seven advisers on his Strategy Group had ever before been in a statewide campaign. A good part of the Governor's next five years would be invested in trying to develop the party into a service organization that voters might trust 365 days a year, not just tolerate on election day.

The working burden of the campaign fell upon the Romney Volunteers. Though set up to be a campaign auxiliary appealing to Independents and Democrats, this band of irregulars became increasingly Republican and had to take on most of the work normally done by regulars. The man Romney picked to recruit them was a hefty ex-Democrat, an associate professor at the University of Michigan (political science Ph.D.), John T. Dempsey, 37, who had been a Washington assistant to Sen. Thomas C. Hennings of Missouri. Dempsey had been impressed by Romney while working as a news reporter, then as news director, for Detroit's WJBK-TV. The new recruiter started organizing with a roll of dimes in a paybooth. Instead of following precinct lines, which only politicians know about, he tried to set up a Volunteer committee "in every place that thought of itself as a community." Sample: The Romney Volunteers of the 19th Postal District. With a plain-spoken manual of instructions (e.g., open a bank account), the man-and-woman pairs of co-chairmen—185 chapters in 83 counties —quickly built to a claimed membership of 80,000, about 27,000 of them very active. They erupted with uncommon energy into bumper-sticker days, telephone solicitation, press-releasing about their activities, organizing rallies, and that constant Romney business of finding undecided voters to whom the candidate ought to send a personal letter.

The distinctive emphasis in their work and the cause of their passion was hidden by efficient but fairly standard campaign techniques. A hint of it came in the Romney-blue questionnaire that they distributed by hand. Alongside the candidate's picture, it asked, "Will you spend 4 minutes—and 4 cents—to improve the State of Michigan?" The questions asked the voter's opinion on tax reform, constitutional change, the causes of unemployment in the state and seven other issues. In the original draft, the questions had been asked objectively as if on a public opinion survey. But Dempsey and the research staff decided it would be phony not to put in Romney's views on the issues. So, in effect, they asked the voter to agree or argue with Romney. The response was almost violent. The first printing of 15,000 sheets came flooding back in the mails, often with contributions, in such volume as to swamp the volunteer secretarial force who were tabulating, answering requests for additional information and sending back Romney thank-yous. When the candidate began quoting from the comments written on the back of the questionnaires, the feedback picked up, and the mailbags brought in several hundred returns a day. Out in the lonely crowd, there seemed to be a bunch of people who wanted a chance to talk back as much as they wanted mother love and wide roads.

The crowd included union members who sensed that their political machinery had slipped out of their control. By bringing such awareness to the surface inside the membership, Romney drove leaders like Gus Scholle into angered errors. Any candidate who made them look like a vested interest inside the union hall was obviously a fraud. Inside the Republican club, Goldwater had leveled the same charge of phony against Romney's argument about business domination. "The reactionaries don't trust George either," says Scholle, taking comfort in company. When Romney, against cautious advice, had debated Scholle on TV over constitutional issues, the labor leader had lost control and thrown a reapportionment map in his foe's face.[1] "Calm down, now, Gus," Romney soothed, aware that the intemperate outburst had made Scholle look like a terrible-tempered labor boss.

Romney was able to reach union workers in part because of unorthodox campaign timing, as the next chapter will explain, but mainly because of political instinct. It began to happen in July when, accompanied by a group of girls in Romney-blue dresses, he went to the annual Wyandotte parade in the downriver industrial city south of Detroit. Democratic officials refused him a place in the parade on grounds that only elected officials were allowed. He accepted the ruling without protest, "but with all those people along the route, I told the girls we'd just walk along the sides handing out literature. We saw a lot more people than we would have seen if we had been marching." Later, at the national convention of Negro Elks, he happened to end up leading the parade, he remembers happily, "until the exalted ruler of the organization arrived and took over. . . . I dropped back in the middle of the line."

The payoff came at the AFL-CIO's big Labor Day parade: "I got in front of all the union bigwigs and led the whole show," he says. Marching in white shirtsleeves, obviously having a high old time, he only smiled and shook more hands when clumps of officials in union hats booed him.

The parade ended at the Fairgrounds for the Labor Day picnic that had been a political ritual through the years of labor rise from bloody heads to brass hats. Republican candidates had traditionally requested invitations to be on the

[1] Perhaps Romney did not play fair. Both sides knew that Scholle expected to win by triggering the legendary Romney intensity. That has been the strategy, a losing one, of almost every opponent he has faced in politics. But Romney prayed hard the night before, he admits, "that I would not lose my temper." Demon temper struck the other side of the table.

speaker's stand, knowing that they would, just as traditionally, be turned down. It was Democratic day. Romney had gone through the please-ask-me routine. But now he paid his dollar at the gate and sat near the back among the rest of the ordinary people. The point was all too clear. The fatcats were up on the podium making speeches against the fellow out there talking man-to-man with the people. Not patronizing, he did not hesitate to argue it out with anybody in the mood to talk. Photographer Tony Spina of the *Free Press* took a picture of him with one foot propped up on a back bench looking wistfully up at incumbent Swainson and the other dignitaries. Wire-serviced around the world, but especially in Michigan, the picture said more than a thousand Republican orations against labor bosses.

Walter Reuther knew Romney too well to make the mistake others made of attacking his character. Reuther kept his fire on the Republican party and said that Romney would be the "prisoner of a bunch of 18th-century politicians . . . GOP reactionary diehards will make hamburger out of Romney's white horse before he gets the saddle off."

But the UAW's television commentator, Guy Nunn, put Democrat Swainson on for a half hour of berating Romney, who was watching at home with the Strategy Group. Incensed at the personal attack, Romney overrode the cautious advisers again (somebody always wants to protect him) and drafted a demand for equal time. To underscore his point that UAW members were forced to pay through dues for political propaganda that all did not agree with, he sent along a check for $1,421 to cover the cost of his time. The check bounded back and forth through four days of headlines before Reuther prudently contributed it to the American Heritage Foundation. Nunn was less prudent. Too sure of his skill, he made the mistake of cutting off Romney's refutations of the Swainson charges—and on his own program lost a shouting match to an underdog full of genuine indignation. Nunn, though a competent pro, declined so fast that he soon was taken off the UAW air.

Human cussedness began to break up a tidy system. Two local unions invited Romney to talk. "The curtain has been penetrated," he hoped. Not entirely. At another local to which he was invited, he was turned away at the door with the threat of a fistfight. But each incident angered somebody. President Warren Creekmore of UAW Local 280 at Continental Motors Corporation found his own signature printed on union literature backing Swainson, attacking Romney. Creekmore protested, joined the Romney Volunteers—and lost his job. "I was forced to choose between the political dictates of the international union, "he said, "and the dictates of my own conscience."

The count on election night seemed at first to follow the time-honored pattern. Democrats celebrated and demanded Romney's concession. But as the vote came in from middle-class neighborhoods and the new suburbs, many of them heavy with union families, the tally shifted. Romney won by 80,573 votes, eight-tenths of one percent. He added five percent to his plurality in each of the next two races. By 1966, nearly half the union members in Michigan were voting for the fellow who crashed their official parades and picnics.

# CHAPTER SIXTEEN

# THE RISE OF THE
# TICKET-SPLITTER

———

"Our campaigns are unorthodox and rational," says strategist Walter De Vries. "Unlike Johnson, Romney is a sophisticated interpreter of polling data."

To talk about your way of wooing the voter is as deadly as
to discuss the technical side of making love. These are activities for novices. Only when provoked by stock superstitions—
they abound in campaign lore—does George Romney rumble
for a moment about tactics. I've heard him laugh at the fear
of a candidate "peaking too early," and at "these reporters and
other experts who talk a lot about timing." He has broken
most of the taboos in the book and undercut, by statistical
analysis of campaign experiments, a goodly share of standard
doctrine in today's political science texts.

Romney has relied heavily on computers and other ad-
vanced electronic equipment, and in significant uses has
pushed his state party two to four years ahead of other well-
known Republican and Democratic machines. "You have to
use EDP and everything else, but they are only tools," says

Michigan state chairman Elly Peterson. "You can't stop there." The best-kept secret of the past three gubernatorial races in Michigan has been the GOP experiment with an unorthodox theory of political behavior. Though unfinished, it works.

Romney's action-research has been directed by Walter Dale De Vries, 38, who took his Ph.D. in political science at Michigan State while handling legislation for the Republican speaker of the state's lower house. Like several others in the Dutch-descended set around Romney, De Vries came from Grand Rapids, an hour and a half west of Lansing. He once joked that he was running a school for Ph.D. dropouts in the governor's office; several of the staff got excited by their daily discoveries and lost the taste for the duller side of scholarship. De Vries, though a seal-shaped mound of muscle, has the temperament of an inventive intellect. He now and then ends up exhausted in a hospital still grappling for a surer hold on a problem of strategy. Romney has lightened his administrative load so as to leave his mind free to roam.

The two met as Con-Con delegates, De Vries recalls, "and found that we agreed on almost everything." Because nobody there knew how to run a constitutional convention, De Vries drafted the plan of staff and organization, took over as chairman of the committee on administration. Romney later called upon him for another job: to propose organization and strategy for the 1962 governor's race. Romney adopted most of the specifics and turned De Vries loose with a substantial research budget. "He gave me carte blanche," says De Vries.

The party's traditional reflex was to "get out the Republican vote" in the outstate counties, and leave Detroit and other ever-expanding Democratic centers alone. As the national GOP was to demonstrate again in 1964, Republicans do not easily abandon the illusion that somewhere, somehow, there are loyal underground millions left over from the Twenties.

"Political machines latch on to a technique and won't change," says De Vries. He served up Census data and projections to show Romney where this outstate notion led: to a dead end. The voting records of the past indicated a deeper irony. Since outstate Republicans voted anyway, hard campaigns in rural counties tended only to bring out a latent Democratic vote.

"Our campaign must be rational and unorthodox," said De Vries, to whom those two words are more or less redundant. So he concentrated on the 19 heavyweight counties, the urban areas that by 1966 would have 81 percent of the vote. (In his last state race, Romney polled a record 78 percent of his votes in this urban belt.) The first order of business was to find the people who could be switched into the Republican column.

One answer was obvious: the self-described Independent. He had been around for a long time. In 1940, pollster George Gallup reported that 20 percent of United States voters considered themselves Independents. In 1960, 22 percent called themselves Independent, hardly a dramatic rise. But in those two decades, the Republican percentage of the electorate had dropped from 38 to 25. The percentage of voters who called themselves Democrats had risen from 42 to 53. The GOP, having once had a near-even split, had shrunk until it needed to corral most of the Independents and some of the Democrats to win a major election. The proud party, like little England, resented the loss of its powers. The figures for industrial Michigan made the Independents look like a shapeless third party that leaned toward the Democrats. Republican elders saw little hope of tilting them.

The whole GOP had, of course, been split for years over what to do about the Independents. Liberal Republicans wanted to pick middle-of-the-road candidates to please them; conservative Republicans damned such me-tooing as a sellout in principle. Romney considered the liberal-conservative division a hand-me-down from New Deal days, and resented attempts to place him or anybody else at a point on the line between extreme liberalism and extreme conservatism. "They try to tie a label on you," he says. But the argument over how to appeal to Independents, presumably somewhere in the soggy center, tore the GOP apart in every election.

Beyond this ideological problem, De Vries had another sound reason for not going after the Independent. In much of the literature of political science, the Independent is a dud. You wouldn't want such a slob in your party. A Michigan survey group, using depth polls, wrote a standard work on *The American Voter*. Their conclusion: "Far from being more attentive, interested and informed, Independents tend as a group to be somewhat less involved in politics. They have somewhat poorer knowledge of the issues, their image of candidates is fainter, their interest in the campaign is less, their concern over the outcome is relatively slight, and their choice between competing candidates, although it is indeed made later in the campaign, seems much less to spring from discoverable evaluation of the elements of national politics."[1]

While the Independent sounded bad enough, to the loyal party worker there was something worse: the ticket-splitter, the voter who, no matter which party has his basic loyalty, divides his votes between the parties. Though often confused with the Independent, he is defined by a more practical test: not by what he says but by what he does.

"I don't know what an Independent is," said De Vries. "But I have a behavioral definition of a ticket-splitter. He votes for one party at the top of the ticket and splits to the other party just below."

The splitter has been controlling more and more elections, not only for the Presidency but also for the Senate and for

[1] Campbell, Converse, Miller and Stokes, *The American Voter* (New York: John Wiley & Sons, 1966), p. 143.

governor. De Vries suspected that the splitter might be a very different animal from the apathetic Independent of political science literature. Also, the research data on splitters could be much more comprehensive than on Independents. The Romney staff could begin with actual vote tabulations, precinct by precinct, from elections back to 1956. The lease-time computer could correlate precinct votes with the detailed U.S. Census reports on each tract, giving income level, home ownership and a socioeconomic profile of a neighborhood. "Our conception of Detroit is not of a city but a series of neighborhoods," says De Vries. Both the election results and the Census reports could be tied by computer into opinion polls. All the pollster had to do was to ask the voter what he did in the last election—at the top and farther down the ballot— as well as standard questions (homeowning, etc.) to fit into Census reports.

The pollster was Fred Currier, then 38, vice-president of Detroit's Market Opinion Research Company (MORC), which had built a record of accuracy in predicting elections for the Detroit *News*. Another Ph.D. dropout, Currier had been a student of Milton Friedman, the University of Chicago economist who became Senator Goldwater's 1964 adviser. Equally strong for civil rights and free market economics— "I believe in freedom on both sides"—Currier kept a cautious eye on "the liberal bias in political science." A thin scholar with a large Adam's apple, he might stay up all night any time he found another mind with an exciting insight. He and De Vries had been working together since 1958, when they talked the reluctant state GOP into a few polls.

MORC's first Romney poll, in 1962, showed him trailing Democratic Gov. John Swainson and dragging a sick elephant by the tail. Not even the Republicans seemed, when tested on "semantic differential" polls, to hold their party in lofty regard. But they were with Romney. In spite of conservative criticism from several party actives, better than 90 percent of what De Vries called "behavioral Republicans" were behind him.

There was clear evidence of disgust with both parties as institutions. More than 60 percent of all voters blamed the state mess on "politicians" in general. A strong majority (59 percent in the Detroit area, 54 percent outstate) believed that Romney could clean things up better than Swainson, though only one percent of these mentioned his Republicanism as a reason. They talked about honesty and business experience. Of the minority who favored Swainson as their man for reform, 35 percent did so because he was a Democrat. The GOP, having lost the 1960 election in spite of the state's money crisis, was even losing ground, the polls showed, in the outstate counties.

On May 5, 1962, De Vries delivered to his boss a 15-page strategy proposal. Though he did not yet have the ticket-splitter data, which took separate processing, he banked heavily on what he expected it to show. "We can win—but it will be tough," he wrote. "Romney's greatest asset is that he is not perceived as a politician. He's not a typical politician —why should we make him look like one by using the hoary, sacrosanct, political techniques of the other campaigns?" De Vries worked within the frame of Romney's thought. He proposed that, believing in citizen participation, Romney should send out a questionnaire asking people's advice on state issues. When thousands answered, De Vries and Romney were the unsurprised minority at headquarters. He also advocated a radical break from the tradition of jamming up TV, radio and printed ads at the end of the campaign so as to have the standard saturation in the last few days of desperate politicking. Romney agreed. By running soft-sell spots much earlier, he reached the undecideds during their actual decision process in the dog days of summer, not later, after they had become bored. At plant gates and on TV, Romney also reached deep enough into worker ranks to make the union leaders nervous. So they tried to keep him physically away from the members, a serious error.

"He's like a tank," said Currier. "He panics the opposition."

The campaign dangers showed clearly in the early polls. Neither the proposed new constitution nor tax reform, which included an income tax, were popular. They were Romney projects, but he had to blend them into the broader issue of fiscal responsibility and cleaning up the Lansing mess.

The data on ticket-splitters started out interesting and became more so with each poll. Splitters were basically Democrats in Detroit, Republicans outstate. Though on most questions they fell between the straight-ticket Republicans and Democrats, as Independents did, they were a breed apart. They gave Citizens for Michigan, Romney's independent action group, higher marks than did straight-ticket voters in either party. And by their open-end comments, they revealed an emotional tie to Romney's Rambler crusade against the Big Three. In Detroit, the splitters worried even more about the state's financial mess than did Republicans. They favored constitutional reform more than the Democrats. Though little worried about unemployment, a substantial third of them gave Romney's answer about the cause of unemployment: plants were moving out because of the state's uncertain economic atmosphere.

Nine out of ten ticket-splitter families owned their homes, far above the national average of 64 percent. The homes were mostly in the modest bracket, $10,000 to $15,000, but a majority of the splitters had moved up half a class on the sociologist's scale. They tended toward white collar or high-skill industrial jobs, and grouped above the $7,000 income line. By population proportions, they were slightly more Catholic than Protestant. They were also active users of radio and TV, but showed an unfashionable preference for print. They read newspapers. They obviously did not belong to the apathetic breed described as Independents.

Intrigued, the Romney staff fed new poll questions to splitters. On a then-popular test (later invalidated by research) for identifying community leaders, the splitters gave mixed answers. They seemed to listen to their neighbors more than leaders were thought to do, and to talk less. Were they involved in the campaign? Well, a high 7.9 percent were, more than the 6.7 percent for Democrats but less than the 10.6 percent for Republicans. That ended the theory that splitters, like Independents, were lazy and apathetic. Had they talked to a party worker on either side? Yes, indeed—39.4 percent had, against 26.8 percent for Democrats and 29.3 percent for Republicans. They had also talked more to union political agents. Had they met either candidate? They sure had—15.7 percent compared to 11.5 percent for Democrats and 10.6 percent for Republicans. The process was like tapping on a prison wall to find out who was in the next cell. All of a sudden at a staff meeting, ex-Democrat Jack Dempsey, chief of the Romney Volunteers, recognized the mystery people: "They're like *us!*"

That discovery made it easier. The campaign concentrated on ticket-splitter country. While Mrs. Romney kept the 64 outstate rural counties from feeling left out, the candidate worked the 19 heavyweights—with time allotted not only by voting strength of the county but also by its previous record of splits. Units of time in later campaigns were allotted on a three-phase contribution-ratio formula heavily weighted for ticket-splitters. Everything the candidate did was pretested and post-tested by polls. Currier ran 18 polling projects in that first campaign. In addition to constant check on issues—job worries shot up, tax fears fell—he pretested radio spots, TV blurbs, ads, campaign literature, direct mail, telephone

234

calls, combinations of mail and calls, Romney's door-to-door campaigning and major events like television debates. The news was not always good. Though Romney scored well after a shouting session with the UAW's TV commentator Guy Nunn, the sample gave him low marks for his three TV debates with Swainson. He lost two, tied one. But the check of what *votes* were switched by the debates brought him out ahead. That, he felt, was better than critical acclaim as a performer.

"If people want to pick a candidate on the basis of who makes the prettiest speech, we'd better run Lenore," he once said. "She's the best there is. She's a professional."

By knowing with considerable precision what people he had to reach, and what they were thinking, Romney could concentrate his energy where it counted. He sent 27,000 letters to undecided voters who were spotted by the Volunteers. In later campaigns, he used mail solicitation for small contributions, as Goldwater did; he also proved out a direct-dial news-tape service for radio stations, a way to run telethons without opposition jamming, and telectraphonic device for Romney taped-message calls (four cents apiece) to thousands of splitters. Currier discovered in post-election studies that Romney, by his campaign planning, had managed to see twice as many ticket-splitters as his opponent had. A startling 18.9 percent of the splitters said they had changed their minds during the campaign, compared to 7.4 percent for Democrats and 5.3 percent for Republicans.

Summing up '62, De Vries reported to GOP tacticians in other states:

> Forty percent of the voting population were Democrats, and Romney took eight and a half percent of that vote; 35 percent of the electorate split their tickets, and Romney took about 68 percent of that vote; and about 25 percent of the electorate voted straight Republican, and the Governor took 96 percent of

that vote. This meant that over half of the Governor's vote came from other than straight-party Republican voters.

It was an expensive campaign. By the estimates of people who handled money, the total outlay topped $450,000, a new high for Michigan. The next two campaigns cost less: about $360,000 for the governor's race in 1964, $260,000 in 1966 when he worked mainly for other GOP candidates.

If Romney had invented ticket-splitters, he could not have found people more to his taste. Many were alienated voters, but not out of apathy. They seemed to want nothing so much as a chance to have a hand in breaking the Michigan stalemate. To judge by the Romney Volunteers, the most active of the people who responded to the candidate, they had a sentimental streak. Some talked over cocktails about the campaign as their "contribution to this state." Quite a few, reported Volunteer organizer Hilary Whittaker, felt insulted when they were later offered jobs in state government.

Politics became a year-round business. Before the Romney staff finished their post-election study on ticket-splitters, they were researching a new campaign: the referendum to ratify, or reject, the proposed constitution. "We're in trouble," the new governor warned. "Even the members of my church [who knew his Con-Con work] are asking me if they ought to vote for it." Union officers were spreading doubt. Since Romney had worked out the key compromises inside the Republican party between moderates and conservatives, the Democrats were not committed. By the time Currier checked the voters, about one third were undecided. "When people are not sure," De Vries said, "they usually vote no."

So Romney blocked out the constitutional campaign as if he were running for office again. And again he had to depend heavily on the ticket-splitter. The delicate problem was the use of GOP machinery. "Since the constitution was supposed to be a nonpartisan issue," explains one aide, "we had to

236

mobilize the party without looking like it was involved." GOP worker ranks had been expanded. After the '62 election, Volunteer boss Dempsey had demobilized his troops, urging them to get involved in the party. Dempsey himself later ran for Congress. Many moved into the GOP to work on the constitutional drive. Along with the League of Women Voters and the Jaycees, plus every other independent association Romney could get to endorse the constitution, the party became a civic crusader and carried the constitution by a hair's breadth.

New people were also at work in the legislature. Some appeared in 1960 after the state's payless payday, and they came into politics for the same reason that Romney did. The key figure was William Milliken, a young Traverse City merchant who had built his family's department store business to four times its previous volume. Milliken, Yale graduate and handsome enough for his face to be a political liability, won election to the state senate in 1960. He was soon in dutch with the senate lords and the business lobbyists. But millionaires don't push easy. Sounding out allies, he invited a group of eight, among them other businessman-senators, to his house for summer skull sessions on state problems. "The Republican Party should have a program," he declared, a seemingly innocuous remark that marked him a wild heretic. The Traverse City Pact, as the program was called, inspired the senate's traditional Republicans to ridicule Milliken's forces as "Dem-Moderates." They proposed, among other radical things, that the legislature pass a construction safety bill to protect workers on building jobs.

Though Dem-Moderates were obviously considered liberal, the ideology box hid their political function. Milliken would normally have been the leading Republican backer of a conservative senator or two. (He broke pattern partly because his father had also been a state senator.) The party's chief problem was that business sent handymen, often lawyers, to do political chores, and they had to be more conservative than their sponsors. As long as the political parties were down-the-line branches of business and labor bureaucracies, their faithful agents could do nothing but stalemate each other. It did not matter much what facts were brought out in legislative committee, since those facts did not reach the real decision-makers. But when men like Milliken put themselves on the line, the Republican way of doing legislative business had to change. The Traverse City Pact fitted into Romney's program. By 1964, Senator Milliken was to be the Romney running mate for lieutenant governor and heir apparent. Like Romney, he refused to stay in either the liberal box or the conservative box. This Dem-Moderate became co-chairman of the state's new Human Resources Council, an agency geared to the conservative ideal of mobilizing nongovernmental forces to solve public problems.

The Michigan GOP was rising from its sickbed when it went into convulsions—the campaign of 1964 in which Romney chose to "accept but not endorse the national candidate." The story of Senator Goldwater's Presidential bid has been written and rewritten, largely by his critics or his former friends. Some consider it *The Last Hurrah* of conservatism or, with Richard Rovere, just *The Goldwater Caper*. There is, however, substantial evidence that '64 was a step toward a conservatism that could earn the respect of more than 26 million voters. Little noticed by the national press, Goldwater has since endorsed and many of his ardent followers have begun to implement a doctrine that calls for the solution of public problems by independent and local action, rather than the negativism of just trying to cut off Federal efforts. These distinctive efforts paid off in many of the Republican victories of 1966.

The Goldwater-Romney clash was a specific forecast of

238

this turn. Since Romney still refuses to attack Goldwater personally, any interpretation of Romney's action has to be made through people around him, and through studying his way of work. Goldwater insisted that the people had lost control of the system. He joked that Lyndon Johnson had so much power and wanted so much more that Democrats didn't know whether to vote for him or plug him in. With that cowboy look of freedom, Barry chopped away at the all-entangling Federal establishment.

Romney could go that far with him, maybe get there first. But Goldwater posed the issue as if the United States were fast turning into a European police state. "What good is prosperity if you are a slave?" he had demanded in October 1964. And having set the crisis on a quick-draw scene, he seemed ready for instant solutions, abroad as well as at home. Romney could not buy the radical shortcut. His method was to locate specific forms of discontent, as among the ticket-splitters, and turn that energy to specific programs, like constitutional reform and, later, community action. He had spent 20-odd years carefully testing alternatives to centralized power; he was still at it in Michigan GOP and state government. The Goldwater movement's mentality—one roll of the dice to settle the future—threatened steady progress on the goals that Goldwater and Romney shared.

The clincher was civil rights. "We were confronted in Michigan with the question of whether we were going to obviously compromise our position, and lose public respect," says Romney. Fund-raiser Max Fisher, fearful of the no-endorse decision, remembers what Romney told him at the time. "George said, 'Look Max, it's a matter of principle, and whether I go any further in public life or not, I've got to do it.' "

There was a practical side that he talks about even less. His cumulative research, now bound in 30 feet of neat black folders, was too precise to let him ever hope, as many Republicans did, for anything but disaster with Goldwater at the top of the ticket. "Research should raise the reality level," said De Vries, and reality was implacable. It wasn't just that Goldwater was not even holding the straight-ticket Republicans; it wasn't just that the ticket-splitters largely saw Goldwater as trigger-happy. Romney was being asked to double-cross those who believed in what he had said. If he put on the Goldwater label, the voter structure he was trying to cement into something new and solid would come unstuck.

He played it by ear. Along with most GOP governors, he was too worried over the liberal-conservative split in his own state to take a strong hand in the national struggle. When Nelson Rockefeller, fighting desperately in the California primary, talked as if Romney were backing him, Goldwater asked for and got a Romney denial by wire. Four years later, Romney knew better than to expect many Republican governors to go out on a limb for him. For Rockefeller's support, he felt especially grateful: "Rocky knows what it's like to be out where I am."

In January and in June of '64, Romney let a couple of small, flabby balloons go up. On "Meet the Press," he said that "like any American schoolboy," he respected the Presidency too much to turn down a genuine draft. But he added that there's no such thing as a genuine draft; the draftee has to help, and he was not doing that. At the June conference of governors in Cleveland, just after Rockefeller's fatal loss in California, Romney got caught in the riot of liberal Republican confusion. His troubles were mainly brought on by Richard Nixon, who urged him to run so as "to polarize the opposition against Goldwater. . . . That's the only chance we have." A friend who sat in on the talk says that Romney refused flatly to run but agreed, as a favor, not to declare himself out. Ohio's James A. Rhodes joined the claque urging

Romney to stop Goldwater. The same kind of you-fight-him shove made a patsy of Pennsylvania's William Scranton. Meanwhile, Nixon left Cleveland and stopped in Baltimore to prop Romney's head up on the target zone. He told The Associated Press that the convention was still open, and Romney was the contender.

But the so-called contender stayed home to run for re-election, except for his sortie to the San Francisco convention to demand that the party stand for civil rights and against extremists. (His anti-Birch resolution, though roundly defeated, was copied after November by Texas and other state parties.) His gubernatorial opponent was Congressman Neil Staebler of Ann Arbor, a wise politician with a clean record if not a strong campaign style. The smart money set up the problem: If Goldwater lost Michigan by as much as 300,000 —or at most by 500,000—Romney was dead. As it turned out, Johnson would have needed nearly three times the highest plurality mentioned, nearly 1.4 million, to beat Romney. Johnson took the state two-to-one, a plurality of 1,067,463 (Johnson 2,136,615 to Goldwater 1,060,152). Michigan GOP candidates, down to the township level, were mangled. But Romney still got 56.1 percent of the gubernatorial vote, five percent better than his first race and won with a plurality of 382,913.

Why? That kind of showing in the middle of a Republican catastrophe is not easy to explain in terms of campaign techniques, though he improved them, or a two-year record, though he had a solid one. Something else was going on. A clue may be found in some of the dull projects that bored capitol reporters but made news in neighborhood papers and on 40 Michigan radio stations. He had worked, as he promised on the '62 campaign trail, at the clumsy business of giving many more people a say-so in government.

After taking office in '63, he had started with what he called Governor's Conferences. Inviting thousands of professionals and community activists to lend their talents, whatever their party, to the solution of public problems, he chaired the all-day meetings himself. A few were so dull that even he dozed. But most tapped pent-up ideas. The subjects ranged from juveniles to the aging, from crime to tourism, from mental health to traffic safety. At one such session in the Lansing Civic Center, I found intense people from all over the state—civil rights militants, executives, schoolteachers and about 300 others—busily taking notes on new local solutions to old unemployment. He drew on the conferences for legislative ideas, but hoped that their main function would be to provide others with the git-up-and-go to invent their own programs. Other governors held conferences aplenty, but Romney turned the state into a constant, floating seminar of thought and action.

Party machinery did bipartisan duty. Though conferences came one on top of another—he was to hold 134 major ones by 1967—they piled up in the months before the 1964 campaign. In 1966, his campaign manager, John Byington, helped organize 13 regional sessions and sent prospective participants 7,000 copies of a 48-page booklet on Romney special messages about the problems up for study. "Can you imagine any other way to get voters to read the full text?" asks Byington.

"You can only separate administration and politics in the textbooks on public administration and in the inviolate sanctity of the classroom," Walt De Vries argued. "This administration—even though there are five political scientists on the executive office staff—has not been able to separate the two."

Instead of taking government down to the political level, Romney raised politics to the civic level. He gave real authority to citizen advisers. He even ended up in a fight with one of 37 blue-ribbon commissions. Management expert

242

William Seidman of Seidman & Co., one of Romney's unpaid business volunteers in government, persuaded his seven biggest competitors to spend months running an efficiency task force through all departments. They consolidated the state's data-processing systems, started performance budgeting, and in effect gave the Romney administration a good-government audit of approval. Savings now run a couple of million a year.

"We didn't find that the Democrats had been stealing, and some departments were run well," says Seidman. "But there had been a general deterioration in performance."

By 1965, the party's problem was to turn the kind of people who go to Governor's Conferences into permanent Republicans. Talking about such activists, many of them ticket-splitters, Romney says "There are a lot of Democrats and Independents who don't agree with the national Democratic philosophy of Federal pills for all ills. We must find a way to get them involved with our party's projects so that they can gracefully become Republicans." The GOP had to tap action-minded Michiganders all year around, as Romney had been doing in campaigns and in conferences. This duty fell to Mrs. W. M. Peterson, "our own beautiful Elly," as Romney introduces her, the first woman state chairman in GOP history and the second in the country (Democrats had the first in Oregon). After losing a sacrificial race for the United States Senate in 1964, she became Romney's choice for chairman at the '65 state convention. Elly is a joyful woman of generous girth. She and her blonde assistant, Mrs. Joyce Braithwaite, are imaginative professionals who have the kind of political fun once reserved for Democrats.

She nursed the sick party back to health, and by 1967 put it into a muscle-building exercise called involvement. For a test, the party hired John Marttila, 26, a gaunt six-foot-two civil rights worker. He opened an Action Center near the middle of Detroit's black ghetto. Word spread, partly by radio, that people in trouble could call 832-0800. Elly soon reported to Romney on some of the people, about 30 a day, who called:

> A twenty-one-year-old mother had twins. One died and lay in the mortuary for eleven days because there wasn't money to bury it. The Aid to Dependent Children people were boxed in by their rules. We found the child's father, who paid for the burial. . . . A couple 67 years old had worked past their Social Security retirement, and when they needed the money, they couldn't get it. They were starving. A call to Senator Griffin got them the check in five days. We've handled a number of Social Security complaints. . . . We found one old couple with two feet of sewage in the basement. We went after the landlord. . . . We've got a group making a price study to see why the poor are being overcharged, and how to get credit from somebody other than the loan sharks.

Marttila began to use GOP prestige to bridge the gap between slum and executive suite. A Detroit utility company, he found, made a practice of cutting the gas off for tenants in a building whenever the landlord did not pay his bill. Marttila ended that in one day of phone calls. The party could be the *ombudsman,* he insisted, guiding people to the right Government agency and forcing the agency to provide the services promised by law. Public services are so complicated that he had to build a catalogue. Perhaps more important, he could tap nongovernment services like Legal Aid.

Businessmen from both parties came when Marttila called for action committees, some to help struggling Negro companies. GOP officials exposed to the Detroit slums threw together a fund-raising campaign—$5,250 to send their first 150 core-city kids to 1967 summer camps. In one neighborhood, Romney's Human Resources Council encouraged a realtor on a nonprofit experiment in "group marketing." Tenants organized behind his plan to buy up their homes and bring in contractors for mass-production rehabilitation, a block or two at a time. Gaining assurance, half-literate families learned to trace titles to vacant lots that they could turn into play-grounds.

The GOP's first Action Center had been in business only three months when the '67 Detroit riot broke out. By noon the second day, Marttila knew that he had to get food and plenty of it. While he called all Republican party offices in the metropolitan area, Elly Peterson got on the phone to 14 other counties. She turned each party headquarters into a collection center, piling cases of donated food under the elephant signs. As requested, most contributors brought in cartons of canned goods, but "one lovely little old lady baked a plate of brownies." Within the first 12 hours, four truckloads of food were rolling into the burnt area. Here, the Republicans worked alongside AFL-CIO volunteers and a ministers' group, Interfaith Emergency Assistance. Marttila routed the trucks to distribution centers set up by IEA in churches. The first load contained 500 cases of food and piles of clothes for homeless people. Thirteen trucks from outstate counties arrived over the next three days, and more came from the three metropolitan counties.

Sniper fire was not a serious problem, says Marttila. But one Negro mother, trapped in a sniper zone, had to be supplied several times with a feeding formula. Knowing about basic needs, Mrs. Peterson also shipped in 50 dozen diapers. "We quit on the fourth day," she says. "By then, everybody else was there, so they didn't need us." In raising, hauling and distributing the emergency provision, she had called up about 300 volunteers from the GOP's standing force of doorbell-ringers.

"It was a time when party people might have been resentful," says Marttila, "but the response was fantastic." He sent 75 Negro children off to summer camp during the violence; when it was over, he concentrated on kids whose homes had been burned. "We're still pretty small, and the problems are large," says Marttila. "We just don't affect enough people."

Meanwhile, about half of Michigan's 83 county chairmen had started 106 projects that suited community needs. One local GOP ran a Head-start program; another, an art-festival; a third opened the first public library for miles around, and sent out an all-county call for books. Livingston County Republicans found 23 handicapped people struggling to support themselves in a rickety workshop; a better building opened up work for 48 people. Swapping plans with similar GOP activists in Minnesota, Illinois, California and Indiana, Elly called a national conference on urban problems and spread the service gospel to other states.

In these early tests, chairman Peterson watched for the more effective ideas. She had a new weapon hidden away. A couple of young lawyers, thinking along her lines, had already chartered a tax-free Republican Foundation. With it, she could raise money and spread the successful service ideas over the state. For future manpower, she realized, much depended upon young people. She hired a full-time youth director for the state central committee staff. Soon the GOP was holding two-day courses in political action (bipartisan) for student leaders in Michigan colleges.

Romney already had a Student Volunteer Corps going, as well as a talent center for Peace Corps veterans. Under his Human Resources Council, an organizer roamed the state's 40 campuses helping 9,000 students find teaching spots in the slums and among Indians. Romney refused a Poverty Program offer of three dozen paid staffers. "These students are the first whites that the Indians have invited into their homes. People trust them because they are acting on their own," he said. "Even some of the students who rebel are just trying to say 'recognize us and let us have some influence.' They want action, and they want a piece of the action." He did not want them turned into form-fillers. He also lured about 10,000 adults into volunteer duty at mental health clinics and other state centers.

Romney's most basic experiment is too recent to prove much. Called the One-For-One program, it began small by matching 25 affluent families (volunteers) with 25 welfare families (also volunteer). Though eight of the unemployed family heads soon got jobs and reduced their welfare checks, and two families went off relief entirely, Lt. Gov. Bill Milliken, in charge of the program, rejected this single-standard test. He was more impressed by the 16-year-old Negro girl who, encouraged at the way her new white friends knocked down barriers, set her sights on college for the first time. "We may have found a way," says Milliken cautiously, "to break the generation cycle of people trapped in welfare."

It all hangs together, though in a time of urban turmoil it may be too little and too late. Romney has used computers and social science to find the voters who actively resent the institutional traps that limit them. He is turning the Michigan GOP into an instrument that they can use not only to make Government listen but to help mobilize, and humanize, their communities. With 56 paid full-timers on state and county committee staffs, the party can work all year round, not just in election flaps. They are catalysts. "The root source of the nation's strength," Romney says, "is the capacity of the person to go out and do something."

The doing may wipe out the ticket-splitters. Last time round, about half of the voters of Michigan became straight-ticket Republicans.

# CHAPTER SEVENTEEN

# URBAN
# POPULIST

---

"It remains to be seen whether we will make a contribution comparable to that made by Greece or Great Britain," Romney says. "We are an unfinished nation."

Given provocation, George Romney can stretch his expletives beyond the limit of a "hell" or a "damn." He had been known to compare a few of his fellow men with the north end of southbound horses. But for a politician who honestly feels that his country is in serious danger, he retains an unusual calm. He keeps right on talking about "the fundamentals."

This habit he defends with the story of a young lawyer trying his first case before the United States Supreme Court. The lawyer was still laying out the basics of the case when his allotted half hour was up. "Young man," said one of the Justices, "don't you think you can rely upon this Court to know the fundamentals?" Without hesitation, the lawyer said, "No, your Honor, that's the mistake I made in the lower court."

If each politician needs a label, then Romney must be

tagged an Urban Populist. Like the rural Populists of the late 19th century, he reasserts the fundamental need for people to have more direct control over the institutions of daily life. He tangles himself in long sentences about "great revolutionary upheaval" that stopped the drift of the United States into monopoly capitalism. Only by a new diffusion of power, he believes, can we make the city and the suburb a place worth living in—as the rural Populists made country life bearable. In this spirit, he attacks not only the Federal establishment's rigidity, but also the business and labor concentrations that inspire more government control over 200 million people. The city cannot be rebuilt from the top down.

His battle, he believes, is an old one. Ever since the Constitution scattered the sources of power throughout the society, he says, new concentrations have been rising at each opportunity. The result: "Periodically it's been necessary for somebody to come along who recognized the necessity of dividing power. Andrew Jackson did with the banks. Theodore Roosevelt did with the trusts and the monopolies.[1] Franklin Roosevelt did as between organized industry and unorganized labor."

If such a fundamental looks rusty to many people, so does Romney's belief in the prospects for state government. Along with several governors in both parties, he is convinced that the states are literally rising again. The issue is not States' Rights, he argues, but states' responsibilities. The Supreme Court's reapportionment ruling has shaken the dust in many a capital.

[1] The Governor of Michigan's kinship with Populism and its successors is not limited to his Western origin, or to the Teddy Roosevelt biography that thrilled him as a boy. Browsing one day in Romney's study at Lansing, I found a copy of TDR's text on "The New Nationalism," delivered in 1910 at the dedication of the John Brown Battlefield. Romney had more or less ravished the pages by underlining with a ballpoint that was running out of ink.

249

With a dozen or two states ready to redo their constitutions, many of the state governments will, for a few years at least, be more agile than the fat old Federal agencies. State leaders also benefit from the most painful form of inspiration: They cannot stay far away from their troubles. In the '67 Detroit riot, it was Romney who, on the scene, knew that he had to have more troops, while Lyndon Johnson, 1200 miles from the heat, could not know the urgency.

A basic change has put state government out on the political frontier. The alliance between big-city mayors and the Federal agencies, once the key to national politics, is in the process of breaking down. With the sprawl of the suburbs, the core city has ceased to be the decisive unit. That's one reason why the city is sick enough to get so much publicity. As urbanologist Paul Ylvisaker insists, it is the states that, acting alone or through interstate compacts, have to bridge the gap between the city and the suburbs.

This, in fact, is what the legislatures in Michigan and other industrial states have been in turmoil about. With the sharp rise in need for education, public health, recreation and other services that states supply, each appropriation bill has become a battleground across which a new set of lines have been drawn: In place of the traditional urban-rural war, the new split tends to be city vs. suburb. The creative job in domestic politics is to weld a working alliance between these interests that now conflict.

The job of the states cannot be done, Romney argues, without "national tax reform." That means get a bite out of Federal income taxes, not just the present grant-in-aid programs that leave control in Washington. Trying to run state programs by his own rules, Romney lost two battles to Federal agencies and several million dollars in grants. He now assumes that jerry-built grant programs will continue without radical change, so he concentrates on reaching beyond them. The

Federal tax structure is set to rake off a disproportionate share of each rise in the Gross National Product. Democrats like Walter Heller, who was economic adviser to Presidents Kennedy and Johnson, have picked up a Republican proposal for no-strings bloc grants of tax money to the states.

Romney feels, however, that it may be necessary to go a step further into some form of tax-sharing or "piggybacking." Under a general piggyback system, each state would set its own income-tax rate but leave the collection job to the Internal Revenue Service. The taxpayer would be spared the misery of filling out two sets of tax forms, and would have a voice through the legislature in setting the rate from which his state draws its revenues.

Because of the failure of present Federal policies, Romney believes that domestic legislation over the next few years will call for something better than an attempt to revive the alliance between City Hall and Washington—which Lyndon Johnson repackaged as "Creative Federalism." One alternative is to see if real Federalism can be made to work once again, now that the states are back in business. This possibility has been largely ignored, except for the insertion of defensive states'-rights clauses in United States laws. But in three terms as governor, Romney has confirmed his prior belief that "states can again be the laboratories of government."

His administration in Michigan, solid and unsensational, was devoted to catching up after a long season of paralysis. In four pay-as-you-go years, he wiped out the $98 million deficit and raised annual outlays 54.5 percent. He put the bulk of the increase into education—up 68.7 percent—which uses more than half of total state funds. Rather than pour all higher education funds directly into state schools, he added a scholarship program. The 20,700 students now on state scholarships are free to make their own choice among state and independent colleges. In a separate program not based on competitive tests, an additional 9,117 students draw state tuition grants while attending non-state schools. Below the college level, he raised state aid to local schools, and experimented with the public school as a community catalyst. With funds from the Mott Foundation, he backed a Benton Harbor experiment in which recreational and social services are being centered around the schools.

In the same four years, Michigan raised its outlay on conservation 86.9 percent. But since the funds were still pathetically small, Romney had to try seed-money schemes. He made state grants to local government for starting work on sewage treatment; he set up tax exemptions for companies that would spend new funds cleaning up their industrial wastes. To prod local authorities as well as corporations, he took on more anti-pollution enforcers, who put tighter controls on raw sewage in 135 towns. Along the Detroit River and Lake Erie's shore, he set timetables for cleanup by 21 industries and 11 units of local government. He became the first Great Lakes governor to turn on the comprehensive water-planning machinery provided by new Federal legislation, and led seven other states in founding the Great Lakes-St. Lawrence River Basin Commission.

Raising mental health outlays 48.7 percent, he built a network of community clinics for near-home treatment and cut into the waiting list outside state hospitals. He quadrupled state support for general health services. On juvenile crime, he went for greater flexibility in handling cases; judges no longer sentence boys and girls to specific reform schools, but give rehabilitators a choice on how to handle each case. With a new Halfway House program, he ended the practice of dumping delinquents back into society without an adjustment stage. For adult felons, he got business help on an experimental Pre-Release Guidance Center.

"The litany of progress," as the Governor's staff benevolently call their own record, fills a thick folder of one-paragraph summaries. Romney and a Republican legislature passed the first minimum wage law in the history of industrial Michigan. He increased workmen's compensation 60 to 75 percent, and pushed through the state's first construction safety law. But the litany has to be qualified. Many of the measures originated with the Democrats, who also controlled the 1965–66 legislature and on occasion pushed Romney further than he wanted to go. The Detroit *Free Press* muttered that he was "fast becoming the spendingest Governor in Michigan's history."

Oddly enough, it was a tiny bloc in his own party who gave the Democrats their bargaining power at critical moments, especially in a 1967 fight over tax reform. Holding narrow majorities in both houses, the Republicans could have passed their own tax bill but for conservative GOP legislators who, by holding out, forced Romney into negotiation with the Democrats. Just as deliberately, August Scholle, AFL-CIO state president, arrived in Lansing to be sure that his old enemy, Romney, had to pay through the nose. If labor-Democrats could make the new taxes, including an income tax, look like a soak-the-rich program, they would also make Michigan's governor look dangerously liberal to GOP right-wingers in other states.

Romney had a way out. Though determined that "the state must live within its means," he could have accepted the labor-rightist stalemate, and made a show of slashing hundreds off the state payroll in the name of budget-balancing. He was convinced that such a move would improve his chances for the Presidential nomination. "They (labor and conservatives) think I'm so eager to run for President that I can taste it," he growled. "I ought to show them." Instead he published an "austerity budget" showing where the slashes would have to come, and invited Democratic leaders to his office for daily, public negotiations, union-management style. (The House Democratic leader was an experienced union bargainer.) While the fiscal year deadline came ominously close, Romney still waited for fatigue to help him out. "They're not worn down yet," he said.

As the legislature went into overnight sessions, he stayed on call in his office. A tired friend who dropped in at 5:15 one morning found him skipping rope. The tax bill, though not exactly to his taste, gave Michigan a solid revenue base and abolished a business activities tax that had discriminated against new companies.

He had for weeks refused to spend more than token time with The Romney Associates, his Presidential campaign organization, and he canceled their plans for a full summer of entertaining GOP dignitaries at the state resort on Mackinac Island. "I need what time there is to think," he said, and cut the visitor list to a few groups.

For states to be aggressive does not please the radical right any more than it does people who believe that all virtue resides by the Potomac. "It's no more humane for the state to shoot you than for the Federal Government to hang you," argues Richard Durant, 49, 14th Congressional District Chairman (slums to Grosse Pointe) and conservatism's loudest Michigander. "I'm radical enough to believe that if you let people alone, they will take care of themselves." Tracing his political theory back to Frederic Bastiát, French writer in the time of Napoleon III, Durant keeps his headquarters supplied with Birch-backed books (e.g., *None Dare Call it Treason*). He provides the basic research for Romney's enemies in the GOP, and periodically mails out a broadside to 10,000 Republicans in 50 states. Though he is an investment counselor, Durant does not generally mention that industry, which had been fleeing the state in 1961–62, started investing nearly four times as much in new Michigan plants during Romney's second term.

Each GOP state convention is enlivened by a Durant attack on Romney, often a very clever one. The bitterness goes back to 1962 when Durant, then a high official in the John Birch Society, endorsed Romney for governor. The candidate, determined to "make my position clear on extremism," rejected the honor and renounced Birch infiltration tactics. But the regular party has been unable to break the right-winger's hold on his district. The reason is ironic. When a Negro worker needs a job, Durant hunts through companies until he fills the need. He frets about drag-racing tracks for kids in his district. In short, he has built a good example of the service organization that Romney is creating elsewhere in the state.

But is that whole approach irrelevant today? Most things called fundamental, even parties and states that serve voters, now look old-fashioned. The urban age seems to have broken man's tie with his past. While humans multiply at an alarming rate, the phone and the jet and the TV bring their troubles and anger to our doorstep. We have too many neighbors on one small planet. Any evening's news is a documentary against the quaint notion that one person or group can do much with the forces at work around us. Helpless, we look to some supernatural power, generally the one installed at the White House, to do something quick about everything.

And the man up there is generous. "We're in favor of a lot of things," says President Johnson, "and we're against mighty few."

The Great Society, Romney argues, has lost touch with *The Good Society*, the Walter Lippmann book of 1937 from which, some think, President Johnson adapted his slogan. Wrote Lippmann: "It is generally supposed that the increasing complexity of the social order requires an increasing direction from officials. My own view is, rather, as affairs become more intricate, more extended in time and space, more involved and interrelated, overhead direction by officials of the state has to become simpler, less intensive, less direct, more general. . . . For, while a few things can be directed much, many things can be administered only little."[1]

Against the over-direction, Romney argues the political equivalent of the method practiced by the computer programmers. When a novice asks how it is possible to break down pages of math into information bits small enough for a computer to swallow, the veteran programmer responds with a question: How do you eat an elephant? The answer: one bite at a time. Romney rouses people and states to make their bites count, but it takes some convincing. To do so, they need overhead direction that is less intensive, less direct, or as Romney says, "a reasonable degree of economic planning, especially in those segments requiring action by a major part of the society, or more than one nation."

He senses a seething inside the monster institutions. People don't like to be numbers. In the University of California at Berkeley, any one of 27,500 bright (top 12.5 percent) students is reduced to a cipher, more so than any one of the 15,000 members of the West Coast Longshoremen's Union nearby. The masses are no longer on the production line, where the union movement once provided a response to the push-around. The AFL-CIO, down to 18 percent of the work force, means little to the half of its members now living in the suburbs. But something always fills a vacuum. The John Birch Society and other right-wing organizations, rising in the anonymous new suburbs, have made greater headway

---

[1] Walter Lippmann, *The Good Society* (New York: Grosset & Dunlap, 1937), p. 35. Lippmann used "Great Society" to describe the gross problems of the industrialized world and "Good Society" as the prospect for something better, if men could resist the tendency toward tight political controls over the economy.

among workers, I find, than labor chiefs know or care to admit. The right-wingers are a symptom of a social illness that cannot be ignored. In their attack upon big labor, big business and big government, they often sound very much like the more inflammatory advocates of Black Power. Both have a pathological sense that a conspiracy, Red or racist, must be running everything.

Romney, talking one morning about student rebels and city rioters, kept coming back to the strident new emphasis, not just in the streets but among intellectuals, upon the uses of power and its implied handmaiden, violence. He noted that even the dairy farmers, living under regional price-control machinery, have turned to strong-arm tactics. The rhetoric of power leads the mind to escalation; diffusion would lead the other way. If the present trend continues, he wondered, "who's to say that we are not in a crisis situation?"

"Young people, not just the protest leaders, are getting fed up with bigness, with distant power centers that they cannot influence, with individual anonymity and insignificance," Romney said. "The New Left recruits its followers not from doctrinaire Socialists and Communists, but from young men and women who have come smack up against the feeling of complete futility—of total inability to influence the society of which they are a part."

The restlessness around us may be, in Romney's sense, fundamental. Some of it is explicit. "America has got to make the black man a capitalist," says CORE's Floyd McKissick, "and do it damn quick." Well before the Detroit riot, Romney warned, "The lid blew off in Watts and Harlem, and it will blow again and again, until we learn to bring power back to the level where the people themselves—and I mean all the people, not just the rich and influential—can shape their own destinies."

And so he keeps running and running, ringing doorbells

and talking about things that sound old hat. "America needs an economic program to do for the urban, industrial society of the 1960's what Lincoln's Homestead Act did for the rural society of the 1860's," he preaches, leading up to his proposal to encourage wider stock ownership. "Corporate stock today plays largely the same role in our economy that land did 100 years ago."

And having once again rekindled the American Revolution at home, he believes, we can share it abroad. "Neither foreign nor domestic policy stands alone," he insists, not persuaded that diplomacy is for diplomats. "They are intimately and delicately intertwined. We cannot hope for progress, peace and order among the nations of the world if we cannot bring progress, peace and order to the cities of America. We cannot inspire others if we degrade ourselves."

If the United States is again to be a movement, not merely a power, it will have to move beyond the trenches of its previous battles. Failures have to be faced. As the welfare state has failed to free the slums, so anti-Communism has failed to abolish China. "The United States and the United Nations must prepare for the day when those who govern mainland China feel it is in their interest to accept the responsibilities and receive the benefits of close collaboration within the community of nations," says Romney. "When they're willing to step forward, we must be ready to accept them." And as the United States has moved, in agony, toward a reassessment of Vietnam, Romney has come down harder on the hurtful points. "We not only made a mistake getting involved there in the first place, but we've made a mistake Americanizing the military aspect of the conflict," he says. "Now we are in the process of Americanizing the pacification. I think that will be a bad mistake because I don't think the conflict can be won unless the South Vietnamese do their part." At home and abroad, policy must begin with a fundamental, the respect of human will. Such questions, unlike "brainwashing," do not fit easily into newspaper leads and TV newscasts.

Romney trusts the spirit of man, and hears in the present anguish a warning that something is very wrong. The materialist emphasis, even the calculation of votes by economic blocs, leaves part of the citizen unfed. "I think it was Thomas Carlyle who said that the spiritual side of man determines the material in the long run," Romney mused one morning as he followed a golf ball into the rough. "He's right, I think, though the material side may control in the short run."

All this may make him somewhat unsatisfactory as a political candidate. Since he is asking the voters to join in creating the future, he cannot offer the finished blueprints. But the United States, by adapting old wisdom to the complexity of the new urban age, can earn its place in the parade of history. As the Greeks brought culture, the Romans gave law and the British an ideal of popular government, he believes, so America can offer "a social and economic order suitable for human dignity."

"It remains to be seen whether we will make a contribution comparable to that made by Greece or Great Britain," he says. "We are an unfinished nation."

# INDEX

271